T0184015

Springer Series on Cultural Computing

Editor-in-chief

Ernest Edmonds, University of Technology, Sydney, Australia

Series editors

Frieder Nake, University of Bremen, Bremen, Germany
Nick Bryan-Kinns, Queen Mary University of London, London, UK
Linda Candy, University of Technology, Sydney, Australia
David England, Liverpool John Moores University, Liverpool, UK
Andrew Hugill, De Montfort University, Leicester, UK
Shigeki Amitani, Adobe Systems Inc., Tokyo, Japan
Doug Riecken, Columbia University, New York, USA
Jonas Lowgren, Linköping University, Norrköping, Sweden
Ellen Yi-Luen Do, University of Colorado Boulder, Boulder, USA
Sam Ferguson, University of Technology Sydney, Sydney, Australia

More information about this series at http://www.springer.com/series/10481

Brigid M. Costello

Rhythm, Play and Interaction Design

Brigid M. Costello
School of the Arts and Media
The University of New South Wales
Sydney, NSW
Australia

ISSN 2195-9056   ISSN 2195-9064   (electronic)
Springer Series on Cultural Computing
ISBN 978-3-030-09813-1   ISBN 978-3-319-67850-4   (eBook)
https://doi.org/10.1007/978-3-319-67850-4

© Springer International Publishing AG, part of Springer Nature 2018
Softcover re-print of the Hardcover 1st edition 2018
This work is subject to copyright. All rights are reserved by the Publisher, whether the whole or part
of the material is concerned, specifically the rights of translation, reprinting, reuse of illustrations,
recitation, broadcasting, reproduction on microfilms or in any other physical way, and transmission
or information storage and retrieval, electronic adaptation, computer software, or by similar or dissimilar
methodology now known or hereafter developed.
The use of general descriptive names, registered names, trademarks, service marks, etc. in this
publication does not imply, even in the absence of a specific statement, that such names are exempt from
the relevant protective laws and regulations and therefore free for general use.
The publisher, the authors and the editors are safe to assume that the advice and information in this
book are believed to be true and accurate at the date of publication. Neither the publisher nor the
authors or the editors give a warranty, express or implied, with respect to the material contained herein or
for any errors or omissions that may have been made. The publisher remains neutral with regard to
jurisdictional claims in published maps and institutional affiliations.

Printed on acid-free paper

This Springer imprint is published by the registered company Springer International Publishing AG
part of Springer Nature
The registered company address is: Gewerbestrasse 11, 6330 Cham, Switzerland

Acknowledgements

Acknowledgement and many thanks are due to the creative practitioners who generously gave up their time to be interviewed. Their voices provided crucial insights and perspectives that have shaped and enriched the book: Joe Agius, Simon Barker, Patrick Cook, Clare Grant, Sue Healey, Alon Ilsar, Andrew Johnston, George Poonkhin Khut, Andrew Lancaster, Simon McIntyre, Ilija Melentijevic, Roger Mills, Manolete Mora, Rhiannon Newton, Bree van Reyk, Andrew Schultz, Greg Sheehan, and Nalina Wait.

Many thanks are also owed to Chris Heine and Fiona Pearce who read drafts of this book and provided invaluable encouragement, critique and guidance.

Contents

List of Figures

List of Tables

Chapter 1
Rhythmic Experience

> All interactions that effect stability and order in the whirling flux
> of change are rhythms (Dewey 1934/2005, p. 15).

> Periodic phenomena attract our minds like flowers (Moriarty
> 2002).

Abstract Our world is composed of rhythms. We walk in rhythms, gesture in rhythms, speak in rhythms, breathe and think in rhythms. We also read rhythms from the environment and people around us. Sitting inside by a window, we can tell the strength of the wind just from the movement of trees and their leaves. Before we see the beach, we can tell the ferocity of the surf just from the sound of its crashing waves. Any disturbance in a habitual rhythm signals itself strongly. Our attention will be drawn towards the person in a crowd whose walk is hampered by an injury or a tight joint. The distant rhythms of people speaking will signal their foreignness well before their words can be distinguished. A change in the rhythmic ripples of a pond will alert us to the presence of fish and we will feel the shift in the vibrations of our car's engine when a cylinder misfires. Rhythm plays a major role in all forms of human expression whether it be music, dance, theatre, art, architecture, film, literature or computer games. It communicates to us, attracts our attention and has emotional impact. We can be soothed by a rhythm, aroused by a rhythm, captivated by a rhythm, made sad or joyful by a rhythm. It is this expressive power of rhythm that is the focus of this book and, in particular, the way that rhythm can be used by interaction designers within the design of playful computer applications.

Human computer interactions all involve rhythm: the rhythm of action and response that is implied by the very word interaction itself. When interactions occur in sequence, their patterned cycles of action and response form rhythms that can be sensed, interpreted, learnt and performed. Such rhythms will attract and engage our attention. These rhythms communicate in ways that, although deeply interrelated, can be separated from the meanings of the events that pattern their flow. Interactive rhythms give a shape and character to user experience, one that is perhaps not always consciously acknowledged but is most certainly felt. Rhythm also patterns the free

© Springer International Publishing AG, part of Springer Nature 2018

B. M. Costello, *Rhythm, Play and Interaction Design*, Springer Series on Cultural Computing, https://doi.org/10.1007/978-3-319-67850-4_1

movement of play, pulsing within the structured boundaries that define a play experience and separate it from the realities of life. Without this rhythm there is no play, no movement. The rhythms of play influence how long a play experience will last, providing an energy that sustains essential oscillations between playful investigation and exploration. Rhythm is, then, well worth paying attention to, especially for designers of playful interactive systems.

Paying attention to rhythms within playful interaction design means paying attention to movements of all kinds. There are the movements of physical bodies, cultural practices, daily lives and expressive performance. There are the movements of attention and of engagement and disengagement. There are larger structural movements that form trajectories across space and time and the transitions and textures within them. And at the beating heart of it all, there are the movements of repetition and difference, the movements between predictability and novelty that drive the dynamic vitality of any playful interactive experience.

As someone who is both an interaction designer and a researcher, I have written this book with practice and practical design strategies at its core. Accordingly, the research process began with creative practitioner interviews which then directed later theoretical research. Many of the practitioners and theories come from design traditions that, compared to interaction design, have a longer history, and depth of engagement, with rhythm. My task was to select, distil and communicate the practitioners' design strategies in ways that would resonate with contemporary interaction design practice. Current interaction design does, of course, deal with rhythm in various ways. As a small sample, there are the rhythms of real-time control that Swink discusses (2009), Jesse Schell's interest curves that pattern game experiences (2008) and the aesthetic quality of rhythm that Löwgren proposes (2009). These and other approaches to rhythm in interaction design are collected here and, as their relationships with the practical strategies of other traditions are explored, new creative strategies for working with and conceptualising rhythm in interaction design are developed. Creative strategies that will, hopefully, continue to resonate and grow long after you have read the book. For rhythm is always about a movement within space, time and energy and that movement makes it a vital resonant force in any design practice.

1.1 Outline of the Book

This book explores the qualities of rhythm, concentrating on how rhythm is experienced and can be created within interactive applications. The focus is on play, often using digital games as examples, but also draws on and discusses many other types of interaction design. The book developed out of a series of interviews with eighteen creative practitioners and eleven of these appear as sections in the book, shaping the themes of its chapters[1]. The eighteen practitioners all use rhythm in their work and

---

[1] See Appendix A for biographies of the eighteen interviewees.

all offer valuable strategies for working with rhythm in interaction design. Twelve of them come from design traditions with a very established rhythmic practice, those of dance, architecture, music, film and theatre. The other six interviewees are interaction designers whose practice involves working with the rhythms of play in various ways. Although some of their ideas may be familiar to you, viewing them through the lens of rhythm and across these different traditions provides a fresh perspective that should also suggest new approaches for your own design practice and give you what an early reviewer called "many small delightful moments of recognising connections." As you will see, the classifications I have just made between design traditions are not quite as neat as they look. Many of the interaction designers are also musicians and performers. Some of the creative practitioners do work that intersects with interaction design and several of them practice across more than one design tradition. Within both groups, improvisation is a common practice. This focus on improvisation springs from a particular interest I have in rhythm as something that can be both performed and played with. For it is out of this play that one of the most exciting things about working with rhythm emerges: the way that its energies can work to sustain engagement, not just in a puppet-like fashion but in a manner that involves the vitality and creativity of expression.

Part one of the book addresses the experiential qualities of rhythm. We begin with a chapter exploring the influence culture has over the experience of time and rhythm. An interview with ethnomusicologist Manolete Mora, a musician and researcher of Asian and African musical traditions, highlights these cultural practices and the way that culture can accent our rhythmic performance. As we examine the cultural practices of listening and performing, we also look at the functions of rhythmic synchrony within society, both discussions revealing potential strategies for interaction designers. Chapter 3 then focuses on the rhythmic movement of the human body and the types of knowledges that the moving body produces and communicates. An interview with composer and drummer Simon Barker introduces us to this theme and leads us into an exploration of the issues involved in designing digital rhythms for the scale of the human body. In the next chapter, online educational designer Simon McIntyre asks us to consider the way the rhythms of our designs might intersect flexibly with the daily rhythms of our users' lives. This chapter looks at practical methods to develop an understanding of the rhythms of daily life before exploring the intersection between daily rhythms and the rhythms of digital technologies. Chapter 5 is the last in part one and takes a detailed look at the performative practices of rhythm. Dancer Nalina Wait describes her work with rhythm in live improvised performances and the practical strategies that help her to prepare for this type of performance. We then explore the practices of performing in time and improvising playfully with a rhythm, focusing on how these practices might translate into interaction design and what pleasures they can evoke.

In part two, the focus shifts to strategies for designing with rhythm. Chapter 6 begins with an interview with director, performer and dramaturg Clare Grant, who stresses the importance of structuring the first moments of engagement, the moments where someone is swept into a work. As she points out, designers also need to consider how to let go of their audience and, consequently, the chapter explores strategies for staging the rhythms of both entrances and exits. Working with the different qualities of attention then becomes the focus of Chap. 7 which is centred on an interview with interactive artist and designer George Poonkhin Khut. George Khut uses human biorhythms in interactive systems to explore the connections between body and mind, and develop specific qualities of attention. We then focus on the unifying power of larger rhythmic structures in Chap. 8 and investigate strategies for designing the dynamics of trajectories. This theme is introduced by game designers Patrick Cook and Ilija Melentijevic, who speak about the way they use rhythm to provide structure and develop possibility spaces in their games. Chapter 9 examines strategies for designing rhythmic textures and transitions. Classical composer Andrew Schultz introduces this theme, describing transitions as "the trickiest thing" in composition and discussing the process he goes through to develop rhythmic ideas in his work.

In Chap. 10 we focus on predictability and the particular satisfaction and stability predictability can bring to a work. In common with the practice of choreographer Rhiannon Newton, whose interview leads us into this theme, our discussion investigates the boundaries between repetition and difference. The chapter ends with a section on strategies for challenging rhythmic habits and creating uncertainty. Next, we look at rhythm as a producer of vitality and interaction designer Andrew Johnston describes the rhythms of control he uses in interactive systems for creative live performance. This chapter examines the concept of mechanical repetition and its performance equivalent the automaton, both usually seen as lacking vitality. We then focus on the creation of instrument-like dynamics and rhythms that produce the lively, vital movement of play. Chapter 12 concludes the book with a summary of the rhythmic design strategies that have been uncovered in our investigation.

As you move through these chapters, the book will introduce you to seven more interviewees whose strategies for designing with rhythm also shape the investigations throughout. You will meet architect Joe Agius, composer and film director Andrew Lancaster, choreographer and film maker Sue Healey, musician and telematic improvisor Roger Mills, percussionist Greg Sheehan, drummer and electronic instrument designer Alon Ilsar, and composer and percussionist Bree van Reyk. The chapters in this book will, in total, produce a detailed definition of rhythm, of rhythmic experience and of the way they operate together within playful interaction design.

1.2   Introducing Rhythm and Rhythmic Experience

If rhythm can be thought of as inherent in the flow of action and also as confining, shaping, organising the flux, we are concerned here with both process and product. (Goodridge 1999, p. 44)

Take your mind back to the last time you were part of a large audience enthusiastically applauding a performance. Think about the moment you started to clap, the decision you made about how loud and how fast to do it, the building thunderous sound as every member of the audience joined in and the moment that you decided to stop clapping. What you have just imagined is an example of a rhythmic experience. Your clapping produced a rhythm and, as you clapped, you listened to the rhythms that others were producing. You may have gradually synchronised your clapping to their rhythms until a moment occurred when the combined applause merged into one loud distinct rhythm. As people became tired, this applause would then have tailed off into individual rhythms. By clapping you were playing a rhythm but you were also opening your perception to (attuning yourself to) the rhythms played by others. You were controlling your physical body to reproduce a cultural rhythm learnt in childhood and then perhaps surrendering some of that control to synchronise with the rhythms of the rest of the audience.

Similar rhythmic processes occur as game players click, press or gesture to control an avatar, producing sequences of precisely timed movements. These players must attune themselves to the rhythms of the game and control their bodies to perform them. The possibility space of gameplay can also provide opportunities for players to control and play with the order and timing of these game rhythms. Rhythmic experiences like these, then, involve opening your perception to a rhythm so that your body can learn to perform it. During this performance, you might synchronise with the rhythm or you might play expressively around it but, whatever you do, you will be producing a pattern that then organises the temporal flow of your experience. As Goodridge points out above, rhythm is both a process and a product. Rhythm involves actions and events that unfold across time. It also gives a perceivable shape and form to that unfolding. Rhythm is simultaneously temporal, experiential and expressive.

Rhythm's role in organising the experience of time involves creating "shapes within which time becomes audible" (Thaut 2005, p. 15). Those shapes come not from the character of the events themselves but from the patterning of the durational intervals between them (Fig. 1.1). Musical theory defines this interval as beginning at the start, or attack point, of an event and ending at the start point of the next event—in musical terms this is known as the inter-onset interval (London 2004, p. 4). A musician can, therefore, vary the duration of each note event and still be playing the same rhythm because the inter-onset intervals are unchanged. Equally, a rhythm can be played fast or slow by varying the duration between the inter-onset intervals. The dynamics of these durational patterns revolve around a temporal interplay between difference and repetition or beginnings and continuations. Always in rhythm, whether musical, physiological or social, "regularity and repetition are balanced by the opposite principles of change and unsteadiness" (Schmitt 2012, p. 3). At a micro level, this interplay between beginnings and continuations is perceived as cycles of strong and weak beats or accented and unaccented parts. This perceptual structure provides "a sort of grid on which music is drawn", a grid that in musical theory is called meter (Jourdain 1997, p. 123). Meter, as my interviewee ethnomusicologist Manolete Mora explains, gives structure to music:

> A pulse in music is generally consistent, like the ticking of a clock. It's the way we carve up time. But then the way we give structure to that is by accenting certain pulses. Say we had a pulse that went like this [clicks fingers at similar intensity and spacing]. It's

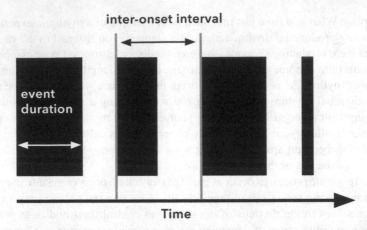

Fig. 1.1 Diagram showing the duration of the events of a rhythm (shown as black rectangles) and the duration between the start points of consecutive events which is called the inter-onset interval (the distance between the two grey lines)

> undifferentiated there is nothing else there. But once you start giving accent to that [one click is now louder/more intense than the others] we have meter…

When we experience a rhythm, our perception will cycle around these metrical accents. They attract the focus of our attention and any expectations of repetition. This focus then chunks and structures our perception of rhythm into cycles. Thus, we will hear repeated cycles of "tick tock, tick tock" in a clock pattern but not "tick tock" followed by "tock tick" (London 2004, pp. 21–3). Such rhythmic cycles of expectation and anticipation can create tension and heightened arousal when expectations are raised but not met. This occurs, for example, if we hear silence or see no movement when we expect an accented rhythmic event. The play between these patterns of "tension and release, arousal and de-arousal" helping to create the affective experience of rhythm (Thaut 2005, p. 5).

Our ability to perceive rhythmic patterns is a vital biological skill associated with evolutionary survival and the ability to detect and interpret movement of all kinds. Neuroscientist Levitin argues that:

> …it would be difficult to imagine an advanced species that had no ability whatsoever to sense vibrating objects. Where there is atmosphere there are molecules that vibrate in response to movement. And knowing whether something is generating noise or moving toward us or away from us, even when we can't see it (because it's dark, our eyes aren't attending to it, or we're asleep) has great survival value. (2006, p. 44)

Perception of these kinds of environmental rhythms involves focusing our attention on their pattern, predicting and anticipating when the next rhythm event will occur. Such anticipation and prediction of future rhythmic events is facilitated by oscillatory circuits in our brain (Thaut 2005, pp. 6–7). These circuits fire in response to periodic patterns. They allow us to synchronise our perception to a rhythm and their rhythmic capabilities constrain the durational patterns we can perceive. The shortest gap between rhythmic events that we can perceive is around 100 ms. For shorter gaps than this we cannot tell which event was first, although we might be able to distinguish more than one event. The longest gap that we can form into a rhythmic pattern is around five to six seconds (London 2004, p. 27). Gaps longer than this are difficult to remember with any accuracy and, without accurate detail, we will have trouble detecting repetition or difference within a rhythmic pattern (Hasty 1997, pp. 79–80). In general, we will also tend to group similar or close rhythmic events. We will not only actively search for regularity but will hear regularity in some things that are irregular (Drake and Bertrand 2003, pp. 25–6). Thus the perceptual capabilities of the human body influences the character of the rhythms we perceive.

The perceptual process of attention is an integral part of experiencing rhythm. Paying attention is a process that allows humans to cope with the incredible detail of the world by enhancing some information and inhibiting other information (Smith and Kosslyn 2006, p. 103). Although we might think that attention is something we control;

> ... if you pay attention to paying attention, you quickly sense that rather than you directing your attention, your attention is directing you. It pulls you into your coming perception, which dawns on you as attention's next-effect. Attention is the perceptual automatism that consists in tagging a change in the perceptual field as new and potentially important and building awareness on that change, for the very good reason that it may signal a necessity of a response or an opportunity for action. (Massumi 2010, p. 1)

Attention operates in tandem with the events in the world and this means attention is something that can be either thrust upon the perceiver or voluntary. For instance, we can have our thoughts interrupted by a loud sudden birdcall or we can choose to listen to a bird singing. Our attention can be drawn to things we wish to avoid and also drawn to things we are attracted to. We can smell rotting garbage and cross the street. We can also smell a sweet flower and move closer to the bush. These two pairs of attentional qualities, captive/voluntary and aversive/attractive, operate across a continuum of attention that can be "conscious and focused" or "unconscious and environmental" (Ash 2012, p. 8–9). For example, we might be unconsciously aware of the drip of a tap while we prepare dinner or consciously focused on each drop when its rhythms interfere with our desire to fall asleep.

Experiencing any rhythm requires both perceptual attunement and a synchronization of attention, a process described by the term "entrainment". A rhythm must be attended to in order to be perceived, and in this attending, we need to synchronize "some aspect of our biological activity with regularly recurring events in the environment" (London 2004, p. 4). The biological activity may involve listening or seeing but might also involve physical movement. The tapping of a foot or clapping along to music, for example, can help someone perceive a rhythm. Experiencing a rhythm, then, involves an opening of our perception as we attend to it and a focusing of our attention as we synchronize with it. The body is intimately involved in the experience of a rhythm and this involvement can be simultaneously voluntary and involuntary. We can choose to listen to the dripping tap but, having opened our perception to it, the rhythm of its drips can then take control of our attention so that we can no longer shut it out, our attention bending with the rhythm of the tap like a leaf bends to the rhythm of the wind. A similar interplay between voluntary and involuntary, controllable and controlling, conscious and unconscious appears in metaphors frequently used to describe these entrainment processes. Rhythm is described as something that can possess and contaminate but also as something that can entrance and enhance. Rhythm can enslave us or we can control it with the expressiveness of a performer playing a score.

Rhythm is, then, something that patterns the flow of experience and binds memory and attention to cycles of prediction and anticipation. To experience a rhythm involves opening our perception as we synchronise to these cycles and surrendering our attention to their control as we become habituated to them. When a rhythm is performed, the cyclic flow of rhythmic experience is also something that we can expressively play with. It is the expressive potential of rhythm that makes it a particularly useful tool for interaction designers. Rhythm provides a way for designers to structure the flow of interactions and to create an embodied experience of time. It operates across the whole macro structure of an experience but also in the micro relations of each action and reaction. Rhythm can communicate to users and can also be a way for users to communicate back. It creates patterns that will guide users through an experience and patterns that can similarly be perceived and interpreted by an interactive system. Rhythm emphasises both change and continuity, difference and repetition. The shifting patterns of rhythm create mood, tension, intensity and a feel or groove that can colour and shape user experiences. All of this makes rhythm worth including as an integral part of our creative processes in interaction design. Worth including and especially important, if we are to come up with a wider range of rhythms. Currently, there is just one genre, argues one of my interviewees, interaction designer Andrew Johnston, and its rhythms are "unsatisfyingly ungroovy." We need to develop a lot more rhythms within our interaction designs. Thus, a key aim of this book is to inspire you to create this wider range of rhythms in your own practice.

References

Ash J (2012) Attention, videogames and the retentional economies of affective amplification. Theory, Culture and Society 29(6):3–26

Dewey J (2005) Art as experience [Original pub 1934] Perigee edn. Penguin, New York, USA

Drake C, Bertrand D (2003) The quest for universals in temporal processing in music. In: Peretz I, Zatorre RJ (eds) The cognitive neuroscience of music, 1st edn. Oxford University Press, UK, pp 20–31

Goodridge J (1999) Rhythm and timing of movement and performance. Jessica Kingsley Publishers, London, UK

Hasty CF (1997) Meter as rhythm. Oxford University Press, New York, USA

Jourdain R (1997) Music, the brain, and ecstasy: how music captures our imagination. Harper Collins, USA

Levitin DJ (2006) This is your brain on music: the science of a human obsession. Dutton, New York, USA

London J (2004) Hearing in time: psychological aspects of musical meter. Oxford University Press, New York

Löwgren J (2009) Toward an articulation of interaction esthetics. New Review of Hypermedia and Multimedia 15(2):129–146. https://doi.org/10.1080/13614560903117822

Massumi B (2010) Perception attack: brief on war time. Theory & Event 13(3):1–6. https://doi.org/10.1353/tae.2010.0003

Moriarty B (1998–2002) Entrain. http://ludix.com/moriarty/entrain.html. Accessed 13 Jan 2006

Schell J (2008) The art of game design: a book of lenses. Morgan Kaufmann, San Francisco, Calif; Elsevier Science, Oxford

Schmitt J-C (2012) A history of rhythms during the middle ages. The Medieval History Journal 15(1):1–24. https://doi.org/10.1177/097194581001500101

Smith EE, Kosslyn SM (2006) Chapter 3: attention. In: Cognitive psychology: mind and brain. Pearson Prentice Hall, pp 103–146

Swink S (2009) Game feel: a game designer's guide to virtual sensation. CRC Press Taylor & Francis, London

Thaut MH (2005) Rhythm, music and the brain. Routledge, New York

Part I
Experiencing Rhythm

Chapter 2
Culture and Time

> *... every culture 'constructs' the human body differently...* (Iyer 2002, p. 388).

Abstract Our ability to focus on and perceive rhythmic patterns, whether they involve aural, visual, tactile, kinaesthetic or any of our other senses, is a basic human skill that transcends culture and history. We all have a common ability to attend to rhythm yet our culture and its historical context has an impact on which rhythmic patterns we can perceive and produce with ease. The rhythmic traditions of the musical culture we are born into give us an internalised ruleset that makes it easy for us to hear any rhythm from our own musical culture, to play or dance along with it and to enjoy its emotional nuances. Ethnographic research suggests that these cultural rhythmic rulesets are not just musical. From birth, we become acclimatised to all kinds of rules and meanings in relation to rhythm, from the rhythms of walking down the street to the rhythms of social interaction. Developing an understanding of the impacts of on rhythmic experience is important for designers of interactive applications because of its potential impact on the end user behaviour. This impact applies not only for those applications aimed at a specific cultural context but also those aimed at the many different cultures within a global audience. An interview with ethnomusicologist Manolete Mora sets the scene for this exploration of the impact that culture and time has on rhythmic experience. As a researcher of musical cultures across South East Asia, China and Africa, Manolete Mora's interview introduces us to the three themes of this chapter: the impact of culture on perceptions of time; the many different cultural practices of listening and performing; and the socio-cultural uses of synchronicity.

2.1   Time Can Be Anything We Want It to Be: Interview with Manolete Mora, Ethnomusicologist

Manolete: Rhythm is about time. It's about how you divide up time and the character that you give to time. Of course, that's all very specific to given cultures, circumstances and genres of music. For instance, in the field of jazz and popular music rhythm plays an integral part in how we think of the groove—the overall quality or feeling tone of the music. So, we could think of a jazz groove, a swing groove or a salsa groove—any particular genre you care to choose—and it would have its own set of characteristics. My colleagues would probably frown on me applying the word groove to the music of Johann Sebastian Bach or Mozart but they also have their own sound and groove—which is about rhythm.

Most of my work has been done in Southeast Asia, Southern China and West Africa or Ghana and so I've been in touch with cultures that really place more importance on rhythm. By that I'm not saying that in Western music there is an absence of rhythm, of course there's not. It's just that, compared to other dimensions and parameters of music, rhythm seems to play less of an important role in the West. In Western music, particularly Western classical music, the emphasis is on meter built around binary divisions two or four. Once you get beyond the Western tradition, to the classical traditions of North India in particular, rhythm and meter is incredibly complex. You'll get divisions of 11, or seven, or juxtapositions of five and seven, things like that. So you can, to some extent, characterise different cultures musically by the way they treat meter.

I remember once talking to a Javanese specialist musician when I was an undergraduate student. I was entrusted to pick him up at the airport and on the way back to the university I turned on the radio in the car and Mozart was playing. And I said, "what do you think of this music?" and he said, "Oh very boring." "Why?" I asked, and he replied, "Well the rhythm is always the same. The tempo is always the same, it never changes".

I learnt subsequently, while studying Javanese gamelan music, the extent to which rhythm and time is very fluid and fluctuates. It speeds up and it slows down. It's an important characteristic of the music. And this gentleman explained it to me in terms of life and the daily cycle. When you wake up in the morning, for example, your mood and the speed at which you move around is different to when it's midday or the burning sun in the mid-afternoon or in the evening. So, the music mirrors that.

In contrast, the western experience of time is very linear, very progressive—we are here and we are going there. It always has that shape to it. It is always going somewhere, which is towards a definite climax and ending. Also, Western musical practices often divide a meter into certain units and we see meter through a sense of time that is based on divisions.

Other cultures tend to have what is called an additive rhythmic approach. That rhythm—and structure in rhythm and time—is created by adding things together rather than dividing. And it seems to me that the regular recurring nature of Western practice has a lot to do with the invention of time, in the Western sense—the absoluteness, carving up time very meticulously and in regular way—and divisions within the clock and the invention of the metronome. They seem to go together and it's somewhat more removed from natural experience and from nature.

The way time is reckoned was one of things that intrigued me about the peoples I worked with in Southeast Asia. Traditionally they didn't have watches and clocks. Nor did they have the calendrical system that we do. They only had four days—yesterday, today, tomorrow and the day after tomorrow. They didn't measure things precisely. They had no notion of 1 o'clock, 2 o'clock, or whatever. How they related long periods of time and short periods of time was just through relatedness. It was all related to some common and re-occurring event—a fraction of a second was the blink of eye. One way in which they measured 15–20 min, for example, was how long it took rice to boil.

Many of the musics that I am talking about are cyclical or they consist of this idea of return, like a cycle rolling along or like a ball on and on and on. For example, Balinese gamelan time is felt in terms of a cycle that's like the daily cycle. We know there's going to be a sunrise and a sundown and there are certain times in the day that will be consistent. But it's the way they are filled in that can be slightly different. There will be variations but there is a basic pattern to it. And what gives Balinese gamelan that incredibly dynamic quality, an exuberant quality, is the complex rhythms that go with it. Those complex rhythms are actually a combination of two rhythms that fit together. The Balinese think of them as like male-female counterparts. These two rhythms, by themselves are complex enough but when you put them together, they fit together like jigsaw puzzle. It's that which produces this tension and energy.

They refer to this rhythmic duality as kotekan, which is the combination of the two rhythms. Each rhythm has a different name—one is nyangsi and one is polos. One of them tends to accent more the on-beat and the other tends to accent more the offbeat, which is what makes them complimentary. But there will be moments in these two separate rhythms where they are aligned at the same time. So, that's where you get accent and you get stress and emphasis. It's quite an extraordinary thing.

The Balinese have imbibed this concept of rhythm from when they were young children and it's extraordinary the way they can make this spontaneously. If you tap out a rhythm, somebody will be able to come up and provide you with the counter rhythm. It's amazing and they do it intuitively. They don't have to sit down and work it out on paper. It would be a lot of work for someone from our culture to try and learn how to do that. That's because if you take a certain style of music, the quality of being able to make it sound authentic or sound right is a little bit like the accent that comes with a language.

You develop an accent naturally as a child. In fact, the first thing you hear is intonation and patterning. It's not the grammar so much. It's all the sounds and the patterns. Yet it's the last thing we learn consciously if we take up a new language and it's the hardest thing to get. You can learn the grammar and the vocabulary but the accent is always what is going to distinguish you from a native speaker. Music works in the same way. You can learn all that stuff and then when you get down and play with people from that culture, you can hear the differences. It's getting the accent that takes a long time. It involves a lot of listening and a lot of imbibing over a long period of time to become unconscious.

But there is something kind of natural about synchronising to a rhythm. Many psychological studies show that when people want to empathise with one another, or want to communicate, their gestures will be similar—they will coordinate. We want to synchronise with others who we want to relate to, so it is no accident that one of the eternal functions of music (of which there are many) is synchronisation for labour, for work. Where a group of people get together and they coordinate their labour through singing. It makes work efficient and it makes it more pleasurable too. You know, the classic work songs of the American South during the slave period working on the slave plantations or the chain gangs in prisons. It's all about coordinating labour and bonding. So, rhythm and synchronicity are vital for harnessing group effort. This is one of the important functions that music provides.

There is a favourite example that I play to my students, a recording of a post office at the University of Accra in Ghana. Normally when mail comes through it goes through a process where it is sorted, franked and shuffled and then moved onto the next person for various other tasks. Well, in this particular place, and all over Ghana, they actually create music while they are doing this—creating rhythms as they stamp and shuffle. If you listen to this without the visuals, it just sounds like people singing and making music together on percussion instruments. But it is actually work.

I suppose there is an imitative dimension to synchronising with others. You want to be with someone—in a sense, you want to transcend your difference. You will work with somebody else rhythmically. That's what happens in the best jazz, rock or blues ensembles, or a string quartet, people actually give up something of themselves and work together as a unit, as a group. Bringing their energies, their labour, and their psychic energy together to create something quite unique and whole.

There are certain types of music where precision and synchronicity is required to make it work, and there are other kinds of music where being slightly out of sync is actually a quality of the music. Charles Keil an American musicologist wrote a very influential article in 1987 called

Participatory Discrepancies and the Power of Music. His thesis is that it is not people playing exactly together that makes the groove of jazz or blues or soul music, it's the way people create tensions by being slightly out of sync. Keil talks about how, for example, in a particular jazz group you might get a drummer who is slightly behind the beat and the bass player might be slightly ahead. And it's that tension, that sense of danger and risk that is involved when they are not exactly in sync, that creates the excitement and tension in the music. So, you can work against it. If you're playing in a jazz group where the groove is set up by most of the musicians and you are improvising, well then you will create tension by working around that—by deliberately playing against it. I guess harmony is created by the oneness and tension is created by working against it. That's what good improvised music does, it works the tension surrounding those discrepancies.

Playing exactly in time is not always what you are looking for. If you look at say practices amongst African-Americans, this is very common. You don't hear that kind of unison performance in Black Pentecostal churches, you don't hear that in jazz. You don't hear it in those traditions because there is the interesting sense that everybody brings to the rhythm something slightly different—but they work together. Through this they create an interesting kind of music and experience of time that marks out time in a regular way but it's done with a great deal of tension and interest.

You can make time do whatever you want through music. Depending on the number of events that are happening in it, it can feel elongated or it can feel short—all sorts of things... I think that is one of the things that music does—it really makes you aware of that relativity of time, the phenomenology of time. How time can be almost anything we want it to be.

2.2 Cultures of Time

Nowadays, it is rare to find a place in the world that does not organise at least a part of the rhythm of the day based on the 24-hour clock. Nevertheless, individual cultures still hold many different temporal concepts and traditions that run alongside, intersect, and/or disrupt this clock-time. As Manolete Mora pointed out, one area in which these cultural differences often reveal themselves is in the temporal dimensions of music. In his interview, he describes two different approaches: one found in European musical culture where time is seen as abstract and absolute, as it is in the 24-hour clock; the other found in musical cultures, like those of the Balinese gamelan, where time is linked to the cycles of nature and everyday life.

The way that European musical culture conceptualises and abstracts time is derived from a mathematical perspective. In this tradition, time is something absolute and can be quantified and divided into discrete units. Musical theorist Christopher Hasty links this way of thinking to a desire to understand and control time, arguing that time;

> ...becomes comprehensible and manageable if we can abstract it from the continuous becoming of events that take place 'in' time and, in effect, regard time as a sort of space - an enduring or persisting order for the dating and coordination of discrete events. (1997, p. 10)

In European musical traditions this abstract, spatial view of time is reflected in the way in which musical notation divides time into notes, bars and time signatures. Rhythms emerge from the division of bars into a series of equal beats, with these beats acting as a basic ruling pattern that is perceived by the listener—whether or not the melody coincides with this pattern or plays around with it (Sachs 1952). Thinking of time in a spatial way, as Manolete Mora points out, leads to musical structures that tend to be linear and relatively static in tempo. The linear thrust of these musical forms is always "going somewhere" and leading to a defined endpoint.

In contrast, the musical culture of Balinese gamelan is based on a concept of time that is more closely related to nature and to the scale of human activities. For example, a musical work might contain rhythmic structures based on biological time-scales like the rising and setting of the sun or the daily waxing and waning of human energy. The musical structures that emerge from this way of thinking are usually cyclical and fluid in their tempos. A fluidity that reflects the variations of tempos in everyday life. As Manolete Mora puts it, "there are certain times in the day that will be consistent. But it's the way they are filled in that can be slightly different". The fluidity within these rhythmic structures is created by adding together grouped patterns of different lengths—a process that musical theory calls additive rhythm. While the divisive rhythms of the European tradition act to regulate their musical forms, these additive rhythms act to configure the music they create (Sachs 1952, p. 392). Their cyclic structure, rolling "like a ball on and on", rarely leads to a climactic end point rather, as Manolete Mora says, the ending is "more a decision that this is going to just finish here".

For interaction designers who create works that are both non-linear and cyclical, this additive approach to composing with rhythm aligns well with many of the creative problems around form and pacing in an interactive context. Indeed, it is already common practice to present users of interactive systems with modular rhythmic patterns that either they or the computer can combine together in response to interactive input. It is also increasingly common for interaction designers to create cyclical rhythmic structures, which mimic natural rhythms, like day night cycles or the growth and decay of plants [see for example, the games *The Elder Scrolls V: Skyrim* (Bethesda Softworks 2011), *Minecraft* (Mojang 2011) or *Don't Starve* (Klei Entertainment 2013)]. A lot of valuable inspiration can therefore be found in the compositional practices of cyclic musical traditions like those found in Bali, India or Africa. Many of us, however, are also designing for an audience raised in a culture with predominantly linear rhythmic forms. Forms that proceed to a climax and end definitively. Those users will have been raised with the steady beat of 4/4 rhythms and will find other rhythms not only difficult to perceive and perform but rhythmically unsatisfying. So, while additive rhythmic structures with fluid tempos might suit an interactive context, we often have an audience that expects a climactic ending and is habituated to regular rhythmic patterns based on a 4/4 beat.

The ubiquity of the 4/4 beat was an issue raised by many of the practitioners I interviewed, no matter whether they were working in music, dance, theatre or film. As percussionist Greg Sheehan observes, even within Indian musical culture, with its vast range of 120 different time signatures, meters based on four still exist and are popular. For example, he says that in Indian music the "most popular and common [time signature] is Teentaal, which is 16 beats—four, four, four, four." Some of the practitioners I interviewed choose to work with this habitual beat and others choose to subvert it. All, however, accept that their audience is culturally conditioned to the 4/4 beat and that this, as choreographer Sue Healey puts it, creates a "dulling of our senses" that means we are "unable to feel different rhythms".

This type of rhythmic cultural conditioning has been found to operate at many different levels of our lives, not just those relating to music and dance. For example, while cultures based on the Gregorian calendar quantify and divide time into days, months and years, the South-East Asian traditional cultures observed by Manolete Mora have only four possible types of days—"yesterday, today, tomorrow and the day after tomorrow." Viewing time as a cycling of events across the short span of four days not only impacts the type of temporal structures that these cultures create in their music but also their perceptions of the patterning of events within everyday life. Where calendar-time is driven by a sense of a day as a finite quantity that progresses to create an ever-expanding future, viewing time as a four-day cycle emphasises not progression but return and leads to a different perception of the pace of life.

An interesting example of the effect of different cultural models of time is provided by anthropologist Edward T. Hall who describes how American Hopi Indians have a concept of time with so little sense of temporal progression that they live in a kind of "eternal present" and value slowness over speed (1983), p. 37. Conversely, the quantification of time in calendar-based cultures, he argues, gives the people in these cultures a strong sense of the importance of progression and leads them to put a high value on speed. For those in a calendar-time culture, the Hopi way of life appears very slow and purposeless. Yet for the Hopi with no sense of future or past, it is hard to understand the calendar-based culture's belief that time is something that has a value and can be wasted or saved. When people from these two cultures meet and try to communicate, their different perceptions of time are likely to result in miscommunication and misunderstanding (ibid., p. 36). As Hall describes it, the rhythms of communication within cultures operate on a "message velocity spectrum" with each culture having its own message speed in which they feel most at ease. Once a person from a particular temporal culture "is 'tuned in' on a given frequency, messages on any other frequency might as well not exist" and misunderstandings will occur (ibid., p. 63). For example, if a fast 'act now or not at all' culture meets a slow 'think for a long time and then act' culture, any pauses in communication will get misread by the fast culture as agreement (ibid., p. 186). Where one culture hears the pause as contemplation the other hears it as a choice to not voice a disagreement. This miscommunication is the result of their mismatched rhythms.

Hall believes that many of the world's cultures can be categorised in one of two cultural approaches to time, monochronic or polychronic. The first focuses on the time-scale of the individual and the second on the longer, multiple and repeating time-scales of interrelated generations, their linear versus cyclical characters echoing the two musical cultures we discussed earlier. Hall describes the way these temporal characters influence all aspects of each culture's social structures. In a typical monochronic culture there is a separation between an individual's home-life and their work-life to the extent that social networks from one domain rarely intersect with the other. Whereas, in a typical polychronic culture there is no distinction between social networks at home or work (Hall 1983). Thus, decisions made in a monochronic culture will tend to be based around their impact on the individual and those made in a polychronic culture will more likely consider the impact of the decisions across a network of related people and across both future and past generations. Monochronic cultures allow themselves to be regulated by schedules and tie this scheduled time to their individual sense of status where 'time equals money'. In polychronic cultures, schedules are more flexible and are often trumped by the demands of human relationships. Here we see the ancient Greek distinction between the quantitative sequential time of Chronos and the qualitative time of Kairos, which refers to the opportuneness of the timing of an event—the 'right' time for something to occur (Thaut 2005, p. 16). A monochronic American will get personally offended if they are kept waiting for a scheduled appointment, while a polychronic Brazilian will take it in their stride, accepting that it may not yet be the opportune time. Hall describes each as being "in the grip" of a different pattern (ibid., p. 77). As above, when cultures from different temporal scales intersect, their mismatched rhythms can lead to miscommunication and misunderstanding.

For designers of interactive applications who may need to work across cultures, or within a culture of a different temporal character than their own, these differences in perspective are important. An application that tries to control the rhythm of scheduled events based on clock-time may work well in a monochronic culture but not in a polychronic one. Similarly, an application that emphasises social relationships across both work and home may work well in a polychronic culture but may not in a monochronic one. And an application intended to appeal to both cultures may need to design in tools and modes that allow for flexibility in these areas so that one culture can adjust schedules based on relationships and the other can separate the social aspects of home and work. Consider, for example, the changes that Facebook has made to accommodate different definitions of 'friend'. It is worth pointing out here that culture is never static. As Hall's characterisations of temporal cultures are based on studies from the 60–70's, we can be sure there will have been shifts in the character of his categories and the way in which they are practiced. The key point is that a person's cultural perspectives on time will not only influence their ability to perceive rhythms within an interaction design but also impact the rhythms that they feel most comfortable practicing and the meanings that they draw from them.

2.3 Cultural Practices of Listening and Performing

> We cannot turn off our ears — the ears are always taking in sound information — but we
> can turn off our listening...How you are listening, is how you develop a culture and how a
> community of people listens, is what creates their culture. (Oliveros 2003)

From the moment we are born, our cultural experiences give us different templates for listening to rhythms and different ways of performing them. Studies by neuroscientists show that the rhythmic traditions of the musical culture that we are born into shape "our neural pathways" causing us to "internalise a set of rules" from that musical tradition (Levitin 2006, p. 27). Thus, we can easily recognise and perform rhythms from our own culture but may not recognise or be able to perform rhythms from another culture. As Manolete Mora observes, it is very difficult to communicate the rhythm and grooves of a culture to those outside it. Even if, after many hours of practice, we learn to perform a rhythm from another culture, we will probably still have an accent that will distinguish us from someone born into it. We need a "facility" to perceive a groove, a "requisite perceptual orientation" and an "embodied perceptual structure" (Roholt 2014, p. 73). This is the hidden thing that those who have it cannot explain and do not notice that they have. Without it we might be able to perceive a rhythmic nuance but won't perceive its effect or feel (ibid.). Even within our own culture our "learned perceptual sets" and lack of expertise in a particular domain might make us interpret or perform a rhythm in a way that an expert might label as "wrong" (Duke 1994). These learned templates are the temporal patterns that Hall described earlier as having us in their grip.

Listening to and performing rhythms is, then, a deeply cultural practice and it is in the moments of this practicing that culture is created. As Emmerson points out in relation to music, the different genres of musical cultures are defined by their practices of listening and performing because "it is in these practices that their existence as works comes into being" (2007, p. 33). Similarly, Roholt argues that a successful live musical performance is "due to things the musicians do *and* things the audience *does*"; there needs to be a complimentary mesh between the listening templates of the audience and the performance rhythms of the musicians for a performance to work well (2014, p. 74). In contemporary interaction design practice, we think in a similar way about the mesh between our interactive applications and their users: an interactive work comes into existence only in the moments that it is interacted with; and the success of that existence is tied to the relationship between the habits, abilities and expectations of *both* the user and the system. In interaction design it is perhaps more obvious that both sides of this relationship are performing and listening.

The way humans listen alters over time in response to changes in our environment and the technology with which we surround ourselves. Societies with the technology for making metal will be able to distinguish between not just the sound of rock and the sound of iron but also between the sound of a knife and fork, and the clink of a handful of coins. A person in the iron-age would have had little trouble understanding the sound of a metal gong, but would have had no template to understand the sound of plastic (Emmerson 2007, p. 17). Our place in history also alters the speed at which we can listen. Classical music composer Andrew Schultz observes that people are now "able to listen more quickly" and attributes this to the wider range of sounds we hear compared with 300 years ago. Similarly, others point to the fast speed of modern life and its impact on listening practices, with modern art audiences described as "twitchy", "disinterested" and "agitated" (Thompson 2010). Dancer Nalina Wait has observed a speeding up of her own rhythms of attention—these days she will "just read the introduction, then skip through and find the points". There is, she says, now a "much faster pulse of attention", one that that requires less time before it needs "a shift". She is always ready "for something new" or "for a change." But as both Andrew Schultz and Nalina Wait point out, it is because of this speed that the modern audience can also crave slowness and enjoy a rest from the pace of the need for new information all the time.

Our place in history and culture does not just impact the rhythms that we understand and the speed we can (and enjoy) listening to them. It also impacts what we do as we listen—the performative aspects of our listening practice. During his collaborations with Korean musicians, drummer Simon Barker observed a difference between the listening practices of Australia and Korea. In Australia, he says, any audience participation is "frowned upon except for applause", whereas in Korea "people are screaming and clapping and saying all these things to encourage you." The lack of participation by the Australian audiences echoes formal European traditions, which focus on the "contemplative" and reject "body rhythm and expression" in musical listening practices (Emmerson 2007, p. 65). These European traditions emerged out of religious culture and are related to the religious shift from the participatory dancing of the Pagan "maypole" to the seated stillness of the Christian "altar". Emmerson describes how this rejection of bodily rhythm also influenced musical performance, for example, the plainchant of Christian monks where "[e]ven breath was harnessed…quite beyond the normal periodicities of regular breathing" (ibid.). Concert halls designed for listening to music that follow this European tradition are built for a seated audience and their acoustics assume the audience will be quiet and still. In contrast, spaces designed for listening to rock music often have no seating and assume that the audience will dance and sing along. Where one practice listens with their mind, the other listens with their body "the classical audience *rapt*, the rock audience *abandoned*" (Frith 1998, p. 125). Each practice has its own template for the types of behaviour the listening audience performs and how the social structures built around each practice (both human and man-made) work to reinforce those expectations.

Another cultural dimension that impacts both the way we perform and listen to rhythms is our culture's attitudes to gender. In many cultures, there are distinctive ways of moving that are associated with either masculinity or femininity and as with all rhythmic templates these are internalised from a very young age. A young American girl, for example,

> …learns actively to hamper her movements. She is told that she must be careful not to get hurt, not to get dirty, not to tear her clothes, that the things she desires to do are dangerous for her. Thus, she develops a bodily timidity which increases with age. (Young 1980, p. 153)

These rhythmic templates may mean that such a girl will not have the rhythmic skill to throw a ball as fluidly as an American boy, but it might also mean that in another rhythmic domain like that of dance she will move more fluidly than he will. Gender has also been associated with the rhythms of physical movement in interaction designs. For instance, the rhythms of masculine bodies are described as suiting the small focused movements of mouse, keyboard and game controller while the open performative bodily practices of the Wii are seen as suited to the rhythms of female bodies (Kirkpatrick 2011, pp. 131–2). I have seen a similar difference between male and female performance rhythms when watching two Australian players try out the same VR game with hand controllers. The male player stood in one spot barely moving, with his arms quite close to his body. The female player moved very expressively waving her arms around and stepping around the space. The game itself did not require either style of movement and, in fact, the more expansive movements of the female player were an issue because the VR headset she was wearing was tethered by cables. So in this case, the technology delivering the game worked to inhibit this female's performance practices. As these examples show, interactive applications draw on habits of rhythmic experience developed through other applications or through other rhythmic aspects of user's lives, such as dance, music or gesture. How easily we can listen to and perform their rhythms depends on how well the application synchronises with our cultural bodily practices. These rhythmic practices are often gendered and, as we saw earlier, will also be shaped by our culture's templates for listening and performing.

2.4 The Socio-Cultural Uses of Synchronicity

Being able to synchronise with the rhythms of another is an important marker of belonging within a culture (Turino 2008). If we can't gesture, breathe, dance or perform in sync with others we are marked as different and shown to be lacking in social competence. Cultural rhythmic incompetence is as obvious as a foreign accent in speech and can indicate our status as an outsider or be a way of purposefully communicating difference. But if we do synchronise with someone else, the action, as Manolete Mora says, has an "imitative dimension" that rhythmically binds two people together allowing us to "transcend" our difference. Rhythm is a cultural form of communication and our ability to listen and perform rhythms in synchrony impacts our capacity to relate to others and marks our status as a member of a particular culture.

Our participation in rhythmic culture begins right from when we are babies. Babies synchronise with their primary carers, wriggling and vocalising along with the rhythms of their speech. These movements and sounds show a level of rhythmic synchrony similar to that observed between a pair of adults in conversation and are described as having the complex phrasing and patterning of a musical score (Gibbs 2010, p. 197). The rhythms of adult gestural movements of hands, head and blinking eyes synchronise with rhythmic beats in speech patterns and occur at tempos of around 600 ms. This rhythmic tempo of 600 ms aligns with the common human tempos of the heartbeat and the pace of walking (Loehr 2007). Adults speaking also synchronise the blinking of their eyes to rhythmic beats within their speech, leaving their eyelids closed until just before the next beat in their rhythmic conversation—in effect marking the rhythmic beats with each blink (ibid., p. 204). Each of us has internalised these complex gestural rhythms so that we not only perform them without thinking but can perceive and interpret them in the performance of others.

Rhythmic gestural communication practices are not always cross-cultural. Where Anglo Americans will gesture on one side of the body or the other, American Indians have a syncopated rhythm; "A gesture starts with one hand, shifts at midpoint, and is completed by the other hand. The two sides of the body work together in phase with speech" (Hall 1983, p. 184). Hall also reports that Japanese speakers will sometimes control their breathing in synchrony with the person they are speaking with and will leave pauses in the content of their conversation to allow time for reflection. Listening to an American speak can leave a Japanese person feeling breathless because there is no space left for thought and no attempt to synchronise breath (ibid., pp. 164 and 208). Cultures will have distinct rhythmic practices that they have learnt to perform and through these they will have developed specific preferences for synchronising with rhythms. When two cultural rhythms interrelate, a mismatch in rhythmic synchrony can lead to misunderstanding and social unease.

Sometimes mismatches in rhythmic synchrony are not caused by cultural differences but are caused by digital technologies and the impact they can have on rhythmic practices. Choreographer Sue Healey describes the experience of trying to give a dance workshop across a Skype video connection to an audience in Hong Kong. Her biggest issue was not the barrier of communicating to people who spoke many different languages, it was a rhythmic mismatch caused by the random delays in the Skype transmission. She describes how the delay and the impact that it had on the rhythms of communication made her feel frozen, unable to move and perceive:

> …that delay. I have never experienced anything like it. I felt like I was paralysed. They could hear me really well but the delay in time between their response to my question and the delay in me being able to see what they were responding to, was the hardest thing for me.

Hamilton describes a similar type of mismatch when he voices his frustration with the combat controls in *The Witcher 2* (CD Projekt 2011), describing how "the animations play out in conflict with my button inputs, and the whole thing winds up feeling like playing a guitar duet over Skype" (Hamilton 2011). The frustration he expresses is not due to an inability to manipulate the controls in order to achieve a game outcome. It is caused by a perceived lack of synchrony between the physical rhythms of movement he is opening to within the game and the visual rhythms that these movements are triggering. There is a mismatch in rhythmic synchrony that blocks his potential captivation by this rhythm of the game.

Some researchers associate the capacity for rhythmic synchrony with sexual selection. A study of Jamaican dancers proposed that the most attractive were able to both sync with the rhythm of the music and provide a counter rhythm (Dean et al. 2009, p. 357). The complexity of each dancer's rhythmic performance communicated his or her physical competence to potential sexual partners. Other researchers associate rhythmic synchrony with social-bonding, maintaining that the capacity is useful for providing non-verbal compassionate support in an emotionally-charged counselling context. By observing the patterns in rhythmic body movements counsellors can read the emotional state of others and communicate non-verbally through the body rhythms they themselves display (Yopst 2015). The use of rhythmic synchrony to create social relationships is also commonly associated with social-bonding in work situations and is often used to coordinate labour. As Manolete Mora observes, rhythmic synchronisation can make work more enjoyable and efficient, especially during coordinated teamwork. It has also been observed that individual cultures have different capabilities for group synchronisation in team contexts and that those cultures with a particular rhythmic sensitivity are often more effective team workers. Recalling a personal experience of rhythmic synchronisation on a Spanish building site, Hall says; "It was as though our small work crew was a single organism with multiple arms and legs that never got in each other's way" (1983, p. 163). Given the value of coordinated labour, it is no surprise, then, that we find people advocating the use of rhythmic performance for team-building (Sommers 1993) or stressing rhythm's value as a management tool for choreographing the temporal patterns in a workplace (Atkinson 2008).

The facility for rhythmic synchrony in teamwork is also involved when musicians play together. When this works well, as Manolete Mora describes it, the musicians exchange energies and give "something up of themselves" to achieve a greater whole. The level of in-the-moment attention needed to synchronize with others while playing music requires a focussed attention and an awareness of other musicians to create a heightened sense of togetherness and shared identity (Turino 2008, p. 43). Percussionist Greg Sheehan describes playing music in this way where:

> ...if you're doing it [playing music] selflessly and you're serving the music and you're serving the people that have come to watch you, and the other musicians, it's almost like a bigger thing can just come through you.

Similarly, McNeill describes a process of "muscular bonding" that occurs in collective rhythmic movement and suggests that it leads to an expanded and collective sense of self. He relates how while entraining to a military drill with fellow soldiers he was "conscious of keeping in step so as to make the next move correctly and in time" and that this created a pleasurable "sense of personal enlargement...becoming bigger than life" (1995, p. 2). A comparable sense of an expanded collective self can occur in multiplayer gaming environments where participants describe the pleasure they get from sharing a common goal on team missions as a "megafized feeling", one that creates a satisfying sense of shared collaborative involvement (Calleja 2007, p. 248). Even in first person player experiences, where teamwork is only between the player and the computer, there can be "a melding of one's real body and one's surrogate body"; a surrogate body that often has skills that human players do not (Gee 2009, pp. 68–71). These extra skills can give a prosthetic sense of expanded bodily capabilities which can create a sense of personal enlargement. The rhythmic synchrony of collective movement, then, leads to a sharing of identity that expands the boundaries of the individual self.

Within collective synchronous musical performance, Turino distinguishes between two traditions. One focuses on the presentation of an artistic product, with the experience being judged by the quality of the musical form the performance produces. The other tradition is participatory and focuses not on any end product but on the quality of the collective participation—on the "doing" of the performance and the social synchrony within it (2008, p. 28). Focus on social synchrony therefore impacts the rhythmic form of music played in these participatory traditions. Layers of rhythmic repetition are used to encourage and allow for synchronous participation by all members across all skill levels. The multiple layers accommodate different levels of expertise and mask individual contributions, making it easy for anyone to join in and, at the same time, reducing the risk of embarrassment from a poor performance. In participatory performances that involve both musicians and dancers, musicians also have a "responsibility" to play at a tempo that is "comfortable" for those dancing to ensure that no-one is excluded (ibid., pp. 33–38). This temporal relationship between dancers and musicians is illustrated by a story told by percussionist Greg Sheehan. He was about twelve and playing drums at old-time Irish dances, accompanying his Mum on piano:

> One time, everybody was dancing and having a great time and when we had a little break, I asked;" Mum, how do I keep time?" In other words, how do I stop from going from really fast to really slow or vice versa. She said: "It's easy, you just watch the dancer's feet!" It was a beautiful answer. [he laughs] But of course it was a typical Irish/Australian answer because obviously the dancers are listening to *us*! We're creating the tempo, but once we set it up you can just watch the dancers. If you take the common denominator of all those people doing a [he taps a waltz rhythm on the table], they're just subconsciously right in the groove — it's not back, it's not forward, it's just right in the centre of the pulse.

In a participatory performance, the musicians provide a tempo for the dancers but the dancers also provide the tempo for the musicians—and the two rhythms must work together to create a collective whole.

This same tradition of participatory performance, Miller argues, is behind the pleasures of playing *Guitar Hero* and *Grand Theft Auto* are both video games but I haven't referenced as they are both series with multiple versions and Kiri Miller does not specify an edition of the game. In her text they are not referenced at all. Moving in synchrony with the repetitious rhythms gives her a similar sense of "sharing visceral common knowledge" that she gets practicing yoga, ballet, or a musical instrument (2012, p. 222). Other types of games, for example, team-based digital games also involve the rhythmic social synchrony of participatory performance. Without it the players cannot play well together and the game collapses. The social synchrony of gameplay has more impact over the quality and duration of a play experience than the score or type of game, because, as De Koven observes, if players "aren't playing well together, nothing works" (2013, p. 29). The process, the *doing*, of the gameplay is where the driving play energy of the game lies. Like participatory performance, the quality of the experience is judged by how much participation there is and how players feel, not by how they look or sound as they play. Interaction designers creating works for multiple users, multiple skill levels or with a focus on social outcomes, therefore, have a similar need to invite the type of collective participatory performance that Turino identifies.

Through our participation in the rhythms of the cultures we live in, we learn to listen to, interpret and perform many rhythms. Our rhythmic capabilities are therefore an expression of our position within those cultures—rhythmic inflections marking us as insiders, outsiders or immigrants. The ability to synchronise with the rhythms of another is a form of communication that binds us together socially and leads to an expanded and collective sense of self. We do not only synchronise with the rhythms of other humans. We synchronise with all elements of the world around us, from the cycle of the moon, to the chirp of cicadas or the swish of a windscreen wiper. Someone from one culture may think about and interpret a specific rhythm very differently from a person in another culture and these different conceptual templates can lead to miscommunication and misunderstanding. A mismatch in rhythmic synchrony whether human-to-human, human-to-nature or human-to-technology can also lead to miscommunication and misunderstanding. At the very least, such a mismatch will lead to a sense of unease and frustration. Designing with a focus on rhythmic experience requires a sensitivity to these cultural dimensions of rhythm and an awareness of strategies that allow for participation across multiple rhythmic cultures.

References

Atkinson D (2008) Dancing "the management": on social presence, rhythm and finding common purpose. Manag Decis 46(7):1081–1095

Bethesda Softworks (2011) The Elder Scrolls V: Skyrim. Video game, Windows, PlayStation, Xbox. Bethesda Softworks, USA

Calleja G (2007) Digital game involvement: a conceptual model. Games and Cult 2(3):236–260

CD Projekt (2011) The Witcher 2: Assassins of Kings. Video game. PC, Xbox. CD Projekt, Poland

Dean RT, Byron T, Bailes FA (2009) The pulse of symmetry: on the possible co-evolution of rhythm in music and dance. Musicae Scientiae 13 (2_suppl):341–367

De Koven B (2013) The well-played game. MIT Press, Cambridge, Massachusetts, USA

Duke RA (1994) When tempo changes rhythm: the effect of tempo on nonmusicians' perception of rhythm. J Res Music Educ 42(1):27–35. https://doi.org/10.2307/3345334

Emmerson S (2007) Living electronic music. Ashgate, Great Britain

Frith S (1998) Performing rites. Harvard University Press, USA

Gee JP (2009) Deep learning properties of good digital games: how far can they go? In: Ritterfield U, Cody M, Vorderer P (eds) Serious games: mechanisms and effects. Routledge, New York, pp 67–82

Gibbs A (2010) Sympathy, synchrony and mimetic communication. In: Gregg M, Seigworth GJ (eds) The affect theory reader. Duke University Press, USA, pp 187–205

Hall ET (1983) The dance of life: the other dimension of time. Anchor Books, USA

Hamilton K (2011) The unsung secret of great games—and how some games get it so wrong. kotaku. http://kotaku.com/5808033/the-unsung-musical-secret-of-great-gamesand-how-some-games-get-it-so-wrong. Accessed 28 Apr 2013

Hasty CF (1997) Meter as rhythm. Oxford University Press, New York, USA

Iyer V (2002) Embodied mind, situated cognition, and expressive microtiming in African-American music. Music Percept 19(3):387–414

Klei Entertainment (2013) Don't Starve. Video game. PC, IOS, Android, Xbox, PlayStation, Wii U. Klei Entertainment, Canada

Kirkpatrick G (2011) Aesthetic theory and the video game. Manchester University Press, Manchester, UK

Levitin DJ (2006) This is your brain on music: the science of a human obsession. Dutton, New York, USA

Loehr D (2007) Aspects of rhythm in gesture and speech. Gesture 7(2):179–214

McNeill WH (1995) Keeping together in time: dance and drill in human history. Harvard University Press, USA

Mojang (2011) Minecraft. Video game. PC, IOS, Android, Xbox, PlayStation, Wii U, Nintendo. Mojang, Sweden; Microsoft, USA; Sony Interactive Entertainment, USA

Miller K (2012) Playing along: digital games, YouTube and virtual performance. Oxford University Press, New York, USA

Oliveros P (2003) An interview with Pauline Oliveros. American Mavericks. American Public Media, Online

Roholt TC (2014) Groove: a phenomenology of rhythmic Nuance. Bloomsbury, New York, USA

Sachs C (1952) Rhythm and tempo: an introduction. The Musical Q 38(3):384–398

Sommers DI (1993) Team building in the classroom through rhythm. J Manag Educ 17(2):263–268

Thaut MH (2005) Rhythm, music and the brain. Routledge, New York

Thompson N (2010) Contractions of Time: On social Practice from a Temporal Perspective. e-flux journal (20)

Turino T (2008) Music as social life. University of Chicago Press, USA

Yopst CG (2015) Choreographing compassion: a clinical adventure of rhythms. Pastoral Care & Couns 69(2):60–67

Young IM (1980) Throwing like a girl: a phenomenology of feminine body comportment motility and spatiality. Hum Stud 3(1):137–156

Chapter 3
Moving Bodies

> ...a beat lands on your joints, it docks on the junction between
> your joints and articulates itself onto your joints, it seizes a
> muscle, it gives you this tension, it seizes you up, and suddenly
> you find your leg lifting despite your head...It's almost like your
> feet are gaining an intelligence at the expense of your
> head...that's the signs of a bodily intelligence switching itself on
> (Eshun n.d.).

Abstract We are used to thinking and speaking about knowledge as something primarily produced by abstract thought, despite being aware that knowledge also resides in our practices, in our doing as well as our thinking. Practical bodily knowledge and its relationship to rhythm is the focus of this chapter. We explore the bodily intelligence involved in rhythmic experience, its relationship to the ways we can move our bodies and the ways these bodies can be in turn moved by it. As we will see, this type of bodily intelligence communicates but does so in a different way to words. It speaks of anticipation, expectation, speed and temporal relationships. It speaks of flux and flow, and patterned durations. Our interaction designs can both speak this language to our users and listen to what their rhythmed bodies are saying. To evaluate these aspects of our designs we need to choose methods that tap into our own bodily intelligence as well as that of our participants. We also need to attend to the impact our interface rhythms might have on the human body as it moves. Leading us into this discussion is an interview with Simon Barker, a composer, drummer and lecturer in Jazz studies who has spent several years working with traditional Korean musicians and shamans. Not surprisingly, given his practice, Simon Barker's interview focuses on the relationship between rhythm and bodily movement: a relationship that he says is integral to understanding rhythm and the knowledge it produces. The three sections that follow Simon Barker's interview expand on the theme of bodily movement to discuss: what kinds of knowledge are involved in rhythmic movement? How can this type of rhythmic knowledge be communicated and analysed? And what are some of the factors designers need to consider when designing rhythms for moving bodies?

© Springer International Publishing AG, part of Springer Nature 2018
B. M. Costello, *Rhythm, Play and Interaction Design*, Springer Series
on Cultural Computing, https://doi.org/10.1007/978-3-319-67850-4_3

3.1   The Movement Is the Rhythm: Interview with Simon Barker, Drummer and Composer

Simon: There's so little understanding of a common language that you can employ
to really articulate what happens in rhythm. Talking about rhythm purely
on a theoretical level doesn't mean anything because rhythm is movement
and sound. Western notation pretty much always rounds things off to the
nearest something or other so, the real feel, the swing, the microtiming of
all these elements, which is what we're trying to manipulate, are not there
in the notation. It's very different to harmony where you can look at notes
on a stave and understand the relationships and almost hear it. You can't
read rhythm, you can't feel it by looking at it, you have to do it. So, if you
talk about rhythm on a purely theoretical level, it can quickly get beyond
the realm of the possible—it's just too abstract. The issue with rhythm is
how you manage this idea of communicating things, which seem simple
but actually require bodily knowledge to manipulate.

So, rhythm is movement and there's a few ways to understand that. All of
them, to me, require some level of connection between body motion, natural movement and rhythmic results. At the moment, there's a lot of focus
on microtiming or expressive timing. I guess in the mainstream you hear
it mostly in R&B music and contemporary Hip Hop where there's slight
micro adjustments to the way the beat is divided up. You can try and understand microtiming theoretically but there's another way—understanding
microtiming through movement. Body pendulums of different lengths produce different microtiming results. So, you can understand how to manipulate rhythm through simple body pendulums and you can get it down to
extremely fine microtiming differences.

Another way of understanding rhythm as movement is thinking about
attaching body motions to certain places within the beat. So if it's the down
beat, it literally feels like it's down. If it's in the middle of the pulse it
feels like it's up. If it's just before the next pulse, like the last sixteenth
note, it feels like you're falling forward and so if you practise rhythm with
these very specific movements in mind you're attaching a motion to it. That
means it's not just an abstraction to which you're trying to attach a feeling.
You have definite body motions that you can work on in order to develop a
deeper understanding of a particular place within the pulse.

A third way of understanding rhythm is through understanding the way
people move when they play certain kinds of music, such as Korean music.
There's certain movements that you find common to certain rhythms and
if you understand the movement it's like you understand the rhythm. The
movement is the rhythm.

For example, in Korea there's a piece called Tasūrūm. It's a common fundamental farmer's music rhythm. And when people talk about it, they talk
about it as a cycle. For example, if you imagine a circle facing outwards

from your body and the down beat is at six o'clock and there's a high note which is around two o'clock and then there's a skip note which happens at around five o'clock. Really the only way to understand this rhythm is to be in motion with the other musicians. When you learn it, you learn it theoretically in a pulse of three but when you play it it has nothing to do with that. It's a different feeling and it comes from this cyclic movement. It's fascinating—you can get people who have never played the drums to sing this rhythm if they all get in the same motion together.

You see the same thing in African-American music too, so whether it's R&B or soul music or jazz, there's a motion. Whether you call it swing or groove or feel—if you discount the body motion, the movement that lead to it, I think you're missing a core element of the whole thing. I think in the west we separate rhythm and movement as if the movement is somehow hierarchically inferior to the rhythmic material. These days that idea is shifting. The movement may actually be the primary access point to understanding how the rhythm works.

If you watch me perform, the motion when I play is very organised. It's not just body motion. It's a complete technical approach. So, from every aspect of how I pick up a drumstick, and drop it, to using my feet—every element of that has been slowly developed to ensure that the motion is natural. I'm trying to remove myself from the action of making a sound. Any slight movement that's not natural I try and get rid of it. It's a really slow process. The broad picture may be just of a body moving but it's all about how you produce sound on a very micro, technical level. You don't have to know that if you're listening but the primary element is removal of the self from making a sound.

A lot of what people do with rhythm is to make the listener hear it in a certain way by doing something that forces the listener to hear the rhythmic structures that certain way. For example, manipulating hemiola[1] can create the illusion of two simultaneous pulses, or a constant shifting from one pulse rate to another. Sometimes, as a performer, you're trying to make people feel like they know what's going on but you're actually doing something else that at some point will create an uncertainty, and then in that uncertainty is the aesthetic experience and physical feeling into which you're trying to draw the audience.

For me the Shaman music traditions, a lot of the music from South America, much of the music from Africa and the great African-American jazz drummers is about these illusions where you're just not sure what's going on, and that's the beauty of it. There's a mystery but it's conscious. They're trying not to give you all the information in a way that you can understand. There's an uncertainty, it's a middle ground, it's an illusion, but it's conscious. For me, manipulating those illusions is what rhythm can do. Harmony can do

---

[1] Hemiola refers to three beats of equal value occurring in the time normally occupied by two beats.

certain things and create certain emotions but rhythm can do something else.

When I'm composing, I write a piece in my head and then I improvise with it. The idea of the piece is transitions from one thought to another and how you manage them in a way that produces certain kinds of effects. So, it's not so much the material, it's what shapes you can create that work certain kinds of feelings—feelings of just not being sure about what anything is. There's a tendency to want to show what it is, especially if it's complicated. You want to say, "hey, look at this amazing thing", but for me, that produces music that is not as interesting. So, the problem is trying to find the mystery and the way of transitioning from one thing to another. It's like a puzzle, learning how to do it with new language.

A few years ago, I started putting a whole range of drum set vocabulary studies online as a source for drummers to learn about some of the rhythmic areas I was having fun with. It was a really eye-opening experience. Because it's very complicated and the only way to write it is in a way that looks complicated. So, if you're not sure what you're trying to do with it, it gets confusing and can lead to an interpretation that is removed from the physicality of playing the material. It can quickly turn into complex "mind knowledge", instead of remaining as a form of "body knowledge". To me, communicating things as embodied rhythm happens one conversation at a time. Simply uploading materials as notation without that deeper conversation into movement can lead to a lot of confusion.

Some people spent a lot of time trying to do it but they didn't know what the idea was. For me there is a very clear idea of what the materials could be but for other people there was a real disconnect. They were working on this stuff without any sense of what it could be. It was just purely language with no aesthetic attached. Now that's fine, but I'm not sure how positive that is as a thing to offer. I don't feel that part of my process is telling people what the language is. If by chance there is some interest in some of the materials, I feel much better about communicating rhythmic things as a form of action and embodied practice, with other forms of transmission coming in once the material has been communicated on a physical level.

I'm working in a university and my job has a research component. A lot of my research is trying to communicate the processes I employ developing these languages around rhythm. But the idea is not to teach people the thing that I do: it's to show ways of developing process. So, the point is not for them to learn my process, it's to know that developmental processes work and provide some templates for developing your own. To say, here's a way of organising yourself to move forward with process, now go and do something different, not this. That way we can collectively share procedural knowledge but not content.

For me it would be horrible if someone just went and copied my material because there's nothing there. I mean, it's not about the notes, it's about how you organise them. But if they take the process and do something else? Well, that's really interesting.

There's all sorts of ways of moving forward with organising rhythm. Some of my ideas have come from studying in Korea. Like if you play something and then you add a note at a time to make it denser, you end up with a way to create complex rhythms. Likewise, if you just ram different rhythms together and then try a few different procedural things, ask a few certain kinds of questions of it, you'll end up with a whole bunch of options. So, there's a range of processes…They're more just templates for thinking about—if I hear something, what can I learn from it in order to do something else?

I love manipulating rhythmic language when I improvise. Some people may think that's not really improvising, but the sounds I like generally involve layers of rhythm—strange relationships to changing pulses which you can't just make up on the spot. So, I'm really into improvising as a form of manipulating language—constantly working on fundamentals then slowly bringing in new ways of organising rhythm and getting it in your body so that you can manipulate it spontaneously. It's a long slow process of learning to manipulate rhythmic language and rhythmic materials in real time. That's how I think about it.

I've got many ways of organising very micro differences in rhythm through motions. So, there's something I'm singing, there's a pendulum going on and there's some kind of technical thing. Once those three cycles come together, you can generate this way of working. They're kind of like entrainment studies, but with the music I play, I hope the audience can somehow hear the movement in the music. And if there are elements of phasing or ambiguity in there, I hope there is some kind of physical reaction to it…or even just a feeling of uncertainty. I like the idea of trying to bring the audience into certain feelings of movement, waves of energy, or tension and release that may be embedded in multiple rhythmic forms happening simultaneously. I love it when audience members have very strong physical responses to the music that I'm involved in.

3.2 Movement as Rhythmic Knowledge

Simon Barker's practice as a drummer has given him insight into the ways that rhythm and bodily movement are deeply interconnected. As he puts it, rhythm is "an action based thing" and can only be understood and communicated by experiencing it physically and performing it with your body in some way. Another musician, trumpeter Roger Mills, echoes this, telling me that you can't fully understand a rhythm and be able to perform it "until you feel yourself physically experiencing it." Both musicians regard rhythm as something that cannot be understood abstractly or intellectually, arguing that the knowledges within rhythm need to be understood through the moving body. Similar ideas are expressed by Tiger Roholt in his book *Groove: A Phenomenology of Rhythmic Nuance*. Roholt argues the incidental rhythmic movements made by musicians when playing their instrument, movements like foot tapping, swaying or finger snapping, are an active mode of rhythmic listening. The musicians are "moving to the music's pulse in order to grasp the rhythm" (2014, p. 87). The incidental movements are not needed to produce sound but are a way of hearing the grooves that they, and perhaps fellow musicians, are producing. The movements are not a passive effect of the rhythms in the music, that is it is not a case of the music making the musicians move. Rather, they are an active way of understanding and "fleshing out" the grooves (ibid., p. 6).

Neuroscientists have known for a long time that there is a connection between rhythm perception in music and the same parts of the human brain that are activated in order to move the body. More recent research has shown that this is not just a matter of an external rhythm causing the body to move (or to feel like it is moving). It is a dynamic multi-sensory relationship where "listening inspires movement" and "moving guides and informs listening" (Phillips-Silver and Trainor 2007, p. 534). One study that illustrates this relationship was conducted where non-musician participants were given different movements to perform while listening to an ambiguously accented rhythmic structure. The rhythm of the movements they made influenced not just their interpretation of accents in the rhythm they moved to, but also their interpretation of accents in similar rhythms they heard afterwards. The researchers concluded that "movement can determine the beat that we hear and feel" (ibid., p. 544). Another study compared the perceptual skills of trained percussionists, DJs and non-musicians. They were all asked to perform a task that involved memorising and recalling a rhythm. This was the kind of task that musicians who are not percussionists can find difficult to do. The DJs performed as well as the trained percussionists, their enhanced perceptual skill being attributed to the movements they made as they practiced their craft, mixing and matching beats across turntables. For all participants, if they were prevented from moving while they performed the task, their perceptual abilities were reduced. Bodily movement, then, was found to play an important role in developing the skill involved in rhythmic perception. It also worked to reinforce the perception of a rhythm and aid its recall (Butler and Trainor 2015, p. 128).

When we experience a musical rhythm, the bodily movements involved extend beyond the arms, limbs, torso or head. As dancer Andrea Olsen points out, sound "resonates in all the body tissues" and vibrates through our bones (Olsen and McHose 2014, p. 105). Similarly, the rhythmic bodily intelligence that Kodwo Eshun describes in the quote at the start of this chapter includes the muscles, joints and, as he later writes, also the skin:

> …there's often a lot of sounds where the percussion is too distributed, too motile, too mobile for the ear to grasp as a solid sound. And once the ear stops grasping this solid sound the sound very quickly travels to the skin instead - and the skin starts to hear it for you. (1998, p. 181)

When we hear with our skin, says Eshun, we will describe music using metaphors that relate to sensations of the skin, for example, describing the music as hot or cold. Music and sound are not the only vibratory phenomena that can have this multi-sensory effect on us. The physical body can be moved by all kinds of vibrations and forces. Our tissues and bones shudder as we operate a drill. Our stomach lurches as the car we are travelling in goes over a bump. Our skin feels the pressure of a twirl as we dance. Our muscles contract as we watch someone fall hard onto the ground. And our perception of the rhythms within any of these situations involves the whole body actively in resonance with the world. When we watch other things move, move ourselves or feel our body being moved by the forces of gravity, magnetism or inertia, we develop knowledges about movement and rhythm. All these bodily engagements shape our understandings of rhythm and produce the kinds of metaphors we use to think about and describe our experience of temporal rhythmic flow in aesthetic forms (Johnson 2007, pp. 247–54). Thus, we talk of rhythm in relation to physical motion—it speeds up and slows down. We talk of rhythm as something that has a trajectory or path that we can enter or exit, experiencing it spatially like a landscape with points that are in front of or behind us. We also talk of rhythm as something that acts like an external force upon us: it can push or pull, make us float or drag us down (ibid.).

Bodily movement is also involved when players interact with digital games, whether they are using a computer mouse, game controller or touch screen. The actions digital game players perform involve temporally precise body movements that can be likened to those musicians perform as they pluck, strum, beat or bow their instrument. Digital gameplay movements have a rhythm and although there is usually no need to accent the beats within this rhythm, observations of game players show a level of bodily movement and effort far beyond that required by the interface or game;

...players reel and swerve, duck through tunnels, lean forward and grind buttons to accelerate, holding controllers in a vice-like grip. According to the simple flow of energies into and out of the registered interface, there is no 'feel', yet players demonstrate and report corporeal experience. (Newman 2002, p. 415)

Similar to the musical studies described above, if players are prevented from or made to feel self-conscious about their movements, the intensity of their experience is weakened (ibid.). Thus, whether they are mimicking the swerve of a space-ship or leaping to echo the movement of a character avatar, digital game players are using bodily movement to grasp the rhythms of the game in a similar way to musicians. Such game players will also use metaphors of bodily movement to describe their felt experience of these rhythms of control, for example, describing them as slow, fast, floaty or laggy.

There are parallels here to Simon Barker's description of the way bodily movement influences the perception and understanding of a rhythm and, crucially, the felt quality of the rhythm that is performed. He describes the feeling of a particular Korean drum rhythm as coming from the cyclic movement of the musicians as they perform it. As he describes it, this is a rhythm that can't be played correctly unless you have the right physical motion. The movement of his body as he performs the rhythm is "a core element of the whole thing." There are three aspects to the bodily movement involved in this description. There is the movement involved in producing sounds from the drum at a particular temporal moment and the movement involved that causes some beats to be accented. Added to these two movements, is the third type of movement (described above), the movement that allows the musician to grasp the rhythm as it unfolds. Without any one of these movements, the performed rhythm will have a different character. The knowledges involved in bodily movement are, then, integral to the perception, understanding, performance and experience of a rhythm. We not only understand rhythm through movement but also need to move in order to understand it; and the way in which we move will impact the quality of our experience.

3.3   Bodily Communication

The type of knowledges that we are talking about here are not the kind that can be articulated precisely using language or notation systems. This is because the knowledge is about and *of* movement. Any representation of such knowledge must mimic movement's flow and be able to accurately represent its temporal nuances. This requires a subtle level of detail about relationships, contexts and practices that is beyond the defined vocabulary of a language or the distilled symbolism of a notation system. As Simon Barker points out, you can't feel or read grooves and microtiming by looking at musical notation: you need to perform the rhythm and when you do "it's very clear". Thus for him, it is the moving body that can most accurately represent and communicate the nuance and microtiming of a rhythmic flow. Choreographer Yvonne Rainer came to a similar conclusion after allowing her dance Trio A (1965–) to be learnt by others from a video-recording. One day she saw a version of it that was "unrecognisable" and realised that the video did not transmit the subtleties of the dance. Next, she tried a detailed choreographic notation system, Labanotation, but again she found that dancers who had learnt from this score needed "not just fine-tuning but gross adjustments" (Rainer 2009, p. 17). Accepting the impossibility of transmitting the complex rhythmic practice of this dance through either video or notation she instead trained and named five dancers as "transmitters" of the dance. As one of the five dancers puts it, "learning and doing this dance" creates an understanding of it "that nothing you read or see about it can" (Catterson 2009, p. 11). Only the close proximity of live body to body communication was able to transmit the detailed kinesthetic knowledge of Rainer's dance.

This type of kinesthetic knowledge work is much more common than you might think and is often performed tacitly in professions where, unlike in dance, bodily movement is not so integral. For example, a study of the hand gestures and other movements structural biologists use in their work revealed that they use bodily movement to think through the movement of molecules and to communicate this knowledge to others. Biologists were observed using their bodies to "feel through the tensions, forces and affinities of their molecular models" and to test out hypotheses (Myers 2012, p. 154). If they had instead created a 3D animated representation of a molecular movement, they would have locked down a specific process and timing. However, because the biologist's theories about the patterns within the molecular movement were still being formed, a locked or fixed representation was not useful. Using their moving body to represent ideas was more useful because it allowed the biologists to experiment playfully with temporal flow and rhythms of movement. One biologist choreographed a dance to describe a particular molecule saying "there was just no other way to communicate the mechanism. I had to dance it" (ibid., p. 175). When dancer Nalina Wait speaks to me about "body to body absorption", she is referring to this process: the way in which watching someone move can communicate the weight, timing and rhythm of a movement and allow you to absorb that rhythmic knowledge into your own body.

We can see similar processes of body to body communication occurring in the way interactive artist George Khut describes how he teaches his students to think about rhythm in interaction design:

> I act out certain rhythms like expansion and contraction…I'll use my hands to talk about certain kind of rhythms…It's like dancing in a way…I'm communicating that things have a certain quality of movement.

George Khut's students develop understandings of rhythm as they watch him move, with these movements communicating rhythmic nuances that he cannot express through language. His hand gestures communicate metaphors of rhythmic movement that his students can then apply to their interface design. In another example, choreographer Suc Healey tells me how, when she is trying to communicate a particular rhythm to her dance students, she will first play the rhythm while asking the dancers to move the part of their body where they feel the pulse. Once the dancers have found the location of the pulse, she will then get them to find it in other parts of their body, adding parts one by one to build up a pattern of rhythmic communication. Her process focuses on developing a whole-body awareness of a rhythm: "it's not just tapping a foot. It's exploring, really embodying that pulse." The movements then become rhythmic metaphors that develop knowledge, as Simon Barker explains, by "attaching body motions" to a beat to provide a "deeper understanding of a particular place within the pulse". These body motions give the beat its feel.

Developing such a deep understanding is not a simple linear process. While learning how to bake sourdough bread, which must be shaped in a certain way if it is to rise, I found a YouTube video demonstrating the rhythm my hands needed to perform to roll and fold the dough correctly. I would watch the video and then try to shape the dough. If my bread failed to rise or I was having difficulty performing the rhythm, I would return to the video to watch again. Then I would try shaping the bread once more. Each cycle of observing and doing would reveal more subtleties in the rhythmic actions that needed to be performed until finally, after a run of successful loaves, I could truly say that the rhythmic knowledge was in my body and I no longer needed the video.

A similarly cyclic process occurs in Sue Healey's description of a moment when her student dancers were having trouble understanding and embodying a rhythm. She had shown them the rhythm by dancing it herself and they had then tried to dance it many times "but it hadn't gone in." What finally worked was making them sit down while she danced the rhythm one more time. This shift in role from dancer to observer drew their attention to the nuances she was trying to communicate and finally "they were able to embody what they'd seen visually and alter accordingly." What these examples reveal is the way that rhythmic communication involves cycles of embodied understanding, cycles of doing and observing. Moving from observer to performer and back again focuses attention on different details of a rhythm. The cyclic process also reinforces the idea that a rhythm needs to be completely embodied before its nuances can be understood.

3.4 Analysing Embodied Rhythmic Experience

If we want to focus more intently on rhythm in our practice as interaction designers, we need to find ways to analyse and evaluate embodied rhythmic experience. However, many of our usual methods rely on language (for example surveys, interviews or focus groups) and, as we have seen above, the abstractions of language may not be particularly useful or revealing in this context. A further possible methodological issue relates to the ephemeral quality of the lived experience. Rhythmic experience is not only intensely embodied but also has complex transient dynamics of all in-the-moment experiences and, as Hasty argues, this means it can't be captured meaningfully through analysis or measurement. We can look at the markings on a block of wood and experience them as rhythmic but, although we might be able to come back and view these markings again, "what we cannot return to is our experience of rhythm as we attend to the markings" (Hasty 1997, p. 12). Rhythmic experience is not contained in the markings but occurs in the moments our perception attends to them. Thus, we cannot say that rhythm resides in an object, however we can say that "an object holds potentialities for rhythmic experiences" (ibid.). If we do try to measure a rhythmic experience, Hasty concludes, all that these measurements can do is produce a new and different rhythmic experience.

Simon Barker's observations about his attempts to share some of his drumming knowledge online reveal similar frustrations. His complex notations of rhythms were too "removed from the physicality of playing". They were "mind knowledge" not "body knowledge" and led to interpretations far removed from his aesthetic intentions. After this experience, he decided that a better approach would be to communicate rhythm by first using "action and embodied practice" and only later, once this embodied understanding had developed, introduce other more abstract representations. This was because the abstract representations could only be understood by those who had the bodily knowledge to flesh them out. He notes that along with bodily knowledge comes an understanding of process. It is that "procedural knowledge" that is the crucial thing, Barker believes, that must be communicated about rhythm within his practice. This process and the "ways of developing process" are also the aspects of rhythmic experience that he finds most valuable in his creative context. With an understanding of process, people are more able to take his ideas and create something different. Even if, as Hasty asserts, it is impossible to precisely capture, reproduce or represent a rhythmic experience, Simon Barker's account points to some ways that rhythmic experience can be understood, shared and used to produce knowledge.

Ethnographers who study dance traditions provide another approach for analysing rhythmic experience. Their method uses a mix of qualitative movement analysis and what Deidre Sklar calls kinesthetic empathy (1994, pp. 14–15). One day, while researching a particular ritual dance from South America, Sklar tried to copy the dance moves:

> I imitated not just the formal elements of the basic three-steps-stamp-and-kick pattern, but the particular way that the men performed it. They bounced stiffly through the first three steps and then let themselves plunge more deeply into the stamp. The weightiness of that stamp created a climactic pause and then rebounded them back up into the flicking, syncopated kick on the last half-beat of music. In my own body, I recognized the dynamic of the step to be a chugging build up of energy with a final liberating intensification and release. (ibid., p. 16)

Through this process Sklar found she was able to develop a deeper understanding of their rhythmic performance, one that she emphasises could not have emerged from observation. This embodied understanding is what she refers to as "kinesthetic empathy". Developing such kinesthetic empathy is about participating in "another's sensory experience of movement" (ibid., p. 15). This is a method, then, where the detailed observations of qualitative movement analysis provide the "what" of the dance that is being observed and the process of developing kinesthetic empathy provides the "how". The method involves a cyclic development of embodied understanding, one that oscillates between observation and participation, similar to many of the examples we have already discussed.

Another method that provides some inspiration is one I have often used in my studies of the audience experience of interactive art, a method known as video-cued recall (Costello et al. 2005). In this method, a video camera records the participants' bodily interactions with an artwork. As soon as possible afterwards, the video is replayed for them and participants are asked to retrospectively report on the thoughts and feelings they had while they experienced the artwork. During their report, a second recording is made, synchronising their report with their experience video. Both recordings are then analysed by the researcher. This method is valuable for revealing some of the nuances of live embodied experience. It involves a shift from participation to observation when the participant moves from experiencing to reporting, however, it only involves one iteration of this shift. To adapt the method so that it is more suitable for capturing the nuances of embodied rhythmic experience, our discussion above suggests that it would need to involve more cycles of participation and observation. It would also need to involve the researcher as a participant in these cycles, in order for them to be able to develop the kinesthetic empathy described by Sklar.

I tested out some of these ideas in a recent comparative study of rhythm in game interactions (Costello 2016). During the first cycle of participation, I played both games so that I could begin to develop embodied knowledge of their rhythms. The game sessions were recorded in three ways: a recording was made of the game's audio-visual content; another recording was made of my body interacting; and a temporal record was captured of mouse clicks and key presses. Shifting to observation mode, I then recorded my immediate thoughts and feelings about my experience in a written diary and did this while watching the video recording of my bodily interaction. A second cycle of participatory gameplay was then recorded followed by a final observational stage of analysis. In the final stage, analysis also involved creating representations of the temporal record of mouse and keyboard interactions. A visual score was produced but, taking on board Simon Barker's comments regarding the limitations of notation, I also represented these interactions in three other ways: two data sonifications and an embodied performance of the visual score.

The data sonifications represented each mouse press and release as a sound. The first sonification mapped game action event durations to pitch and sped up the temporal playback. This representation emphasised the start point of each event and the rhythm of the intervals between them. The second sonification used a single pitch for each game action but played the pitch for the whole duration of a mouse event. In this instance, the sonification time scale matched that of the gameplay. This approach emphasised rhythms of action intensity within the data. The third representation involved an embodied performance of the visual score, using a series of finger taps on a table top in sync with the gameplay rhythms that were recorded. Physically performing the interaction rhythms as taps proved useful for revealing patterns of tension and release not consciously felt when immersed in gameplay and not obvious in any of the other representations. Together all three methods built a layered understanding of the gameplay rhythms and their grooves.

The choice of appropriate methods for research is always (and necessarily) context dependent and the methods described above are just one approach within a particular context. They do, however, suggest some principles that can guide the choice of valuable methods for analysing rhythmic experience. As a first step, choose methods that combine embodied participation with observation and plan to conduct multiple iterative cycles of these. Focus on the development of your own embodied understandings before analysing any abstract or symbolic representations. When working with representations of rhythmic data, experiment with multiple representational forms, and where possible, choose those that foreground temporal relationships, maintain the complexity of rhythmic flow and involve embodied performance. Involve research participants in similar cycles of participation and observation and analyse records of participants' movement in ways that allow you to develop kinesthetic empathy. Finally, remain sensitive to the ways in which each method reveals nuances and builds layers of interrelated rhythmic complexity.

3.5 Designing Rhythms for Moving Bodies

Discussing the drumming movements of his hands, arms, limbs and feet, Simon Barker points out that the different lengths of "body pendulums" will produce different rhythmic timings. The scale of the parts of his body, their flexibility and range of motion, all have an impact on his capability to perform and produce rhythms. No matter how much he practices, the physical dimensions and composition of his body will give his rhythms a particular character and, to a degree, limit the rhythms he can produce. Ignoring the possible limits of the body's physical capabilities, can create rhythms that are unable to be performed. As composer Andrew Schultz says:

> Sometimes the sheer rhythmic complexity or speed of something creates problems for a performer. You can actually do things, which in the composer's mind are wonderful and potentially possible, but for the performer, it just defeats them.

Andrew Schultz works with professional musicians and so this defeat is not caused by a lack of rhythmic expertise. Rather, it is a result of constraints produced by the relationship between the capacities of musicians' bodies and their musical instruments. For example, the sounds produced by wind instruments are constrained by the volume of air in the lung, while more percussive instruments like the piano are constrained by the speed that human muscles can move (Iyer 2002, pp. 392–402). Composing a rhythm that requires movements faster than human capability or one that does not consider the time needed to refill the lungs would, as Andrew implies, defeat his creative purpose. There is a parallel here to the way interaction designers must consider the physical design of their interface and its relationship to a user's physical capability. Thinking about this relationship in terms of rhythmic experience means that designers must focus on the scale of the human body, its range and speeds of movement, and the impact these might have on the ability of people to perform the kinds of rhythms their interfaces demand. Get this relationship wrong and you might produce an application rhythm that is difficult to perform, similar to the rhythms described by Andrew Schultz.

There are several ways in which interaction designs can get this rhythmic relationship wrong. A common one occurs when a design involves rhythms that the human body has trouble synchronising with. For example, there might be a mismatch between the user's perception of motion and the motion being represented on the interface. The motion sickness that can arise from this is a frequent issue in VR environments and first-person shooter games, with gamers swapping motion sickness remedies in online forums and telling stories of enduring hours of nausea to play their favourite game (Jellayrei 2016). A digital interface causes motion sickness because it is out of sync with the rhythms of the human body: the eyes see a representation of motion but the body doesn't feel it. Another common synchronisation issue occurs when designers change the scale and position of a familiar interactive element, causing users to have to adopt new rhythms of movement. Once people are used to the particular rhythm of an interface, anything that changes that habitual rhythm can be very disruptive and cause them to lose sync with the interface. This loss of sync can occur both when the interface representation changes and when the scale of the physical interface changes. For example, choreographer and filmmaker Sue Healey describes how shifting from a desktop computer to a laptop disturbs her habitual flow when editing video. The scale of the desktop with its large screen, and mouse control requires a rhythm of movement that does not easily translate to the smaller scale of the laptop and its trackpad. The different scale of the laptop causes "a lag that muddies everything." She loses the ease of her usual rhythmic flow and winds up feeling that she is "disembodied from it." The scale of the laptop is thus out of sync with the habitual rhythms of her workflow.

The feeling of being out of sync can also occur when there is a mismatch between the rhythms of human breath and those of a digital interface. If these two rhythms are not well synchronised, they can impede human movement. Composer and percussionist Bree van Reyk gives a good example of the potential impact. She describes listening to music while doing her morning exercise, finding that some tempos made exercising really hard:

> I thought that it was because I had to keep my legs moving in time with the tempo. Then I realised later, that I can move my legs separately to the time when I'm listening to music, but I have to *breathe* in time…If I was jogging I'd find that I'd set up patterns of breathing, like four steps in and three steps out.

Musical tempos that did not mesh well with the rhythm of her breathing made exercising difficult. The breath powers all movement and is not only a motivating force for actions, it also "gives accent… dynamic shaping, and creates intensity" (Olsen and McHose 2014, p. 155). I noticed a similar impact on my breathing while playing the 2D side scroller game *Limbo* (Playdead 2010). As my character avatar climbed ladders, swung on ropes and leapt across chasms, I could feel myself becoming breathless as if I was physically performing the actions myself. I realised that I was holding my breath when I performed any actions that required precise timing. As the puzzles became harder and the sequence of precisely timed actions grew longer, the end result was a breathlessness that gave an intensity to my experience of the game. Breath is, therefore, another bodily rhythm with which an interface might be in or out of sync. Breath may also be a rhythm that the interface augments, amplifies or works with to add accent, dynamism and intensity to a rhythmic experience.

Due to the limitless energy of the computer, digital interfaces can ask the body to produce rhythms at speeds and durations that are beyond our human capabilities. Although it would be a rare (and not very long-lived) application that went to this extreme, there are many ways that interfaces can play around at the very edge of these capabilities. Even if an interface has not been designed with this in mind, a particular context of use might mean that its rhythms are fatiguing and physically punishing. An example of this is the rhythmically repetitive movements required to type, move cursors and scroll during computer work. In a work environment, such movements can be put up with long enough for permanent damage to occur. However, in entertainment contexts, where consumers exercise more choice, such physically demanding repetitive movements might not be as accepted. A review of the Nintendo 3DS game *Metroid Prime: Federation Force* (Nintendo 2016) critiqued the punishing rhythmic movements its shooting controls demanded. The reviewer described the way the "claw-like position your hand needs to adopt" combined with "long, carpal tunnel syndrome-baiting boss fights" and left the player feeling like they had just spent a punishing "four hours with a grip exerciser" (Gillett 2016). Reviews like this suggest that as our bodies become more worn by the physical rhythms of our work environments, we might become less willing to accept new technologies that make us move in physically punishing rhythmic ways.

The limitless energy of the computer can also be used to expand the rhythmic capabilities of the human body. Humans can tap a single finger seven times per second at most because our muscles need to relax briefly before they can contract again (Iyer 2002, p. 402). These muscular limitations constrain all kinds of human movement. However, a computer does not need to relax and so can produce rhythms outside these limits. This is something drummer and digital instrument designer Alon Ilsar finds creatively useful. As he plays his digital drumming instrument *Airsticks*, he enjoys the way it allows him to play at speeds his physical body cannot. Ilsar calls this playing in a "space of impossibility". He can produce rhythms that can't be played on a physical drum kit because they are "just so fast that only a computer can play it." As an instrument, *Airsticks* expands his creative possibilities but, he says, there is a downside to rhythms that don't involve direct muscular interaction. Unlike a physical drum kit, *Airsticks* has no surface that is struck. The instrument works with two hand held controllers that register the angle and direction of the drummer's wrist movements. Therefore, it has none of the haptic feedback a drummer would usually get from the action of their drum stick hitting the drum skin.

Haptic feedback is something Alon Ilsar admits he does sometimes miss. In my interview with Alon, he recalls an experiment he once did with dancers. The dancers would hold onto his arms and accentuate the movements he made while playing the *Airsticks*. After a while they would start pushing back against his movements. This "felt really good" while he was performing slower less percussive movements because it gave him haptic feedback that felt like he was "bowing a string." Without the dancers, he had none of this haptic feedback, only the intangibility of sound and his mental model of the space of interaction. There is less detail in the information these can provide, much less, he says, than "the complex rippling effect that occurs when striking an acoustic drum", revealing how the muscular rhythmic contact of the human body with another resonant object or person is potentially rich with tangible embodied knowledge.

Such tangible embodied knowledge is a component of any touch-based digital interface. As with Alon Ilsar's experiment with dancers, the rhythmic nature of a particular touch action will have an impact on the felt quality of a rhythmic experience. Game designer Patrick Cook describes the way this can work using two of his studio's touch screen mobile games as examples. In one game, the input involved binary taps on the screen and this, Cook says, created an obviously percussive and foregrounded rhythm. In another of his games, the player keeps their moving thumb on the screen such that the rhythm is felt as more of a flow. There is a rhythm there "but you kind of melt into it a bit more—it's more of a subconscious feeling." As his colleague Ilija Melentijevic notes, the physical engagement of a touch interface makes it "easier for people to feel" the rhythmic patterns. With another mobile game that lacked such a direct rhythmic connection between gesture and action, Melentijevic consciously added a sound element to "compensate for that physical disconnection" and ensure that the player could sense the rhythmic patterns of the game. Touch interactions can, therefore, not only reinforce interface rhythms but the types of movements they involve can create rhythms and influence the felt rhythmic experience of a design.

A recent study compared touch, keyboard, tangible and gestural interactions using participants grouped into three age ranges, child, young adult and older adult. In keeping with the discussion above, the mode without any tangible physical connection, gestural input, was both the least efficient and the least liked. Interestingly, although the keyboard was the most efficient mode of interaction, all three groups said that for ease of use they preferred interacting through the touch screen (Carvalho et al. 2016). The study did not provide any firm conclusions as to why touch was the preferred mode, but it is possible that the reported ease stemmed from the way this mode combined tangibility with the most direct, unmediated match between body rhythms and interface rhythms. This possibility is supported by the results from another study that showed a similar preference for movements closely aligned with the rhythms of the participant's bodies. In this study two methods of non-tangible gestural interaction were compared: a 'point at the screen to click' gesture was compared with a moving gesture that mimicked the path and rhythm of an on-screen animation. Most participants reported a preference for the rhythmic movement. They liked having control over where they held their arm and the ability to move their arm wherever was most comfortable for them. Needing to hold their arm relatively static and aimed at a specific spot for the pointing gesture was fatiguing with participants reporting muscle strain and tiredness (Carter et al. 2016). The pointing gesture required a duration of muscle contraction that stretched the capabilities of the human body. The moving gesture was more comfortable and pleasurable because it worked in sync with the rhythmic capabilities of the human body.

Designing rhythms for the moving body, then, requires a focus on human scales of duration, speed and range of movement. Such design practice asks us to pay attention to the different ways that the body can sense rhythms, whether through sight, breath or muscular resonance. It demands that we attend to the ways that moving bodies can develop rhythmic habits and also attend to any possible disruption of these rhythms. Taking on this perspective means we might need to think about, for example, the way the scale of a child's body will generate different rhythms to that of an adult. Much like the experience of matching stride to a much taller or shorter person as we walk together, our interfaces might need to accommodate these differences or risk falling out of sync. These insights also apply to the methods we might use to evaluate rhythm in our designs. We need to acknowledge the way we move our bodies can be a way of developing new knowledge, a way of thinking. A design perspective that focuses on rhythm cannot be separated from the body and the ways the body interprets rhythm through movement.

References

Butler BE, Trainor LJ (2015) The musician redefined: a behavioral assessment of rhythm perception in professional club DJs. Timing & Time Percept 3(1–2):116–132. https://doi.org/10.1163/22134468-03002041

Carter M, Velloso E, Downs J, Sellen A, O'Hara K, Vetere F (2016) PathSync: multi-user gestural interaction with touchless rhythmic Path Mimicry. Paper presented at the proceedings of the 2016 CHI conference on human factors in computing systems, Santa Clara, California, USA

Carvalho D, Bessa M, Magalhaes L, Carrapatoso E (2016) Age group differences in performance using diverse input modalities: insertion task evaluation. Paper presented at the proceedings of the XVII international conference on human computer interaction, Salamanca, Spain

Catterson P (2009) I promised myself I would never let it leave my body's memory. Dance Res J 41(2):3–11

Costello BM (2016) The rhythm of game interactions: player experience and rhythm in Minecraft and Don't Starve. Games and Cult. https://doi.org/10.1177/1555412016646668

Costello B, Muller L, Amitani S, Edmonds E (2005) Understanding the experience of interactive art: Iamascope in Beta_space. In: Interactive entertainment 2005, University of Technology Sydney, Australia, 23–25 November 2005. Creativity & Cognition Studios Press, pp 49–56

Eshun K (n.d.) Abducted by audio. Cybernetic Culture Research Unit. http://www.ccru.net/swarm3/3_abducted.htm. Accessed March 2013

Eshun K (1998) More brilliant than the sun: adventures in sonic fiction. Quartet, London, UK

Gillett N (2016) The month in games: virtual reality falters, while Mario makes a play for the smartphone market. The Guardian, UK, 24 Sept 2016

Hasty CF (1997) Meter as rhythm. Oxford University Press, New York, USA

Iyer V (2002) Embodied mind, situated cognition, and expressive microtiming in African-American music. Music Percept 19(3):387–414

Jellayrei (2016) FYI about overwatch FoV and motion sickness caused by FPS's. Overwatch forum, vol 26 (May 2016). Reddit.com. Online: https://www.reddit.com/r/Overwatch/comments/4l79ti/fyi_about_overwatch_fov_and_motion_sickness/

Johnson M (2007) The meaning of the body: aesthetics of human understanding. University of Chicago Press, Chicago

Myers N (2012) Dance your PhD: embodied animations, body experiments, and the affective entanglements of life science research. Body & Soc 18(1):151–189

Newman J (2002) In search of the videogame player. New Media & Soc 4(3):405–421

Nintendo (2016) Metroid Prime: Federation Force. Nintendo 3DS. Nintendo, Japan

Olsen A, McHose C (2014) The place of dance: a somatic guide to dancing and dance-making. Wesleyan University Press, USA

Phillips-Silver J, Trainor LJ (2007) Hearing what the body feels: auditory encoding of rhythmic movement. Cognition 105(3):533–546. https://doi.org/10.1016/j.cognition.2006.11.006

Playdead (2010) Limbo. Video game. PC, PlayStation, Xbox, IOS, Android. Playdead, Denmark; Microsoft Game Studios, USA

Rainer Y (2009) Trio A: genealogy, documentation, notation. Dance Res J 41(2):12–18

Roholt TC (2014) Groove: a phenomenology of rhythmic Nuance. Bloomsbury, New York, USA

Sklar D (1994) Can bodylore be brought to its senses? J Am Folklore 107(423):9–22

Chapter 4
Daily Cycles

A game may be a beautiful object, with beautiful strategies and perfect balancing. But a game must compete with laundry, work, dinner appointments, and with the attraction of other emotional experiences. (Juul 2010, p. 7)

Abstract The previous chapter focused on the rhythms of the human body at a micro personal scale. In this chapter, we explore the larger macro rhythms of humans interacting with the people and environments in their everyday life. Our discussion draws inspiration from the design processes of architecture and the sociological method of rhythmanalysis. Both these traditions consider rhythmic experience across multiple scales and perspectives, including the intersection between biological, social and political rhythms within human life. They suggest ways that designers can approach creating applications that carefully consider the impact of interactions across multiple users and their associated networks of friends and family. The two traditions also give us some insight into the types of rhythms that can be created when digital technologies resonate alongside the linear and cyclical rhythms of daily life. An interview with award winning online educational designer Simon McIntyre, Director of Learning and Innovation at the University of New South Wales, Australia, serves as a perfect lead into the exploration of the larger macro rhythms of human interaction. Simon McIntyre has designed for a wide range of online educational contexts and talks about the ways in which rhythms of learning intersect with the rhythms of his student's everyday lives. Following Simon's interview, we explore processes for understanding the range and qualities of rhythms involved in everyday life. We then look at the rhythms of digital technologies and how they can intersect with, disrupt, augment or blend with these everyday rhythms. We also consider what it might mean to take on board Simon's key message—to design interfaces that allow people to interact at their own pace and with their own rhythms.

© Springer International Publishing AG, part of Springer Nature 2018
B. M. Costello, *Rhythm, Play and Interaction Design*, Springer Series
on Cultural Computing, https://doi.org/10.1007/978-3-319-67850-4_4

4.1   Let Them Find Their Own Rhythm: Interview with Simon McIntyre, Educational Designer

Simon: I don't think I've ever said the word rhythm to myself when I'm designing an online course—but for me it's really important because in education we talk about scaffolding learning. You gain new knowledge and you get to test this knowledge and apply it in new situations. Then you reflect on it so that you can build on that again. Often when we're designing online or any curriculum, we look at that cyclic rhythm of finding out new things, testing, throwing ideas around, doing something with it and reflecting. Then we take it up another notch in the next cycle. Learning is rhythmic in that way. In terms of the user experience in online courses—we tend to find that if we don't have a rhythm of where students know to look for new information, where they submit things, where they look for their feedback, it gets really confusing. Often, we would actually build in this rhythm of okay it's a new week, you know what's coming so you know where to go. There would be instructions that were really detailed the first time they did it and then we would make those thinner as we went. People just got used to navigating and being at home in the online space in that way. So, it becomes a custom in a way. It becomes like the village law of the people in that space because they know that this happens here and this happens here.

Another form of repetition is in the conventions that come from other forms of interaction that people are actually used to. With mobile apps, for example, people get used to what swiping one way means and what lifting things up from the bottom means, and so you actually carry those familiar rhythms into the way you present information. That makes a big difference. Some of the older technologies are harder to do that with but I think that's something that we need to consider as well—how people digest information, how they're familiar with interacting and finding information out there. We repeat that rhythm in what we do.

Completion rates of MOOCs [Massively Open Online Courses] are woeful. Only 10 per cent of people finish. I think that's because they're designing a university style course from beginning to end for people who don't work that way anymore. I think the thing is, from the student perspective, to not try and force one rhythm on every single type of student that's coming into that space. You need to provide the infrastructure to enable them to find their own rhythm. A lot of people lose interest when we try to force a rhythm on them particularly one that doesn't fit with all the other things they're doing.

What we tried to do with our MOOC was have a structure there for people who want to go all the way down to the bottom depth and apply the ideas and so on. But people could also choose the order they did things in. They could completely ignore things if they wanted to. They could pick and choose what bits to do, to look at, to engage with and there were many different ways to pass the course. Not everyone has to do the same thing. In that way, we let people build their own rhythm—based on their own goals, their available time and where the interactions led them, I guess. There was a flexibility within that rigid structure for people to create their own rhythm.

I think there's often a chasm between the designer's perspective on what people will do in an online space versus what people really do in that space. In the university setting, for example, if there's a fully online course, and say it's not well designed, people have this vision that because they put a discussion forum in their online space, everyone's going to be in there and it's going to be fantastic and it doesn't happen. Why is that? I think we've got to be realistic about the reasons and the motivations, about why people are coming into this space in the first place.

In our MOOC, what we found is that those who were active in the discussion areas found themselves. They found their own rhythms, if you like, in terms of who they hung out with—likeminded people—and they went through it that way.

I've done MOOCs where they've said, now go and say what you think in this forum. Quite frankly, I just don't think they'd thought about that very well—because think about the numbers of people in there! You can't really have a conversation because if you post something it's gone. You might be able to quickly interact with someone as they speed past but then it's too fast, too rapid to actually do it. They're trying to funnel so many people into one little thread.

I found it a bit disingenuous most times and personally I didn't really spend a lot of time in there once I went in and was confronted with 1000 different threads, some with one post. It was just a bit much. I wouldn't call it conversation because it's everyone just putting their flag there to say, I've done this. It's a series of single statements that might string together. That's why we made the choice to have the forum there but leave it up to the people who wanted to populate it. You could get by without even looking at it. We didn't care. That was up to you. What we actually found interestingly was that new centres were being built. People started saying "Hey any secondary teachers from Spain here?" There were regional, there were sector based things—"Anyone from Brisbane?" All that sort of stuff. Those are the things that grew and stayed there—versus things that were tied to what we considered were important learning milestones. It was more of a legitimate social construction I guess.

I got to know a lot of names in that MOOC because these people just rose to the top and they became the authorities in these areas. They were posting more than we were because they just owned it and it was real. I think that's why it actually worked, because we weren't forcing it in that way.

Although the modules in our MOOC had a common structure, the flexibility came in what people chose to do. You didn't have to do that before this or anything like that. We found some people just went through everything in a linear way. Other people watched the videos and did the activities in one module, completely skipped another module, or just watched the videos. This meant that, in a way, the rigidity went away. We didn't sledge people with reams of content. It was about core ideas and then you could build on it as deep as you wanted to.

The activities in each module were designed not as a summative recall of what you just listened to but they were all scenarios and self-reflection questions. They made you realise what you did and didn't know and what you were comfortable with and what your surroundings were. We organised responses to the quiz activities so that you got an individual set of recommendations for further reading. That might be a link to a great YouTube video that explains something. It might be an open access journal article. And you felt like it was responding to you.

Part of the feedback when you finished an activity was a report that showed you, not just what you answered, but what everyone else who did the activity answered in graph form. You would see that, wow, a lot of people actually think this.

I did that because when I did MOOCs myself, it was like, I know there's 17,000 people in here somewhere. Where are they? I had no sense of what it is. The graph would give you that sense of placement in the scope of things. You would get your recommendations and you'd build a library of the links that you had for each module that were relevant to you.

People really liked it. We got a lot of feedback from people saying it felt like these activities (which were just basic quizzes) were about them. Or they'd say, "I learned so much for what I do." That's what we really wanted the MOOC to be—that everyone could have a personal learning experience even though the content was built the same. The activities were a way of centring the content around them. You self-explored and then you got stuff that was where you needed it to be. That was probably the thing that went down the best with people who were doing it.

The course wasn't designed to provide the final answer for those people but to provide the launch pad—so now they know what they're looking for when they go off and continue to learn. I think that's what made it good for the people who went through it and enjoyed it in that way.

One mistake we made in our first iteration of the MOOC was to have a weekly email that said, "Hey welcome to week one. This week's all about this". Afterwards, we realised it was the wrong approach because we had designed something flexible but then, through these emails, we presented it in a more traditional linear format.

In the second email we never talked about week one, week whatever. What we did was post things in response to what was happening in the course. So, it was more, "Hey a lot of people seem to be interested in this particular topic. Have you seen this new thing that's happening—whatever it is?" We really tried to design something where people could establish their own rhythms.

When I taught online under-grad and post-grad students, I used to be very worried about a regular weekly rhythm, I really did. I was like—where are you? You haven't done anything—if, for example, by Tuesday there weren't enough posts in the forum. Over time I just started to chill. Because I started my Ph.D. and I realised that when you are under pressure, you know, you ebb and flow. It's all spikes of activity based around when you can do it, when you've got the brain power.

So, I sat back a bit and just let it happen and watched the natural rhythm. In the end, I learned when to give a little push and when to stop. I was getting feedback from the students saying, it's amazing, you're always there. But, to be honest, I may have been there a third as much as I used to be but they feel that I'm always there because I am able to co-ordinate my activity with them when they most need it.

What I'm working on now is moving away from the bums on seats for 12 weeks, or fingers on keyboards at a certain time, and really starting to look at the outcomes, bringing people out of their usual spaces into temporal learning communities—whether it's physically on campus or whether it's online—and actually try and let them find their own place. Shifting to a supported online open structure where the content is all there if they want it but we anchor that at key points through the curriculum to give guidance as well. We encourage them to work with people who are not in the same class, who are not in the same year and in spaces where there are experts they can learn from as well as the lecturer.

I guess my takeaway point is that we need to shift from determining rhythms for people to actually designing systems that enable people to determine their own. Because these rhythms now have to intersect with so many other rhythms of our lives. The traditional linear approach is like turning the tap on so it drips and people have to wait to catch the drips to get a glass of water. That doesn't work anymore. We have to make sure they can control the flow and get what they need.

4.2 Understanding the Rhythms of Everyday Life

As interactive applications become ever more mobile, their rhythms are becoming enmeshed with more and more aspects of our daily lives. Simon McIntyre suggests that this might require a shift in thinking for many interaction designers. A shift away from determining the rhythms of users, towards creating more flexible rhythmic structures that allow users to create patterns that are in sync with the rhythms of their everyday lives. To do this effectively, designers will need a creative process that can give them a detailed understanding of the scale and scope of these rhythms. Such design processes already exist in the design traditions of architecture. As my interviewee architect Joe Agius points out, the rhythms of the everyday permeate all thinking in architecture. When Joe Agius approaches a building design, he will focus on rhythm at many different scales. At the human scale, he needs to be conscious of not only daily cycles of human activity but also of seasonal and yearly cycles, focusing on the impact they all have over the use and experience of a space. Joe Agius considers the way a human body might relate to the exterior of the building and the possible rhythms involved in pedestrian movement around and through it. In an urban environment, he will also consider the relationship between the building and the rhythms of its neighbours and their human inhabitants. Then at a larger scale, Joe Agius will look at the experience of the building within the broader landscape. For example, he will ask of an urban building "How does it sit within the morphology of the city?" and "What does it overshadow or not overshadow?" For Agius, another important perspective will be thinking about the building as potential creator of rhythms within its environment. As he says:

> From my point of view buildings should always give more than they take to their neigh-
> bourhoods and their cities, and that's largely about how a pedestrian might experience a
> building walking past it. That doesn't necessarily just mean having a nicely detailed façade
> but it's about enlivening and enriching the experience on the street. So how does it do that?
> Obviously, a café contributes more to a street than a substation, so placing things on the
> street in the right way to support street activity is important.

Architectural design, then, considers rhythms at multiple scales, temporal dimensions, and perspectives. Architects pay attention to the way their designs might intersect with existing rhythms and, perhaps most importantly, actively consider their design's potential for generating rhythms. Interaction designers who want to create designs with a more flexible relationship to the everyday rhythms of users will need to emulate this holistic approach.

Another useful perspective we can draw on to help us develop design processes for understanding the scale and scope of rhythms within everyday life is that of rhythmanalysis, a method developed by Lefebvre and Régulier (2015 [1985]). Conducting a rhythmanalysis involves analysing the everyday intersections between the biological, social and political through close observation of individual, multiple and overlapping human rhythms. Tim Edensor, builds on this method in his 2012 book *Geographies of rhythm: nature, place, mobilities and bodies*, and describes how the value of rhythmanalysis is found in the way it can reveal not only what might be fixed by habit, or repeated through routines, but also the way it can reveal movements, dynamics, interruptions and the subtleties of their rhythmic qualities (2012, p. 3). For instance, a rhythmanalysis of an urban environment might consider:

> …the walking patterns of schoolchildren, the rush hour of commuters, the surge of shoppers,
> the throngs of evening clubbers, the rituals of housework, the lifestyles of students, the
> slow pace of unemployment, the timed compulsions of drug addicts and alcoholics, and the
> timetabled activities of tourists… (ibid. p. 4)

In each of the examples above we see rhythmic intersections occurring between biological bodies, social practices and political structures. The rhythms of the school children's steps are influenced by the energy of their youth (biology), the weight and type of school bags they carry (social practice) and the time of day that the school dictates they must arrive and leave (political structure).

Proponents of rhythmanalysis argue that it is especially useful as a method because of the way it reveals not just structures but, in particular, the "qualities of relations" between things (Nansen et al. 2009, p. 184). Using this method, rhythm generating spaces like the café that Joe Agius describes above can be analysed as places where different rhythms collect together and potentially co-ordinate or synchronise, as places involving "collective choreographies of congregation, interaction, rest and relaxation" (Edensor 2012, p. 8). One such rhythmanalysis, for example, reveals that the elderly can become out of sync with the rhythms of their neighbourhood after they leave the workforce, are less involved in caring for children and begin to walk more slowly (Lager et al. 2016). Another analysis compares the daytime and night-time rhythms of a public urban space, revealing differences in the people who move through it, the ways these people use the space and the policing of their rhythms (Schwanen et al. 2012).

Rhythmanalysis directs us to think in a detailed way about rhythmic intersections and relations between people, society and their environment. To think about where there might be a synchronisation or mismatch of speed and what might happen when these collide. The approach also prompts us to think about moments of flow as well as moments of disruption or blockage. Above all, rhythmanalysis points out the often subtle impact of social and political structures on rhythmic practices.

For Lefebvre and Régulier, a key rhythmic dynamic in everyday life occurs at the intersection of cyclic and linear rhythms, which they describe as operating in an "antagonistic unity" (2015 [1985], p. 85). Cyclic processes, like days, seasons, tides, heartbeats and breath, involve oscillation, rotation and return. Whereas, the linear involves repetition and has a temporal spacing that leads to a sense of trajectory and closure. As examples of linear trajectories, they describe "the fall of a drop of water, the blows of a hammer, the noise of an engine" (ibid.). Where cyclic rhythms mostly derive from the forces of the cosmos or nature, linear rhythms mostly emerge from human social practices. Their unity comes, in part, from the way each creates a measure for the other: the cyclic process of a day creates a measure for the linear trajectory of a work session; and an accumulation of work sessions marks the moments of cyclic return across multiple days.

When the two rhythms intersect, their relationship "sometimes gives rise to compromises, sometimes to disturbances" (Lefebvre 2015 [1992], p. 18). For example, we might compromise by dragging ourselves out of bed in the morning because our work day must start at a particular hour; jetlag might disturb our eating patterns and so we might force ourselves to eat when we are not hungry; or we might need to close the curtains when the evening sunlight of summer falls on our TV screen and disturbs our viewing. Cyclic rhythms, because of their association with nature and constant sense of renewal, are usually regarded as a positive force, whereas, linear rhythms are often "depicted only as monotonous tiring or even intolerable" (Lefebvre and Régulier 2015 [1985], p. 85). I think these are all useful insights for interaction designers. They suggest that we can create rhythmic dynamics in our designs by combining linear completion and cyclic return, enlivening the monotony of repetition with the creative force of renewal. We can think about how to use the intersections of cyclic and linear rhythms as measures that might provide moments of stability or clarity within our designs. Perhaps most importantly, we can carefully consider the way in which our designs might compromise or disturb the linear and cyclic rhythms of our users' everyday lives.

Joe Agius describes this type of rhythmic design as a process of orchestration. He says that architects often need to:

> …orchestrate a public space, be it a park, or a system of streets, or the rhythm of the street lighting, or the street trees, or the paving pattern, or the sequence of main road to laneway to higher order road to mid order road, or the positioning of towers within a terrain or a precinct.

His process of designing multiple intersecting rhythms at different scales involves not only thinking about "how they rhythmically interact" but also "how they feed off each other." In Joe's description, this orchestration is about designing an ecology with rhythmic energies and forces that can be exchanged between component parts. Sometimes his design will focus on creating opportunities for rhythmic energies to combine and grow. Other times his design process will focus on blocking or containing energies in order to shelter and support specific qualities of rhythm. For instance, he describes designing a courthouse building where he deliberately broke down the usual "pulsating rhythm" of such an institutional building to create smaller spaces with a sense of domestic security and safety. In another building, a neuroscience research centre containing multiple laboratories, his design went against laboratory norms to create lab spaces that supported the social rhythms of coffee breaks and had windows to allow researchers working long hours connect with the cyclic rhythms of daylight. Getting this type of design right is, he says, about having a "nuanced understanding" of the ways people use and engage with the space, and of the specific rhythmic qualities that you want to support and shelter. Most importantly, however, you must understand all these elements "at all scales."

In his work on rhythmanalysis, Lefebvre also speaks of the way rhythms can be orchestrated, focusing on how social practices can control and regulate human rhythms. Lefebvre calls this process dressage, likening it to the taming or breaking in of an animal. For him, dressage is a process where the human body bends its biological rhythms to the rhythms of social practice, going through cycles of repetitious training that involve "duration, harshness, punishments and rewards". The "rites of politeness" with rhythms of please and thank you are but one example (2015 [1992], p. 49). Once trained, the body then repeats these rhythms even though they may be out of sync with its own biological ones. Someone may, for example, politely refuse the last portion of cake although still hungry. However, Lefebvre's metaphor of animal training implies a lack of human agency within this process that others have challenged. As Edensor points out:

> …the body also produces place as well as fitting in with it, and it may not keep in step or synchronise with regular beats. And while dressage may produce conformist rhythmic performance, it also has the potential to produce identity and scope for improvisation… (2012, p. 5)

Rhythm shapes the body but the body also shapes rhythm. Thus, there can be control and agency on both sides as well as opportunities for disruption or play. But whatever its character, the concept of dressage indicates that the orchestration of rhythms involves a relationship of power that needs to be carefully thought through, both from an ethical perspective and because the impacts of its design may be different from those intended.

One example of these impacts can be seen in a study of the temporal experience of twenty UK households. The study revealed that the increasing flexibility of working rhythms and weakening of the socio-temporal structures of family time led not to a sense of temporal freedom but rather to a desire to impose new personal structures of control in order to manage this new flexibility. Imposing these structures then, paradoxically, created tensions and challenges that resulted in an increased sense of the "time squeeze" they aimed to alleviate (Southerton 2003, p. 22). In other cases, though, regulation and control can be useful for helping the flow of different rhythms braid together. For example, the way that "traffic lights and other apparatus, speed limits, highway codes, laws, road layout, and the dissemination of good habits" work to control the rhythms and flow of multiple types of vehicles (Edensor 2012, p. 5). In the worst cases, a lack of control over rhythmic flow can leave one "diminished as a human being", as Small reports feeling when he hears music in public places that he has no power to shut out. He describes the experience as "manipulative, intrusive and domineering, like a pacifier forcibly shoved into my mouth to keep me docile" (Small 1998, p. 213). Trying to create a design that flexibly accommodates the rhythms of everyday life therefore requires careful consideration of the ethical and political dimensions of power and agency. To do this well, interaction designers will need to follow architect Joe Agius' advice and develop a design practice that provides a nuanced and holistic understanding of the scale and scope of the everyday rhythms of their users.

4.3 When Digital Rhythms Meet Daily Cycles

Asked to name a rhythm he has noticed in his daily interactions with digital technologies, Simon McIntyre immediately identified email as a common rhythm that patterned his day. At first, he described his daily email use as having a controlled almost repetitive rhythm. He wakes up, grabs his phone and checks "the things you check in the sequence you always check them." In the next breath, he admitted "actually I have no rhythm for email", and laughed as he said that "it rules my life." Many of us feel similarly, digital technologies take over the rhythms of our day, and this feeling can give us a sense of increasing busyness, a sense of life speeding up. However, as the UK study (described above) showed, sometimes the strategies we adopt in response to these digital rhythms contribute more to a sense of life speeding up than the technologies themselves (Southerton 2003). There is no simple one-way relationship of cause and effect between digital technologies and the rhythms of our daily life. The rhythms of any digital technology resonate in tandem with our personal rhythms, the rhythms of those around us and the rhythms of our social practice. All aspects of our daily lives intersect with the rhythms of digital technologies to produce multiple, layered and complex rhythms. The key practical issue for many of us then, is not so much speed or acceleration, but rather how to live with a multiplicity of rhythms across multiple and growing temporal dimensions (Nansen et al. 2009, p. 197).

Nansen et al.'s three-year study of Australian families identified a web of four rhythms patterning the experience of digital technologies within their families' every-day lives. The first rhythm they identify has the quality that Simon spoke of above, a constant and never-ending background drone of multiple streams of digital activity (Nansen et al. 2009, p. 188). These multiple streams blend work with leisure, blurring any boundaries between work and home, allowing work to spread across the whole day. The background drone of digital activity creates a permanent state of expectation that something might be about to happen, that someone might be about to contact you or that you might have to suddenly respond or act in some way (Nansen et al. 2009, p. 187). Alongside this expectation, there is often an associated compulsion to check, watch or listen. The compulsion is likened to the lure of gambling by one of the study's participants, who speaks of a constant sense that "you are nearly there" when surfing the internet, saying that this kept you engaged far longer than you wanted to and certainly longer than you would with finite media. With its "always on" and infinite nature, the drone can also lead to frustration, if the expectation of being able to access a constant, flexible flow of digital activity is stalled, falters or "misses a beat" due to a poor connection (ibid., pp. 198–90).

I would argue that there can be similar expectations, compulsions and frustrations experienced by those who create the media that populates the drone. For example, the way in which professional streamers on Twitch can feel a compulsion to remain live and online because otherwise "they risk having followers peel away to another channel." (Slotnik 2017). Whether you are a producer or a consumer, the drone is something that you can quiet but never completely silence.

Living with rhythms of expectation, frustration and compulsion creates the second rhythmic quality that Nansen et al.'s study identified, temporal routines that "typically started, stopped, switched and interspersed with each other" (2009, pp. 191–2). This start-stop nature of digital engagement was a rhythm noticed by more than one of my interviewees. For example, interaction designer George Khut speaks of an interplay between moments of engagement with digital technologies, moments where "you disappear into this thing", and moments of disengagement where you declare "I've had enough or I've spent too much time." Choreographer Rhiannon Newton also describes a rhythmic interplay but, in her case, this shifts between intense focus on one task and dispersed engagement across multiple tasks:

> I go back through the things that I have open and I do that a few times. Then I ask, what is it that I'm meant to be doing? Then...disappear into that and then enter back out into this screen that presents these various things to me and wander in them for a while.

Rhiannon compares the close spacing of this rhythm on her computer to the more distant spacing she experiences when multitasking around her house. Switching between tasks around the house has a slower rhythm whereas on the computer it's "all just there" and you can switch quickly between, email, Facebook and your bank account, for example. The close spacing of digital tasks makes multitasking both easier and more likely, leading to more opportunities for rhythmic interruption and disruption. However, as Nansen et al.'s study observed, people frequently attend to multiple rhythms at once and some are able to integrate these in a way that is not disruptive or distracting. For example, someone might eat dinner in front of the television and be simultaneously checking Facebook on a tablet and conducting a text conversation on a phone. Younger participants were found to be particularly skilled at this rhythmic integration and described enjoying doing it (ibid., pp. 192–3). The generational difference in rhythmic performance is something one of my own interviewees, dancer Nalina Wait, spoke of when describing the rhythms of her young daughter using a computer application:

> …the speed at which she [her daughter] will experiment with things. I might get it out and I'll go oh, that's interesting and I'll very tentatively look at it. Whereas she has already worked out how it all works and all the secret functions and has no apprehension about deleting everything or losing it or getting caught in a matrix of emails and passwords…

Nalina sees her daughter performing a fast, bold, continuous rhythm that contrasts with her own slow, tentative, halting one. What this suggests is that this second rhythmic quality can be experienced very differently by different people: where some will experience the process of integrating multiple rhythms as disrupted and uneven, others will experience it as a flowing, continuous intersection between multiple temporal streams.

The start, stop nature of Nansen et al.'s second rhythmic quality can be experienced in the micro-moments of engagement but also at many scales—across days, weeks, months and years. When it is experienced at these scales, the rhythmic pattern often takes on the quality of an ebb and flow, of a shifting between waves of densely intersecting and competing rhythms and quieter moments where the waves recede and allow a single rhythm to dominate. The same shifting patterns are identified in Southerton's study as "hot" and "cold" moments within the rhythms of daily life. Southerton's participants describe tightly scheduling events around these "hot spots" so that they could "create time for cold spots" (2003, p. 19). Where hot spots tended to cluster around timed events that were inflexible, cold spots usually had a temporal flexibility. For instance, his participants would schedule a range of things around the morning rush of getting all members of the household off to work and school. This would then give them some time at another point of the day or week where they could be "free" to "spend proper time together" (ibid.). Of course, these descriptions are experiential—to an outsider someone's cold spot may feel like a hot spot. However, what they reveal is that among his participants there was a common framework for assessing the quality of, and organising the rhythms within, their daily lives (ibid., p. 20).

Providing frameworks for this kind of temporal organisation is something interaction designers can also do, or at least try to accommodate. Simon McIntyre's description of dealing with the "ebb and flow" of his students' "spikes of activity" in an online course is an example of this kind of accommodation and night mode on a mobile phone is an example of a more structured design element that gives users the ability to organise the stream of digital rhythms in their lives. Given the increasing number of ways digital rhythms can intersect with our lives, providing such frameworks for temporal organisation should now be a key consideration in the design of all kinds of applications.

The third rhythmic quality that Nansen et al.'s study identified relates to the asynchronous nature of digital technologies. This provides a flexibility that allows people to harmonise their digital rhythms with the other rhythms of daily life, for instance, the biological rhythms of sleep and hunger, and social rhythms such as family dinners, or the "sociotemporal structures" of weekends (2009, p. 196). Some of these opportunities for harmony result from the way digital rhythms are often patterned by the same biological demands and social practices. For example, work emails will slow at night when workmates eat or sleep, and on weekends when they relax. Other opportunities for harmonising multiple rhythms arise from the temporal flexibility of asynchronous structures and the freedom users consequently have to take their "own pace" with the way they produce and consume each stream (ibid., p. 194). Users can time their consumption of certain technologies based on the way its rhythms harmonise with other rhythms in their lives. For instance, the way video-game players might choose short, less intense games to suit their work-life rhythms. As one gamer said, now that he is working he ends up "just replaying multiplayer games" because with those he can "get some satisfaction from a 'couple hours'" (Blyth 2010). Another describes strategising when to make certain moves based on his energy levels, saving important and complex ones for times of the day when he is "most likely to be focused and sharp", and others for when he will be "tired and just going through the motions" (Juul and Keldorff 2010). Other gamers find that the rhythms of "Let's Play" videos or the variable intensities of Twitch streams to be a better fit for the time and energy they are able to devote to games (Vosmeer et al. 2016). Simon McIntyre made a similar observation, saying that he doesn't have "the energy to play games or the time" so instead, when he "can't sleep at night", he watches games on Twitch. The types of participation involved in Twitch, E-sports and multiplayer gaming accommodate a wide range of different rhythms—from those involving actual play to the many forms of audience participation, such as heckling, cheering, commentating or coaching (Downs et al. 2015, p. 95). This, along with their streaming or on-demand nature, gives users the flexibility to choose a participation intensity and temporal rhythm that fits with the other rhythms of their lives.

The fourth and last pattern identified by Nansen et al. involves a similar kind of rhythmic orchestration to that described by architect Joe Agius in the previous section. In this case, the orchestration involves coordinating an individual's rhythms and simultaneously orchestrating the way they might intersect and combine with the rhythms of others. As the number and complexity of such rhythms multiply, there is an increased need for coordination. However, this coordination is made even more difficult because of the instability produced by the flexibility, disruption and endlessness of the previous three rhythmic patterns (2009, p. 199).

Orchestrating these rhythms is one of the areas where digital technologies can be very helpful. Particularly if they can make such rhythms perceivable across differ-ent scales and durations, create moments of rhythmic stability and provide tools for managing and regulating multiple rhythms. Far too often, however, applications ignore the need for such rhythmic orchestration. Simon McIntyre gives an example of this when he describes his experience of a forum with thousands of users, where the sheer volume of posts made it "too fast, too rapid" for meaningful interaction. In response to this and similar experiences, he tries to design in features in his own work that will give his users the stability of a "sense of placement in the scope of things." Game designers Patrick Cook and Ilija Melentijevic also describe consciously designing for moments of rhythmic stability. For instance, one of their games involved continuous fast flowing movement but also had "pegs" that players could "latch onto" and rotate around. Ilija describes how, although players were still moving, the pegs gave them a moment of pause, some time to reflect and develop a strategy for their next move. As we discussed in the previous section, when creating these tools for rhythmic coordination, a designer needs to be conscious of their potential impact on the power and agency of users. For, as a study into the tacit assumptions of health application designers found, it is easy to intentionally or unintentionally reframe users in ways that strip them of their agency. The study revealed how designers of health trackers saw their users as not just bodies that can be tracked but also as bodies that need and desire to be kept "on track." The point of their designs thus became to "nudge" users in ways that "relieve the stress of a person's choice", creating a user profile that assumed and designs that potentially reinforced a level of submissiveness and lack of autonomy (Schüll 2016, pp. 332–3). Simon McIntyre's advice to "not try and force one rhythm" on users is perhaps useful here. As he says, you "need to provide the infrastructure to enable them to find their own rhythm." You need, as performer and dramaturg Clare Grant also observes, to create space for the "separate beingness" of each user and allow them to set their own pace in relation to your design. You also need to follow Joe Agius' example and consider your design as something that can support, shelter, generate and feed rhythms across multiple scales.

We continuously negotiate a multiplicity of rhythms across our daily lives and interaction designs can contribute to these rhythms in ways that might produce a constant state of expectation, feelings of compulsion or frustration, and a sense that the flow of life is being relentlessly interrupted. However, interaction designs can also provide us with ways of orchestrating these rhythms so that we can flexibly manage moments of collision or intersection, orchestrate moments of calm or quiet, and regulate the competing energies of the biological, social and political forces in our lives. To have the power of orchestration requires a level of control and agency, and this is a power that needs to be wielded by both users and designers. As the example of architectural design has shown us, the key source of this power lies in developing a deep understanding of the nuances of the different rhythms in everyday life. Developing tools and processes for making these rhythms not only perceivable but also legible is, therefore, crucial to a design practice that focuses on designing for rhythmic experience.

References

Blyth W (2010) Re: Limbo's completion time—what's in a length? [Web log post]. Gamasutra. http://www.gamasutra.com/view/news/120445/Analysis_Limbos_Completion_Time__Whats_in_a_Length.php. Accessed Apr 2013

Downs J, Vetere F, Smith W (2015) Differentiated participation in social videogaming. Paper presented at the proceedings of the annual meeting of the australian special interest group for computer human interaction, Parkville, VIC, Australia

Edensor T (2012) Introduction: thinking about rhythm and space. In: Edensor T (ed) Geographies of rhythm: nature, place, mobilities and bodies. Ashgate Publishing, Farnham

Juul J (2010) In search of lost time: on game goals and failure costs. In: Fifth international conference on the foundations of digital games, pp 86–91. https://doi.org/10.1145/1822348.1822360

Juul J, Keldorff R (2010) Depth in one minute: a conversation about bejeweled blitz. In: Davidson D (ed) Well played 2.0: video games, value and meaning. ECT Press, Pittsburgh, PA

Lager D, Hoven BV, Huigen PP (2016) Rhythms, ageing and neighbourhoods. Environ Plann A 48(8):1565–1580. https://doi.org/10.1177/0308518X16643962

Lefebvre H (2015) Rhythmanalysis: space, time and everyday life (trans: Elden S, Moore G). Reprint (1992) 2nd edn. Bloomsbury, London

Lefebvre H, Régulier C (2015) The rhythmanalytical project. [Original publication 1985] In: Rhythmanalysis: space, time and everyday life. Reprint (1992) 2nd edn. Bloomsbury, London

Nansen B, Arnold M, Gibbs MR, Davis H (2009) Domestic orchestration. Time Soc 18(2–3):181–207. https://doi.org/10.1177/0961463X09338082

Schüll ND (2016) Data for life: wearable technology and the design of self-care. BioSocieties 11(3):317–333. https://doi.org/10.1057/biosoc.2015.47

Schwanen T, Iv Aalst, Brands J, Timan T (2012) Rhythms of the night: spatiotemporal inequalities in the nighttime economy. Environ Plann A 44(9):2064–2085. https://doi.org/10.1068/a44494

Slotnik DE (2017) Gamer's death pushes risks of live streaming into view. The New York Times, 15 Mar 2017

Small C (1998) Musicking. Wesleyan University Press, USA

Southerton D (2003) Squeezing time. Time Soc 12(1):5–25. https://doi.org/10.1177/0961463X03012001001

Vosmeer M, Ferri G, Schouten B, Rank S (2016) Changing roles in gaming: twitch and new gaming audiences. Paper presented at the DiGRA/FDG 2016—Abstract proceedings of the first international joint conference of DiGRA and FDG, Dundee, Scotland

Chapter 5
Playing Rhythm

> *Our fingers push and pull with the beats and pulses of the game,*
> *using the controller to develop a cadence as surely as a*
> *drummer does when slicing his sticks around a drum kit or when*
> *a pianist bangs out chords with both hands.* (Hamilton 2011)

Abstract When a musician blows a trumpet, a dancer improvises to a soundscape or a videogame player controls a character's movement, rhythms are being played. There are two practices of playing rhythm involved in these examples. There is the playing *of* a rhythm, that is, playing as a performance that keeps time to a beat or score. Then there is playing *with* rhythm, the creative playfulness of an improvised performance. Each practice will involve different rhythmic skills and embodied pleasures. Both types of play are involved in the choreography and improvisational dance practice of acclaimed dance artist Nalina Wait. Her interview gives us valuable insights into practical methods for improvising with rhythm and discusses the pleasures that physical performance can evoke for both performer and audience. These insights from the world of dance are valuable for interaction designers. Dance or music are often used as metaphors for the playing of and with rhythm during human computer interactions. Making a metaphorical connection between digital interaction and physical rhythmic performance might be easily done for games with their varied controllers, common focus on sequenced timing skills and consequently vigorous physicality. However, these metaphors of performative play can also apply to many other types of rhythmic human computer interaction. For instance, many interactive technologies will involve rhythms whose beat and timing we must learn to perform and keep in time with. Many will also involve occasions (whether intentional or unintentional and whether functionally impactful or not) where we might play and improvise with the rhythms of these interactions. And both these types of rhythmic performance will contribute to the pleasures of our user experience. This chapter focuses on all three aspects of rhythmic performance keeping time, playfulness and improvisation, and the pleasures of performance.

© Springer International Publishing AG, part of Springer Nature 2018
B. M. Costello, *Rhythm, Play and Interaction Design*, Springer Series
on Cultural Computing, https://doi.org/10.1007/978-3-319-67850-4_5

5.1 Activating Unexpected Events: Interview with Nalina Wait, Dance Artist

Nalina: I see rhythm as coming from a bodily place. As Emile Dalcroze says, rhythm originates in the body. It's to do with the torque of the torso and the sensation of that is the origin of rhythm. This idea of rhythm speaks to me a lot, because when I think about it, I think about the torque and traction of the organs in-between the pulses as being the motivator of rhythm. That space between the pulses is, I feel, generated through the twist in the body. So for me rhythm is a bodily urge to meet the pulse through that torque traction feeling in the body. And that's also about weight and it's about the tone of the muscles, about the muscles activating to shift the weight of the body. I think that gives a very strong kinesthetic sense in the body of the space between beats. The shift is instigated by the torque and you can feel the time it takes for the weight to travel before the impulse activates the torque, to shift it somewhere else. That's why partner dancing or having close contact with somebody is a good way to teach someone about rhythm, so that it's not just leaving it up to the person to see the rhythm and take it in and try and move their body. But you are actually moving their bodies, so they get a sense of weight. If you hold them and dance so they feel the transference of weight, they get a good sense of rhythm.

Rhythm underpins everything I do. I feel like improvisational impulses come from that feeling of rhythm across time and space. There might be an impulse to do something that's a change. But that occurs in relation to the rhythm of the whole thing that is unfolding. It feels like there is a moment where I feel in my body it is time to make a change. Or it's time to resist a change that is arising. So, rhythm is the framework for the whole thing, although it might be stretched or worked against, because of the tension that it provides. To pull against the rhythm and suspend the moment before meeting the rhythm—it's a useful way to build up a sense of tension for me in terms of a connection to the composition of the work. It's interesting, I think, for people to see a moment they recognise arrive, then transition and then arrive in some other ways—coming together like a picture that starts to make sense. I think that is a definite rhythm that audiences appreciate the satisfaction of. It's very useful compositionally because it's cohesive—having moments of satisfaction is really pleasurable for an audience and also just lands the work. Laughter can also be useful, because improvised dance can get really serious. It's a release in the body to laugh or to feel that you are allowed to laugh or, as an audience member, to not feel that you are supposed to take everything very seriously, but to open up a space where laughter is allowed. I think that's just part of the palette and it's really very useful and refreshing. Building something up and then releasing it, that's a very satisfying rhythm.

Another one of the main things I'm working with is the rhythmic experience of the audience—the rhythm as a framework for the whole dance improvisation. I don't mean a regular rhythm. It might be irregular and punctuated in different ways, but there is a sense of cohesion to draw the audience into the feeling in their bodies about when something needs to happen. There is this satisfaction of getting it or the surprise of something else happening that they weren't expecting. So just working with ways of pulling the audience's body impulses into the scenario. Improvised dance really operates on that level of body to body communication. So, if you are watching an improvisation and you get sensations in your own body that you want to move or respond in different ways, then it's really operating well for you as an audience member. And that feeling really comes from the sensation of the torque or the impulse drive in the body.

In an improvisation, a lot of the time the work is actually about waking yourself up and about waking the audience up—about activating unexpected events. Even on a micro level, trying to play with unexpected rhythms or setting up a rhythm and then shifting it in an unexpected way can be successful—or it feels that way in my sensory experience of doing it, because I feel like I get to surprise myself and also hopefully surprise the audience. That's just a way of working that I've trained myself to do. I'm always looking for strategies to surprise myself, really. To get underneath my own prediction of what might happen next. But as Jonathan Burrows [the choreographer] says "Break the rules on a need to break the rules basis". So, if you are breaking particular traditions or rules, it needs some kind of purpose. Either it's to wake something up or to reveal something or break something down. If a work is constantly breaking things down, it's not relevant anymore because there is no actual thing to begin with that was broken. You have to set something up in order to smash it. Or you can smash it apart and then put it back together.

I often work with improvising musicians and there is usually the ethos that the sound and the movement speak to each other and they communicate, but they don't always follow each other. They can also ignore each other. So, I don't necessarily go with the music. I think it's really great that it's there and that it is strong in its own thing. It can respond to the movement but it isn't accompanying, necessarily—trying to fit in with the movement or follow the movement quite directly. I prefer the sensation of the tension that's held in the space between the music and dance, rather than them coming together, collapsing too much on each other. Because improvised music is unpredictable, it's really exciting to work with.

There are some performances I do that are improvised and yet they're highly structured. I know that I'm working with this particular movement territory and it's going to transform into this one. It's going to move along that trajectory and it's going to amplify at this point. Some performances are particularly structured, but often I will do improvisations where there is absolutely nothing to begin with and the structure comes as the dancing happens.

Even when there is a set structure for an improvisation, all the tiny little decisions of when and how have to happen in real time. That is also in response to just feeling the audience—imagining playing with their attention—focusing, drawing, sculpting, shaping their attention. Because you can have that structure and you can feel like you are losing the audience and that something needs to happen at this point. I don't necessarily mean I want the audience to be totally attentive. I don't mind if people go into a dream state. In some improvisations, I almost want to create that, because sometimes it helps the cognitive mind slip back a little bit. They might drop into a more sensory experience that actually opens them up to experiencing the improvisation on a deeper level.

Sometimes, when doing a group improvisation in particular, there is a sense of waiting or creating a space for the thing to happen and trying not to impinge too much upon that delicate space. And sometimes I feel like it just goes for too long. I often have this big urge to break it or smash it or throw in something—some kind of wildcard—to make it okay to start doing things. That is often a space where I feel like things aren't working, when the impulses are coming, but people are holding back or if I'm holding back.

If I'm feeling the impulses and not acting—it's usually when I've thought about it slightly before the moment. It's actually almost happened then. If you've already thought about the thing that you were going to do and then you do it. It feels like—"ah, no, that was actually a moment ago that had to happen." Now it's past—after the fact or something. It feels like a residue of it. To me that feels like it isn't working rhythmically—when you miss the impulse…To go against an impulse is useful too, but it has to be a very deliberate awareness of the impulse being there and of not doing it. Not just missing it or feeling the impulse and not quite landing it.

I've done a lot of research in nightclubs, going out dancing. A lot of physical exploration with rhythm to music that has a much stronger musical structure; playing physically with syncopating with the music or going against the music… or predicting it—without knowing the song necessarily. With that traditional music structure, the beat is so obvious—you can feel it coming in the body and you know what is going to happen. I really love doing that. But it can easily get boring—if that's all you are doing. I enjoy exploring the range of possibilities of relating to rhythm. Even moving in a three, during a four-beat music or just playing with those sorts of different ways of going with the downbeat or with the upbeat or on the offbeat or the syncopation. That's what I tend to explore when I'm in a nightclub because that's really the only place where the music is repetitive enough to be that predictable in a way. That exploration then informs me when I work with composers or choreographers where the sound might be more of a soundscape. I can then play with those nightclub experiments against a musical score that is less predictable.

I really do feel that all that research in nightclubs gave me a whole palette of ways to physically respond or physically create different tones in the body, different textures of response to particular rhythms. To fall through them, to be really on them, to slide against them. Different ways to work with the framework of the rhythm physically. In part, it is about learning in a muscle memory type of way, strategies to play with rhythm. It's not necessarily a sequence but it is a strategy or part of the palette. It can become muscle memory, but it is also open ended in the sense that it's dancing as a question. As you are dancing, you are saying "What could I do now? Could I do this? Could I do that? What's supposed to happen now?" This listening to the body and the body going "now this" and then going "okay and now what?" So, opening up a channel for the body is a way of training unexpected things to happen.

5.2 Keeping Time

An enemy is approaching, and you must jump at *just the right moment* to land atop and dispatch him. A leap to a moving platform must be timed *just so*. Enemy missiles must be ducked at exactly the right time. Success at *Super Mario Bros.* depends on hard-won interface mastery and a sense of the rhythm of the game… (Costikyan 2013, p. 20)

A key focus of Nalina Wait's rhythmic practice, whether she is improvising or performing a choreographed dance, is the notion of timing, of finding and landing an action at just the right moment. She dances with a delicate sensitivity to the feeling in her body that it is "time to make a change" or time to "resist a change." When the timing of this process goes wrong, she attributes it to "missing" the moment or "not quite landing" the action because she waited until the impulse had crystallised as a conscious thought. The ensuing action then feels too late, like a "residue" of a past event. As choreographer Sue Healey says, rhythm "can't be half-half." It has to be "utterly accurate." To illustrate what she means she shows me a video of some student dancers who are rehearsing and not landing the rhythm accurately. For her, their movements have a sluggishness that is out of time with the rhythm. She says:

If they can't get to a certain point at the exact right time, it doesn't work for me. The rhythm is negated. The rhythm becomes out of sync. It jolts the eye and it jolts the brain. They could be in a different zone of rhythm and it would work…But they just weren't feeling anything. They were inaccurate.

In Sue Healey's description, the students' lack of accuracy is not necessarily due to their inability to hit exactly one point in time. There could be many ways they could play the rhythm and still be, as she says, in the zone. Their accurate time keeping in this circumstance is about being in time with the rhythmic feel of the work and amplifying or augmenting its rhythmic flow. Getting the timing wrong meant their performance cancelled out, overrode or interfered with the rhythm.

Learning to keep time with a rhythm is a skill that involves the body as much as the mind. This is something percussionist Greg Sheehan highlights when he describes really skilful drummers as "dancers" who perform rhythms "from their hips." He says that, although the "mind is involved," these drummers perform a rhythm that emanates "from the centre of the body." For him, it is the body not the conscious mind that leads and keeps time in rhythmic performance. This rhythmic skill relies on the incredible capacity the body has for memorising rhythm. Sheehan is constantly surprised by the complexity of rhythms he can teach musical beginners to remember and perform in his body percussion classes. As he says, "I really do feel it's like the hip will say 'yep hit me right there, right now'." The capacity for bodily memory of a rhythm is crucial for keeping time in rhythmic performance because, as drummer Simon Barker relates, you need to get a rhythm "in your body" before you are able to "manipulate it spontaneously." Once a rhythm is remembered by the body, it can then be recalled with a speed that will allow a performer to land an action with rhythmic accuracy. Such body memory and timing accuracy is also involved in rhythmic interactions with digital technologies. For example, when players learn the often extremely precise temporal windows for performing specific actions within a digital game. Players of the game *Streetfighter IV* (CapCom 2008) are described as knowing the way each "punch has a specific temporal window in which a follow-up move can be performed" (Ash 2012, p. 196). The performance of these punches relies on the same kind of spontaneous manipulation that Simon Barker speaks of. These players and other digital game players use body memory to develop the range of split-second rhythmic sensitivities they need to succeed in the game.

Our discussion so far suggests some ways an interface design might help the player develop and perform such rhythmic sensitivities. For example, an interface could clearly communicate its rhythmic feel so that it can be quickly grasped. It could actively assist the development of rhythmic body memory. It could also focus on keeping time with the physical capabilities of the player. For those applications delivered across multiple types of control interface, these rhythmic design parameters might need a range of different solutions. This is something Nick Adams, a design manager on the Kinect game *Puss in Boots* (THQ 2011), describes as something the design team needed to do when they realised that the gestural interaction they were designing for the Kinect required different strategies of keeping time to those they used for button controllers. Not only did gestures take more time to execute than a button press, but, because they were dealing with whole bodies and not just fingers and hands, there was a much wider range of "shapes and sizes" and "varying levels of coordination and mobility" to be accommodated (Adams 2012). To solve these timing issues, they made the interface respond before a gesture was complete, adding trailing rhythms of animation and sound to mask the pre-emptive timing. They also lowered the threshold of timing accuracy, accommodating a range of interaction timings. In effect, they were creating a zone of rhythm that players could move within. This zone made it easier for players to learn and memorise the rhythms of the game and more likely the game would keep time with variations in player performance.

Performing timed rhythmic movements successfully is about more than just body memory and keen temporal perception. It is also about having a sensitivity to the weight and energetic flow of the body as it moves through space. As choreographer Rhiannon Newton observes, dancers with a really keen "feeling for timing" are able to be "incredibly grounded, but also floating." There is a "quality of ease" to their movement and they are able, it seems, to effortlessly "land" the movement right in the "centre of the beat." Similarly, choreographer Sue Healey, associates rhythmic skill with performers who manage to have a playful suppleness around rhythm, while maintaining the clarity of their rhythmic flow. As Healey puts it:

> ...they don't always have to be just rigidly on the beat. They can meet it, they can pull away from it, they can syncopate. They don't just deal with the regularity of rhythm, they allow this play. And that's the magic...you see the flow of energy. It's just clear...

Such grace and ease in rhythmic movement is, for Souriau, also connected with play and the energetic flow of rhythm. While someone is moving gracefully, he says, the spectator will have a pleasurable sense that the performer's rhythms are freely made and open to any rhythmic variations. Graceful movements also have a freedom of purpose similar to play and this, he contends, gives them more rhythmic variation than functional movements. Lastly, graceful movements will appear to be free from effort and, thus, may involve feats of performance. He gives the example of an Opera singer trilling a long note at the end of a phrase as if there was no need to breathe. The freedom from effort and graceful ease such movements express comes from a sense that the performer is in complete control of the moment when the movement will stop (1983 [1889], pp. 89–91). For Souriau, a graceful performer is someone who skilfully controls the speed and rhythm of his or her movements, often deliberately slowing down or accenting them to show the spectator that "when he proceeds, it is not because he is propelled by impulse, but because he wills it and is in control of what he does as well as the speed at which he does it" (ibid., p. 94). Although there might well be physical effort behind graceful movements, these three descriptions all link skilful rhythmic performance with those performers who possess an effortless control over the speed, energy and flow of their performance.

Personal control of this kind and its relationship to the energetic flow of a performed rhythm is something that can be facilitated by an interaction design. It is also something that a design might get in the way of. This is an issue raised by drummer and electronic instrument designer Alon Ilsar. He describes an experience where he worked with a choreographer on the movements he would perform while playing his electronic instrument *Airsticks*. Ilsar found that being "told to move a certain way" could make him "compromise some of the sound" that he was trying to play. The choreographed gestures felt imposed and the self-consciousness required to perform them destroyed the freedom and fluidity of his rhythmic flow. His performance was constrained and he was no longer able to keep time accurately. Finding the right mapping between the gestures and sounds of his electronic instrument, was in part about finding movements that gave him rhythmic control and enabled him to perform with grace and ease. For interaction designers, Alon Ilsar's example emphasises the importance of giving the user rhythmic control and of ensuring an interface design does not block or impede the energetic flow of its user's performance. It also suggests that doing this well will involve focusing on the grace, ease and playfulness of the physical movements an interface might require.

Another aspect of rhythmic performance that can be useful for interaction design is the idea of rhythmic leadership or time-keeping. In many musical groups, it is often the percussionist who will perform this role, acting as a time-keeper for other performers to follow. The relationship of leader to follower is seldom one where the leader acts like a metronome, forcing exact rhythmic precision on the follower. There can be many types of control involved and all will be centred around feeding and playing with the energetic flow of rhythm.

In one type of control described by percussionist Greg Sheehan, the leader keeps a different time to that he or she wants the ensemble to play. Sheehan needed to do this when he was playing in bands with people who "tended to drag and lose energy." In response, he would play "slightly ahead of everybody" to create a driving energy that kept them all on time. Other musical traditions, for example African music with its complex cross-rhythms, have no single leader. Rather performers need to hear everyone's rhythm and depend on the whole ensemble for keeping time. African music involves a rhythm that is not played or heard: a rhythm that is created in the mind of the listener. This rhythm is the rhythm people dance and it is the reason that Africans will say that they understand a piece of music by saying that they know the dance to it. It is a rhythm that allows the listener to stay "steady within a context of multiple rhythms" and it can only be heard while these multiple rhythms are being played together (Chernoff 1979, pp. 49–51). Chernoff gives the example of an African drummer who, when asked to play alone in order to be recorded, complained that:

> ... he could not 'hear' his variations when he played without a second dondon [a type of drum]. He regarded the counter-rhythm which would tend to throw Westerners off the beat as the only thing that kept him on time and enabled him to hear what he was playing and to be creative. (ibid., p. 53)

Hearing a second rhythm would have made both his own rhythm perceptible and given him a structure that he could play off creatively. Thus, no matter whether it is played by one or many people (or by human or non-human actor/s), the role of rhythmic leader functions to make rhythm perceptible, providing the rhythmic energy and creating a structure that can be played against. This is an important time-keeping role that could be performed by the user/s of an interaction design, by the design itself or by the intersection between their multiple rhythms, and is another way that interaction designs can help users to keep time during an interactive experience.

5.3 Playfulness and Improvisation

A key aspect of Nalina Wait's improvisational practice is the creation of a performance environment that will lead to the activation of what she calls "unexpected events." In interaction design we might describe this process using the word emergence rather than improvisation. Either way, we are aiming to create a system whose rhythmic dynamics produce "new wholes greater than the sums of their parts" (Berkowitz 2010, p. 183). Nalina Wait's interview reveals how improvisers need to have an exquisite sensitivity to the possibilities of what might happen next. Developing that sensitivity is, she says, about developing a palette of "strategies to play with rhythm." Wait describes how she found it useful to first explore these possibilities within the predictable structure of nightclub music. This explorative play then gave her the tools to work in the more unpredictable environment of improvisation. Such live improvisation might be all about making split-second choices but these choices, as Iyer observes in relation to piano playing, "are informed not simply by which note, phrase, or gesture is 'correct,'" but also by the constraints of "which activities are executable at the time that a given choice is made" (Iyer 2002, pp. 408–9). Thus, both freedom and constraint, both predictability and unpredictability are at work during improvisation. As dancer Andrea Olsen puts it, improvisation is a process of "holding uncertainty" (Olsen and McHose 2014, p. 67).

One way that practitioners will *hold* the uncertainty during improvisation is to create constraints around the number of parameters they are working with. Dramaturg Clare Grant describes how, while teaching improvisational performance, she will focus on "patterns of possibility" and then use these to create a set of tight parameters that will "allow the inexperienced people to fly." In her opinion, the "tighter the base is, the greater the freedom." During improvisation, tight parameters will act to channel (but not block) the rhythmic flow of her students' performances.

Drummer and electronic instrument designer Alon Ilsar describes a similar process also involving a restricted palette. He finds that at first restricting his palette makes it harder to improvise but "once you break through that, you realise there's actually a lot more to explore." As Ilsar points out, one of the issues with computer-based instruments is that you are "at the mercy of possibilities." The looseness and large range of the palette on the computer can work against the creative expressivity of improvisation. Working with the constraints of a physical drum kit he finds he is more able to move quickly from the exploratory phase of "what have I got here" to the playful creative phase of "how can I get different sounds out of it." Thus, if you are creating an electronic instrument, he advocates reducing the number of parameters to increase its expressive potential in performance. As these examples reveal, there is a paradoxical relationship between freedom and constraint in improvisation, with constraints providing "the freedom that is at the heart of improvisation" (Berkowitz 2010, p. 180). This is because of the way they facilitate processes of playful investigation. Constraints quickly lead to a shift of thinking; a shift away from the *what* of a situation to thinking about *how* you might act or move within them. Constraints also give the performer a structure that makes it possible to make the split-second decisions required during improvisation.

Although constraints are important, working creatively within them will always involve a balancing act between closing down possibilities and leaving them open and free. For percussionist and composer Bree van Reyk this is "the real challenge". She says that you need to keep an improvised composition "open and free" but eventually it will need to "come into a structure that is repeatable and then can develop." A strategy that both she and choreographer Rhiannon Newton use to help keep this sense of remaining open to and playful around possibilities is to avoid or hold off going to the first response they think of. Newton describes how she will:

> slow down the very initial thing and notice all of the things that could potentially happen along the way of that pathway and maybe allow it to transform, or change or take on something.

Rhiannon Newton finds that this process really "wakes up" her system and creates an "aliveness" or "alertness" that she can creatively play with to produce choreographed structures during improvisation. For practitioners who work in design areas with less of a focus on live performance, many take a reverse approach, working with openness and freedom only after their structure has developed. Architect Joe Agius, for instance, will begin a design with a focus on the constraints and parameters he is dealing with. Once he has a grasp on these, he will then start to "fracture and loosen it up." The beautifully loose, playful visual rhythms in the buildings he designs are "arrived at through peeling away the rigour of the set geometry." Joe Agius's designs start with something fixed and then open up this fixed structure. Both strategies for working with openness involve creating a sustained flow of rhythmic energy by balancing freedom with constraint. Get the constraints wrong and you will "dissipate energy and attention" (Olsen and McHose 2014, p. 68). Provide too much freedom and the same will occur. A game where the rules get changed every five minutes, for example, will eventually collapse because it's "all play and no game, all release and no control" (De Koven 2013, p. 40). With the right balance of freedom and constraint, creative results that are greater than the sum of their parts can emerge out of the sustained and dynamic energy of a playful rhythmic performance.

The importance of sustaining the flow of rhythmic energy is an observation also made by interaction designer Andrew Johnston. Johnston creates interactive live performance systems for musicians and dancers and observes that those that work well to foster expressive creativity combine quick direct control with emergent complexity in a way that sustains the energy of engagement. His first step is to make the connection between a performer's movement and the reaction of a system "simple enough that they understand it straight away." This facilitates that quick shift mentioned earlier: the shift from investigating *what* a system can do, to exploring *how* it could be used. Most importantly for Johnston, once the performer spends more time with a system, they need to be able to "get more back" from the system. To do this, his systems work with the unpredictability of emergent complexity. Andrew Johnston's observations also emphasise the importance of sustaining the energy of this rhythmic relationship, with Johnston's phrase "get more back" suggesting that for expressive creativity this relationship involves a to and fro rhythm of energy exchange between performer and system. A theatre improvisation technique provides a clue to the way such a rhythm can work to sustain engagement across time. A common technique for training improvisers involves pairing actors and getting them to mirror each other, with first one leading then the other. As Uren describes, the rhythm of this process with its fixed leader and follower roles quickly gets "monotonous." When the actors switch to mirroring each other simultaneously, the:

back-and-forth process of constantly trying to correct what can never be a perfect match provides the dynamic action that keeps both improvisers in constant fluid motion… [without a fixed leader] each moment is the natural organic result of the moment before and the process sustains itself. (2007, p. 280)

The design of such sustained engagement and its emergent creative expressiveness depends, then, on providing a restricted palette that will channel but not block the flow of action. This palette needs to give users direct control quickly and provide opportunities for exploratory play. The balance between freedom and constraint in such a dynamic system also needs to involve an oscillation between leading and following. This to and fro then provides the energy that will sustain on-going rhythms of creative and playful emergence.

5.4 The Pleasures of Performance

Players dance, mainly with their hands, in response to games as choreographic scripts and it is through this dance that they derive the pleasures and frustrations of form. (Kirkpatrick 2011, p. 7)

Whether keeping time or improvising, performers and their audience will derive pleasure as they experience the playing of rhythms. These pleasures are what Nalina Wait refers to when she describes drawing her audience into "the feeling in their bodies about when something needs to happen." Wait is speaking about rhythmic anticipation and expectation but she is also speaking about what she calls "body to body communication." This communication, as we discussed in Chap. 3, involves muscles, skin, bones and any other part of the body that can be excited by rhythm. Such bodily communication does not necessarily require physical presence. As Iyer argues in relation to the affective power of music, whether heard live or on a recording, listeners have an empathetic sensitivity to the physical effort of performance. There is, he says, a "sonic trace of the body" in all performed music (Iyer 2002, p. 403). Such sensitivity to traces of physical movement has also been observed in neurological studies of visual rhythms. Viewer's brains show activity in regions that correspond to the performance of gestures an artist might have used to form the rhythmic strokes of the image (Gallese 2017, p. 13). Similarly, spectators of digital games, whether watching online or live gaming events, develop a keen sensitivity to the physical performance of rhythms of gameplay and can identify rhythmic skill within all kinds of traces of the performing body. An example of this occurs in a reviewer's explanation of the prowess and popularity of the pro-gamer Greg 'Idra' Fields. He describes how spectators are impressed by the way "on his stream you can hear the keys being hit hundreds of times every minute." It is not just the speed of the rhythm that impresses but also the timing nuance of its execution, the way "the pressure behind every clack sounds even" (Stanton 2013). For any rhythm based on human performance, this affective power of physical movement forms an integral part of the pleasures it might evoke in a spectator.

Performers of rhythm will also experience pleasures associated with the physical movement of their bodies. These pleasures will, in part, depend on the types of rhythms that the moving body is capable of producing. According to Souriau, there are three muscular causes of such rhythm in human movement. The first relates to the way we cannot constantly tense a muscle and, therefore, all muscular movement involves alternating tension and relaxation. The need for a "compensatory period of calm" after exertion creates a resulting rhythm of alternating "strong and weak beats" (Souriau 1983 [1889], p. 23). The dynamic of this rhythm will also be impacted by the way in which movements that require a lot of effort are performed more slowly than effortless ones. Thus, the speed we can perform these muscular alternations will also depend on the amount of energy we are expending. The second cause of rhythm relates to the way we anticipate a movement before we create it. For example, we will bend our knees before a jump or draw back our arm before throwing a ball. After a large movement, we also might make "a small movement which is like its echo." These anticipations and echoes create a rhythm of weaker notes around the attack of a large or strong movement. Lastly, Souriau says, we have a tendency to speed up repeated movements as our muscles get used to performing them, creating rhythms of acceleration as we begin to perform repetitious actions and rhythms of deceleration as we tire (ibid., pp. 25–6). These physical capabilities create a rhythmic palette of speeds, accents and dynamics that performers can play with to create a rhythmic flow of action.

How performers might play with this rhythmic palette will be influenced by whether certain movements are pleasurable to perform. This quality depends, Souriau argues, on balancing effort with pleasure, and only if the balance falls in pleasure's favour, will we find a movement pleasurable. This explains why we find walking on soft sand, snow, pebbles or slippery ice so disagreeable. These movements require too much effort for the pleasure they bring (1983 [1889], p. 10). In other forms of effortful movement, the pleasure of overcoming a challenge will outweigh the effort involved. Thus, he says, there is "the pleasure of climbing a slope, of pushing aside an obstacle, of clearing a ditch, of walking against a strong wind". A similar pleasure of challenge also explains why we find moving at fast speeds so intoxicating. Fast movements allow us a momentary respite from the weight of gravity that we constantly "fight" against as we move. In order to triumph over gravity, we "abandon ourselves to the whirl of a waltz" and "to the swoop of a roller coaster" and we do this "without restraint, with a certain disregard for ourselves" (ibid., pp. 5–7). This same kind of pleasure occurs in play theorist Roger Caillois' category of vertigo. He associates vertigo with the "pleasurable torture" of amusement park rides and a desire to "destroy the stability of perception." The intensity of this experience is also caused by the way the wildness and lack of restraint of such movements create a pleasurable feeling of "voluptuous panic" (1962, pp. 23–26). The effort here is more emotional than physical. The danger of the speed of movement causing a panic that balances the pleasure of weightlessness.

Another perspective on the human body's rhythmic palette and associated pleasures is that of dance theorist and choreographer Rudolf Laban. Effort plays a major role in his detailed model of movement which categorises effort based on the four fac-

Table 5.1 Rudolph Laban's motion factors and effort elements (adapted from Laban and Ullmann 1980, p. 77)

Motion Factors	Effort Elements		Quantitative	Qualitative
	(fighting)	(yielding)	(functionality)	(felt sensation)
Weight	firm	gentle	Resistance: strong to weak	Levity: weightiness to weightlessness
Time	sudden	sustained	Speed: quick to slow	Duration: momentariness to endlessness
Space	direct	flexible	Direction: straight to wavy	Expansion: narrowness to everywhereness
Flow	bound	free	Control: stopping to releasing	Fluency: pausing to fluid

tors of weight, time, space and flow (Table 5.1). These factors are further categorised into two opposing pairs, each relating to whether the movement can be described as "fighting" the factor or "yielding" to it (Laban and Ullmann 1980, p. 77). Thus, when speaking about the effort of weight, a movement can be firm and fighting against weight with its push or gentle and yielding to the weight. In the same vein, the effort of time can be sudden or sustained; the effort of space can be direct or flexible; and the effort of flow can be bound or free. An important aspect of Laban's model is the way he distinguishes between the observable, quantifiable functionality of a movement and the quality of its feeling or sensation. That sense quality is felt by the performer as they move and can also be communicated to an audience. In relation to this sense quality, the effort of weight is described as operating across a qualitative continuum between a felt "weightiness" and "weightlessness". Time is described as operating between "momentariness" and "endlessness", space between "narrowness" and "everywhereness", and flow between "fluid" and "pausing". It is out of the experience of these qualities that the pleasures of rhythmic movement will emerge: they give "mood" and "colour to bodily actions" (ibid., pp. 73–6). Thus, we can speak of "the 'calming nature of movements in one plane, and the 'rousing' effect of those using three-dimensional pathways" (Goodridge 1999, p. 134). Laban's model provides a useful, in depth palette of experiential qualities for designers of rhythmic interactions. Not surprisingly, it is already in use by designers of robotic movement (Knight and Simmons 2016) and designers of gestural mobile applications (Loke and Kocaballi 2016).

Similar sense qualities relating to weight, time, space and flow also appear in digital game players' descriptions of the performative pleasures of their play. For instance, a player describes sequencing combat moves in terms of their rhythmic impact saying that the "rip and spray of a Gears weapon is like a snare-drum roll, and the active reload is the cymbal crash at the end." Getting the timing and flow of this right is, for the player, "so viscerally, rhythmically satisfying" (Hamilton 2011). Another player describes the way the combat flow of *Doom* (Bethesda Softworks

2016) creates a rhythm that "feels rewarding and fun instead of repetitive and 'chore-like'" (Kriee 2016). This combat flow, as one of the producers of *Doom* explained, has a rhythm that intentionally combines the fluidity of riding a skateboard with the performative speed and variety of Bruce Lee's martial art. Contributing to the rewarding nature of this rhythm, he says, is the way that the game lets players improvise with these rhythms so that "you can play these spaces over and over" (Martin 2015). The visceral pleasures of such video-game rhythms often depend on a tight empathetic connection between player and avatar. Designers of the Kinect game *Puss in Boots* (THQ 2011) describe using this connection to increase the player's pleasure in their performed movements. They exaggerated and improved the rhythmic flair of their on-screen representation, thus confirming the player's biased view that "they look considerably cooler than they actually do" (Adams 2012). The player is then able to produce pleasurable rhythms with less effort and skill. In these descriptions, we see the play of Laban's four efforts; weight, time, space and flow. We also see Souriau's balancing act between pleasure and effort. These players are not just keeping time to the rhythms of the game, they are improvising with them and, in so doing, they are experiencing the pleasures of performance.

Creating interaction designs that focus on the pleasures of the physical performance of rhythms, asks us to focus on ways our designs can support the development of rhythmic performance skills. To do this we will need to consider how our users might use body memory, which movements they can perform with ease and grace, and who (or what) might provide rhythmic leadership. We will also need to pay attention to the flow of rhythmic energy and the efforts it involves, seeking out potential blockages as well as potential pleasures. Playful applications will need to balance freedom with constraint, if they want to work with the sustained and sustaining energy of improvisational rhythm. Playful rhythms involve an oscillation between investigation and exploration. Therefore, our users will need to move back and forth between leading and following the play of rhythm. These movements helping to create the pleasurable intensity of in-the-moment rhythmic performance.

This chapter marks the end of our focus on the way the human body experiences rhythm. As we have seen, this rhythmic experience will be shaped by the historical and cultural use-contexts of our designs. The way such designs choose to traverse and synchronise with these contexts influences their global reach and communication potential. We have also seen how the experience of rhythm is intensely embodied. To truly grasp rhythm's nuances, we must employ bodily intelligences developed through cyclic processes of doing and observing. We must also consider the impact of rhythm at both the micro scale of the human body and the macro scale of its intersection with the social networks and practices of everyday life. Lastly, we have focused here on the performance of rhythm and some of the pleasures this can evoke. Each chapter has offered suggestions for processes, methods and techniques interaction designers might use when designing for rhythmic experience. Many of these suggestions and themes will now be developed further, as we concentrate on exploring specific strategies for designing rhythms.

References

Adams N (2012) Using kinect for high adventure. Gamasutra. https://www.gamasutra.com/view/feature/163515/using_kinect_for_high_adventure.php. Accessed 11 Apr 2013

Ash J (2012) Technology, technicity, and emerging practices of temporal sensitivity in videogames. Environ Plann A 44(1):187–203. https://doi.org/10.1068/a44171

Berkowitz AL (2010) The improvising mind: cognition and creativity in the musical moment. Oxford University Press, USA

Bethesda Softworks (2016) Doom. Video game. Windows, PlayStation, Xbox, Nintendo Switch. Bethesda Softworks, USA

Caillois R (1962) Man, play, and games (trans: Barash M). Thames and Hudson, UK

CapCom (2008) Streetfighter IV. Video game. Arcade, PlayStation, Xbox, PC, IOS, Android. CapCom, Japan

Chernoff JM (1979) African rhythm and African sensibility: aesthetics and social action in African musical idioms. The University of Chicago Press, USA

Costikyan G (2013) Uncertainty in games. MIT Press, Playful Thinking

De Koven B (2013) The well-played game. MIT Press, Cambridge, Massachusetts, USA

Gallese V (2017) Visions of the body: embodied simulation and aesthetic experience. Duke University, Franklin Humanities Institute

Goodridge J (1999) Rhythm and timing of movement and performance. Jessica Kingsley Publishers, London, UK

Hamilton K (2011) The unsung secret of great games—and how some games get it so wrong. Kotaku. http://kotaku.com/5808033/the-unsung-musical-secret-of-great-gamesand-how-some-games-get-it-so-wrong. Accessed 28 Apr 2013

Iyer V (2002) Embodied mind, situated cognition, and expressive microtiming in African-American music. Music Percept 19(3):387–414

Kirkpatrick G (2011) Aesthetic theory and the video game. Manchester University Press, Manchester, UK

Knight H, Simmons R (2016) Laban head-motions convey robot state: A call for robot body language. Paper presented at the 2016 IEEE international conference on robotics and automation (ICRA), Stockholm

Kriee (2016) Re: Whoever came up with the idea for the new chainsaw mechanics in Doom 2016, thank you. https://www.reddit.com/r/Doom/comments/4j8s8j/whoever_came_up_with_the_idea_for_the_new/. Accessed 18 Aug 2017

Laban R, Ullmann L (1980) The mastery of movement, 4th edn. Dance Books, UK

Loke L, Kocaballi AB (2016) Choreographic inscriptions: a framework for exploring sociomaterial influences on qualities of movement for HCI. Hum Technol 12(1):31–55. https://doi.org/10.17011/ht/urn.201605192619

Martin L (2015) Doom interview: 'It's Bruce Lee on a skateboard with a shotgun': Marty Stratton explains what it is that makes Doom so special. http://www.digitalspy.com/gaming/e3/interviews/a655477/doom-interview-its-bruce-lee-on-a-skateboard-with-a-shotgun/. Accessed 18 Aug 2017

Olsen A, McHose C (2014) The place of dance: a somatic guide to dancing and dance-making. Wesleyan University Press, USA

Souriau P (1983) The aesthetics of movement (trans: Souriau M). [Original publication 1889] The University of Massachusetts Press, Amherst

Stanton R (2013) Starcraft II and the bad boy of pro-gaming: The short and sharp career of Greg 'Idra' Fields, videogaming genius and part-time offensive lout. The Guardian UK, 20 May 2013

THQ (2011) Puss in Boots. Video game. Xbox, PlayStation, Wii, Nintendo DS. THQ, USA

Uren T (2007) Finding the Game in Improvised Theater. In: Wardrip-Fruin N, Harrigan P (eds) Second person: role-playing and story in games and playable media. MIT Press, USA, pp 279–287

Part II
Designing Rhythm

Chapter 6
Being Swept in

Check for updates

> *… one might picture each of us and all of us as enveloped in a force field, a cloud of energetic probabilities and potentials. This field does not stop at the skin or at the nerve endings. It is unbounded. Should it encounter a different energetic system, which it inevitably must, they can clash or they can fall into synchrony with many variations in between* (Kaschak 2011, p. 11).

Abstract When users first encounter an interactive application, their personal rhythms need to synchronise with and become attuned to its rhythms. Any breakdown of rhythmic synchrony at this stage can leave users confused, distracted, frustrated or bored. Often, users can't explain this breakdown, apart from having a sense that the application "just didn't grab" them, and it can occur no matter how interesting the work's content may be. At the other end of the scale, the rhythms of a work can grab users so fast that they feel as if they have been taken over and possessed. An experience they might then describe as addictive. The rhythms of a beginning lead users into the patterns within a work, guiding attention and developing expectations about how these patterns might then progress. Their flow has an energy that, when combined with a user's rhythms, pulls the interactive experience ever onwards towards whatever it is to become. Beginnings sow the seeds not just for rhythmic progression but also for its potential resolution or ending. The rhythmic flow of the beginning of a work is also a key focus in the theatre and performance practice of Clare Grant, a director, dramaturg and performer. Grant is internationally recognised as a leader in the field of experimental theatre and has worked with companies across Europe and Australasia. Her performances experiment with the boundaries between audience and performer, and often involve audience interaction. Like this chapter, Clare Grant's interview focuses on the rhythmic processes of captivation. As she emphasises, this process is not just about grabbing attention but also about the quality of the way that you might hold that attention and then let it go. It's about being swept in and out. Thus, it's about rhythmically shaping both entrances and exits.

© Springer International Publishing AG, part of Springer Nature 2018
B. M. Costello, *Rhythm, Play and Interaction Design*, Springer Series on Cultural Computing, https://doi.org/10.1007/978-3-319-67850-4_6

6.1 Rhythm Is the Breath of the Work: Interview with Clare Grant, Performer, Director and Dramaturg

Clare: I've always leant on a definition of rhythm spoken about by Richard
Hornby.[1] I've found it so useful to help us think across whatever works
we were making—whether they were very traditional in form or super non-
traditional. Richard Hornby goes through five things: tempo; rhythm; duration; sequence; progression; and then he uses the word choice—how you
choose to make all those things work together. The tempo is the frequency
of events. Duration is how long each event takes. The sequence, of course, is
the order in which they come—because that affects the rhythm as well. Then
the rhythm is … I guess you'd call it something like the shifting patterns of
how a work progresses, or shifting patterns that lead an audience member
through the experience of an artwork. Progression is what it all adds up to
along the way—incrementally.

So, what does the rhythm do? I think it is that rhythm works with tempo and
duration and sequence, to create the progression—how you experience the
work and how you go through the work as an audience member. I'm always
talking, thinking, making, teaching from an audience perspective. Rhythm
for me is about experience—how the audience experiences the work and
what rhythms are engaged in that.

Progression has been really important for me with performers that I've
worked with, because I'm always asking them—what is the thing that's
being done? What's the enactment here? What is the thing that is taking
place? Progression is the word that articulates the fact that something is
going on and accumulating minute, by minute, by minute—and within that.
It may charge straight to a tight point, or it might revert back, or it might
actually be throbbing in one place for the entire time. That progression is still
determined by its duration or by its tempo and so forth. But it's still about
the thing that it adds up to.

Rhythm is like the breath of the work really. I was wondering earlier today
whether it was the machinery between the audience and the performer where
you can most clearly tell what's happening. So maybe it's a diagnostic spot,
but it's also what carries all the currents and the reversals, the forwards and
the backs, and the stops and the goes. It's often about, 'we've got to pick
it up here', or 'we've got to let them go there' or we must stop here'. And
that's about rhythm.

I'm almost experiencing the work through the audience as soon as I start
to make it. Certainly, in terms of feeling my way into the opening moment,
I'm feeling that through them. What's the first thing they see? What's the
first thing that happens? What's the first object and then what comes next?
How long are they going to stay with that? Do I click the next one in before

---

[1] See the Richard Hornby book Script into Performance: A Structuralist Approach, Applause Theatre
& Cinema Books; 3rd edition (2000).

they've quite finished with that, so that they slide forward? Or do you leave them to savour and finish it?

About 15 years ago I worked with some people who were making an interactive computer work. I was constantly asking them about how they thought about the audience entering the work. The whole day it was all—here's the button that you push and then you get this effect. And I kept asking, why do I want to push that button? How are you going to make me want to push that button? I wanted them to first set it up that I want to press the button, otherwise, I'll probably hang around, but I won't engage until I've been drawn into that point. They assumed that the audience would get in there and just get going, and yet I wanted to be led in first. I said to them, I just find it really strange how you work. About a year later at a big event, a couple of people from that interaction design group were there and they said, you know we've changed our practice since you said that and it's so much more exciting.

So, I think that a lot of the work in creating an original work of any kind is opening it out at the beginning. To think about what you enter into and what you set up at the beginning. What the receiver is flowing through, what information they're getting and when they're getting it—that sequence thing. Quite often, if something is a bit out, it's to do with the performers setting up something that they are conscious of but the audience isn't.

For instance, in a show I was working on recently with some young people, a lot of the rhythms were missing. It was because they'd started out making it with: well what will we do next? What will we do next? It was this mad adventure with all sorts of different pathways that it could take. It was extraordinary how much they were assuming. There were these big gaps or moments where the audience might know what was meant, but their emotional engagement was left behind because the sequencing of that information wasn't plotted as well as it could be. The performers needed to think about the rhythm of the piece as a whole. Fixing those gaps was a lot about giving information and about slowing things down using repetition and emphasis. They had to work with both tempo—giving more information—and duration by spelling it out. They had to basically remember they had an audience there. It was a very strong example for me of the consequences of leaving the weight of the audience behind.

Every single audience is different and that means you need to have your markers, your key points, your information and your sequence really strong, creating a bed for the audience to ride on. And that is about the rhythm of the audience and the autonomy of the audience meeting the infrastructure of the piece. It's also about how all the different rhythms lead you back into that infrastructure as an audience member. Because otherwise you'll float away and think about what's for dinner [laughs] and think, gosh I've got to come back. But also, it needs to be about understanding that progression—what is it you want to have had happen by the end of the show? Trying to understand, closer and closer, what that thing you want to have had happen is, helps you to understand exactly where your starting point is.

You need to think about what are the processes the audience has got to go through? They enter, they pay, they go. It's liminality—because you're passing through one thing and you're going into another. How do they pass through that point of coming in as an audience member and then being part of the world that's being set up? That crossover point where you cease to be an audience member and you cease to be an arriving audience member and you become a participant, or you become engaged. It tips—if it works. Then at the end, you've got the other tipping point of the leaving of the space as well. How do you then allow your audience to leave? How have you unhooked them again so that they can go away?

But the eddies and swirls of rhythms are different every night with different audiences and each audience member is engaged in their own rhythm. I approach that by allowing audience members to take their own pace with a work. I would try to find the core action that was going to allow all those different rhythms and not design something particularly for somebody. But I suppose, if I was thinking about synchronising the audience, I'd focus in on the action again. What is the action you want? Do you actually want everybody to be in that same state at the same time? Or is the action on a different plane, because it doesn't matter whether they are all in the same state.

In theatre, there are many rhythmic cycles you go through. One pattern is being caught up and then being aware, then being caught up again or being surprised and being aware. This is probably what you do as you follow a narrative. You get to know a certain amount and then suddenly, you don't know. Suddenly you're flying, not knowing. Then you get another bit of information and it might lead you here, or there, or somewhere else. I would always aim to be really aware of what I was leading the audience into and try to be aware of an automatic rhythm. I don't know that one can always be aware—but I would put it on myself to keep trying to fight back behind it, to undercut it, or turn it around or lean it a certain way. I suppose that boils down to predictability and where a scene is going. How far down there do you lead it before you say, uh-uh, we're not actually really going there. We're going over here. I would be aware of allowing them to be there and then turning them off, allowing it be there and flicking it somewhere else just a little bit different. You can do anything, as long as you know what you're doing with it. But I guess if the work and/or the audience is dropping into a habitual rhythm, everybody might be comfortable, but the work is not going to take you anywhere.

As a maker, you also sometimes need to challenge your habitual rhythms. There are lots of exercises you could use to do that. For example, Bisoku is an exercise that really breaks down your assumptions about time. I've met it through the body weather practice, which comes out of Butoh dance in Japan. The participants line up and face a certain direction. They're encouraged to create an imaginary horizon like oceans beyond where they are. So, there's a point of focus far, far ahead of where you are, but an equally strong focus far, far behind where you are, which automatically creates a sense of tension between the past and the future. Every millimetre you move forward, you've got to readjust those other parameters of forward and backward. You've got that task of moving forward, but you've got to move no more than a millimetre a second. Of course, it's a little bit impossible. But, it's that thing of just slowing it right down and holding everything in balance all the way through. If you keep your eyes focused on that horizon level, with your inner eye looking at where you've come from, it creates a really powerful present body, a body that's in constant tension with its past, its future and its shifting present.

I've used that exercise in lots of different ways. One way was just to give makers an experience of time that was different—that they might like to lead their audience into somehow. That's probably a predominant way I've used it. To make a piece of theatre from that balance position, you have to be in that position as a maker as well. As an exercise, it's also to help them re-relate or reorganise their relationship to their breathing, to their habitual behaviours, to their habitual sense that everything's going to keep rushing forward.

I like the theatre to make a space for me to think and for me to travel. That I guess is part of what the audience rhythm needs to be allowed to do. They need to be able to fly and come back and fly and come back, and at certain points find themselves all with each other and then separate. But they're all separate beings. Giving that separate being-ness space is probably pretty fundamental to my idea of what bringing people in public together should be about.

6.2 Captivation

Rhythm, for Clare Grant, is the machinery that carries the audience forward and contains the currents and reversals of a work. This carrying and captivation of an audience is something all creative practitioners aim for. We want our audience, in their individual ways, to pay attention to our works and be transported by them. As Clare Grant suggests, it is the breath of rhythm that does this transporting. But to be carried in this way, the audience first has to be entrained to a work's rhythms. They have to go through a process where their perception becomes attuned to, moves in sync with, the intervals and accents of the rhythms in a work, allowing the rhythms to be 'heard'. Entrainment is a two-stage process that involves finding the pulse of a rhythm and then cognitively constructing a relationship of "perceptual prominence" where some pulses are heard as stronger or more important than others. These constructed relationships allow us to perceive the flow of a rhythmic pattern because they create accented metrical structures that our attention cycles around and that produce a "rhythmic context of expectation" (Fitch 2013, p. 3).

Thus, a perceived rhythm organises our expectations and in this sense rhythm captivates us. It captivates our attentional energy and will do so even in moments of silence or stillness, provided we remain attentionally attuned to the "projective possibilities" of the rhythm we are following (Hasty 1997, p. 169). However, as with all things that involve energy, the entrainment process needs to be fed if it is to continue. Entrainment will collapse into distraction when rhythmic events are too far apart and fade into boredom when events are too repetitive (Emmerson 2008, p. 3). In the first, attentional energy is dissipated when it is shared across other events and in the second, repetition requires such a constant state of attention that it saps energy. The energetic flow of an audience's context of expectation needs to be factored into any rhythmic design process and is something that can be played with during a creative work to produce the expressive contours of rhythmic experience.

During rhythmic entrainment, the accented metrical structures that we cycle our expectations around exist only in the processes of perception. They are cognitive constructs that are related to the rhythmic sequence of events being perceived but are not identical to it (Fitch 2013, p. 2). This is because their form is also shaped by the rhythms that a perceiver is physically capable of hearing and the structures a perceiver has already learned, rehearsed and practiced (London 2004, p. 4). As Edward Hall describes it, this is a perceptual process that involves a "release of rhythms already in the individual" (1983, p. 178). Thus, designing with frequencies that occur within common human activities can be a way of speeding up the perceptual process of entrainment, because these are rhythmic structures a perceiver already knows. We see an expression of this creative strategy in the way that many rhythmic frequencies in music match those of physical human movements. There are the "dynamic swells associated with breathing, the steady pulse associated with walking, and the rapid rhythmic figurations associated with speech" (Iyer 2002, p. 392). These movement speeds relate to the first three of the four common frequencies that occur in music, which are 0.1–1 Hz, 1–3 Hz, 3–10 Hz and 10–60 Hz (ibid., p. 393). The fourth and fastest speed is associated with musical microtiming and the most rapid sounds and movements a human can make. Similar to the music described above, artist George Khut also deliberately matches the frequency of human movement in his biorhythmic artworks, designing with the slowest range of these frequencies. Khut creates ten second intervals between events to match the slow six breaths per minute of a very relaxed person. He does this to take advantage of the mirroring habits of social synchrony, hoping to entrain his participants to a similarly relaxed rhythm of breathing. To design with common rhythmic frequencies to which humans are already habituated, is a strategy for making it more likely that people will entrain to the rhythms in a work.

To be entrained to and captivated by a rhythm is a process that some describe as a form of possession. For instance, Robert Jourdain says that we are possessed by rhythm as we listen to music. This feeling of possession is most conscious when a rhythm makes us move and it is as if something "has entered not just our bodies, but our intentions, taking us over" (1997, p. 328). However, whether we are conscious of it or not, any perceived rhythm possesses our attention and compels us to attend to its flow. Jourdain links this sense of being possessed to the anticipations involved in perceiving rhythm and proposes that it can be the cause of consequent ecstatic experiences. When a flow of rhythmic anticipations captivates us, it creates a structured moving pattern of attention that is a pleasurable contrast to the usual disorder of attention within our real world. This ordered attention can then create a coherence that allows us to understand relations between things in a much deeper way than we do in real life. When it does this we might "feel our very existence expand" and even experience ecstasy (ibid., pp. 329–331). In Jourdain's argument, the control a rhythm has over the flow of our attention has none of the usual associations made between possession and a lack of creativity or imaginative thought. Possession is seen as the potential cause of an expanded existence and as a creator of meaning.

Ecstatic experience is similarly linked to feeling possessed by a rhythm in a David Kanaga blog post on the spiritual in games (2012). Although the ecstasy that he describes comes from a different cause, there is a common connection made between possession, expanded existence and creation of meaning. Kanaga first proposes that in order for players to experience what he calls "the divine," games need to be less controlling of player goals and include more free play of meaning. This will, he suggests, allow players to experience an ecstatic divine state that is like the creative fluidity of playing music. Responding to Kanaga's post, Brendan counters that the divine can also be experienced in games that are linear, tightly controlled and have very little play of meaning. He describes playing the game *Super Meat Boy* (Team Meat 2010) and feeling the divine in the rhythms of his repetitive movement:

> … I don't even think about what I am doing and just watch my character move and feel my fingers twitch and am consciously totally detached from what I am doing. Like I am sitting outside of myself going "how is he doing that?" For me, that is a kind of divine, and one I only get from doing the same thing over and over and over again. (Brendan in Kanaga 2012)

Kanaga agrees and describes experiencing something similar while playing *Super Mario Galaxy* (Nintendo 2007). Although there is very little choice in the game, the musical rhythm of "moving through the tightly composed spaces" also gives him some of that pleasurable sense of meaningful free play (Kanaga 2012). In common with Jourdain's argument above, possession by game rhythms is seen here as resulting in an expanded sense of existence and creation of meaning. Although the game actions Kanaga and Brendan performed were repetitive and had little free play of meaning, their rhythms still resulted in a meaningful experience. This suggests that it is possible for a rhythm to create a meaningful experience that operates alongside and can be different to the meanings created by the events that form the rhythm. It suggests that the flow of a rhythm and the way it structures and takes over our attention can create ecstatic experiences that might seem incompatible with our experience of the other elements in a work but that are nevertheless still pleasurable and meaningful.

Possession by a rhythm is not always seen as something that creates positive pleasurable experiences and, especially so, when this rhythmic possession is associated with addiction. In advertisements and reviews for games, you will often find praise for a game's addictive qualities. However, the type of playful addictive possession that is being sold often has more in common with the pleasurable and relaxing state of mindlessly passing time: the game pleasure that Hunicke et al. call "submission"

(2004). Players expect to be possessed by a game's rhythms in a way that allows them to forget the worries of their real-life but not in a way that creates more worries. The destructive state of actual addiction has non-negotiable real-life consequences that play by definition does not have (Juul 2005, p. 36). Play has a protective frame of artificiality around it (Salen and Zimmerman 2004, p. 80)—the notion that we are "just playing." Any play experience can shift out of this protective frame and fully into real life. For instance, you might wrestle with someone and be playing, but push your opponent too hard and suddenly you are fighting for real. Addiction, although it might happen during gameplay, lacks this sense of artificiality. Addiction also lacks the essential freedom of choice that is needed for a play experience and this again puts it back into the realm of real-life. As Bernard De Koven puts it: "[w]hen you have to win, just as when you have to play, the game takes on too much reality" and play collapses (2013, p. 129). This lack of choice also means that addiction is not play, because the experience of play relies on the pleasurable feeling of freely being a cause of something (Costello and Edmonds 2009). Video poker gambling addicts who forego "agentic gratification" and give themselves "over to the uncontrollable, stochastic flow of chance" (Schüll 2012, p. 177) are, thus, by definition not playing because of this lack of free control. A person might be possessed by any game's rhythms in a way that is destructively addictive, but when this happens they are no longer playing. For within a play experience, the player never fully relinquishes free agency or control. To do so would break the pleasurable play spirit and send the player tumbling back into the seriousness of non-negotiable real-world consequences.

The possible lack of agency that exists when someone is possessed by the rhythms of a game is another concern expressed by game theorists. That is, there is a fear that people will start to enjoy this feeling of possession and become more likely to accept being "mindless automatons" in their real lives (McGonigal 2007, p. 257). Jane McGonigal argues against this view, using evidence from her experience designing alternative reality games. The games that she describes take place in real-world locations with players acting as puppets controlled by the game's designer puppet masters. She explains that, although it might appear as if the only task of players is to follow the instructions given by their puppet masters, the way the games unfold in practice involves a more shared relationship of control. In the first such game that McGonigal designed, the 2002 *Go Game* in San Francisco, she and the game's other puppet masters watched in secret as their players downloaded and then completely misinterpreted their first game message. Although she was later accused of getting "a kick out of manipulating" players, she says:

> … the exact opposite was true. We didn't get a rush of power when the players misinterpreted our simple welcome message. We actually felt completely out of control … Yes, we could give the players a set of instructions—but clearly we could not predict or dictate how they would read and embody those instructions. We were absolutely not in control of our players' creative instincts. (ibid., p. 260)

The experience taught her that players are always involved in the play of agency within these games. In later games she designed, not only was this experience repeated but she realised that her players' actions gave clues to the ways they wanted to be directed. By the time she was creating the 2007 game *I Love Bees*, she had adjusted her design process to actively monitor player behaviours. She would then write instructions that gave the players "exactly the stage direction they were implicitly requesting" (ibid., p. 262). The puppet masters were sharing authorial control with their puppets but in a way that maintained the puppets' pleasurable illusion of being possessed. This allowed the *I Love Bees* players to experience the playful pleasure of captivation: the pleasure of feeling like another entity has control over them (Costello and Edmonds 2009). There was a shared agency in this rhythm of control where each was following the other, creating a rhythm of energetic exchange that would have added vitality to the game experience.

This rhythm of shared agency matches the type of twin follower relationship that has been revealed in a study of synchronised tapping (Konvalinka et al. 2010). The study discovered that a pair of people trying to tap a rhythm together in synchrony will operate as a single system, with each constantly following and adapting the microtiming of their taps to the rhythms of the other. In this process, there are no leaders but rather two followers. There is a "mutual continuous adaptation to the other's output" (ibid., p. 2228). Both people tapping are possessed by the rhythms of each other. Both share control over the flow of the rhythm. Interestingly, a single person tapping along with a predictably precise non-responsive computer metronome was no better at synchronising. This shows, the study concludes, that there can be "equally good synchronization with a partner that is unpredictable but responsive" as compared to a predictable but non-responsive computer (ibid.). Konvalinka et al. are interested in human synchronisation because of the role it plays in social interactions (as discussed in Chap. 2). Their results suggest that achieving social synchrony relies on more than just predictability: it is also dependent on there being a responsive interactive flow of mutual adaptability. For instance, being able to dance well with a partner involves being able to predict how they might respond to the beat and how you adapt your dance movements in response to theirs. If you both continuously adapt your dance movements to each other, you will feel a strong sense of social synchrony. The twin follower rhythm described in this study is a rhythm of shared agency that inherently has the "free movement within a more rigid structure" that defines a play experience (Salen and Zimmerman 2004, p. 304). It is a structure of responsive control and has a to and fro oscillating rhythm that, as suggested by the *I Love Bees* example above, can work to increase the playful energy of a game. Designing rhythms of mutual adaptability are, for this reason, a valuable strategy for playful interaction design.

6.3 Entrances and Exits

If you start too fast it can be hard, though not impossible, to keep going. If you start slow you will need strong material to hold our attention. The pace with which you begin is an important part of the contract you make with the audience …. (Burrows 2010, p. 85)

The way that your audience is swept in by a beginning influences how they will respond to the way the rest of the work unfolds. This is because a beginning's rhythm and energetic dynamics will entrain an audience to a certain pattern and tempo of expectation. Setting up these first rhythms might seem like an obvious part of the creative process but, as Clare Grant's experience with interaction designers and young theatre performers shows, the process of leading the audience into a work can be overlooked in the rush of creation. Thinking carefully about the beginning of a work is not just about choosing the first thing that happens but, more importantly, it is about understanding what the audience needs to have happen first in order to be entrained to a work's rhythm. This is something composer Andrew Schultz emphasises.

Andrew Schultz will often begin with an idea and then realise that something "had to be done before that" to lead the audience into the composition. He then thinks about what "people need to hear before the piece starts". Beginnings can also set up patterns of action or behaviour. Interactive artist George Khut does this by staging the initial moments of a work to signal "an appropriate set of behaviours" that he wants his participants to bring to the experience. The beginning of a piece will also set up expectations that later influence how people will perceive it. As composer Bree van Reyk observes, people will categorise a composition "from the first notes" and decide right then what the rest of the work will be like. If the beginning promises something major that it doesn't deliver, it can disrupt the captivating flow of entrainment by breaking these expectations. In effect, it breaks the contract Burrows describes in the quote above.

Playing with the audience's initial expectations can also be done for aesthetic effect. For instance, the game *The Path* (Tale of Tales 2009) purposefully breaks the contract it first sets up with the player. The game, which is based on the Little Red Riding-hood fairy tale, begins by instructing players to stay on the path (Fig. 6.1). To follow this rule, however, results in failure. That failure then teaches players the rhythmic structure of the rest of the game, which revolves around breaking rules not following them (Ryan and Costello 2012). An interaction design might choose to similarly play around with the contract set up by the beginning of a work. However, as in *The Path*, such a design will still need to eventually lead the audience into its rhythms by communicating a graspable tempo of expectations. It is this creation of a "congruence of temporal understanding" between the work and its audience that London views as essential for producing an effective creative work (2004, p. 25). Beginnings are about creating graspable patterns of rhythmic expectations and understandings.

An important observation that Clare Grant makes about beginnings is that getting them right involves developing processes that create an emotional connection with an audience. Effective beginnings, she says, are more than just setting up patterns of information. The audience needs to feel their way into a work and this is an embodied process that takes time and often requires structures to guide it. In order to provide these structures, George Khut pays a lot of attention to facilitating the initial processes of connecting participants to the sensors in his biorhythm artworks. When he does this facilitation well, it creates "a sense of trust" and a "surrendering into" the experience

Fig. 6.1 Screenshot of the opening game instruction screen in *The Path* (Tale of Tales 2009) highlighting the two rules of the game: go to grandmother's house and stay on the path

that will carry people along with the rest of the work. Without facilitation, he has found that his audience won't "necessarily find the right connection". For Clare Grant, creating connections also involves creating "markers" or "key points" that will guide and carry the emotional and attentional weight of the audience through an experience. These markers act as "landmarks" to "invoke cognitive schema", helping an audience to perceive and understand patterns in a work (Levitin 2006, p. 237). They create what Clare Grant calls "a bed ... for the audience to ride on" that allows the audience to maintain its "autonomy" while being led back rhythmically to the "infrastructure of the piece". This guidance, whether through facilitation or markers, will prevent the dissipation of attentional energy that can lead to boredom or distraction.

A work can draw on existing schemas, like the human movement frequencies discussed earlier, but for novel aesthetic experiences these schemas need to first be developed and this takes audience effort and requires repeated exposure to a rhythmic pattern. As choreographer Sue Healey explains, doing this is about gradually opening an audience's awareness to a work's patterns:

> You have to lead the audience in, you have to show them, you have to guide them. And there has to be a simplicity to that and an accuracy. Then the complexity can come through whatever the composition is by the end. I do that with all my work. I try and find that simplicity of logic at the beginning to enable someone to come in and go "ohhh okay now I can take it on".

To do this, Sue Healey will break the pattern down to its simplest parts and reveal each part to the audience, one by one, with each part adding to the next in repetitive sequences. The repetitive sequences then end up creating the final complex pattern.

The simple beginning and additive repetition quickly develops the cognitive schemas that then allow the audience to attune themselves to the logic of the piece. A similar additive technique is used to great effect in the puzzle game *Limbo* (Playdead 2010). *Limbo* has a steady rhythm of introducing players to new actions and strategies that their character can use to solve puzzles. For instance, a player is first introduced to running, then jumping, then climbing, then repositioning objects and swinging on ropes. As the game progresses and more actions and strategies are learnt, the puzzles combine these simple actions and strategies to create ever more complex patterns. This is common technique of game design, one where the rhythm of player mastery needs to almost (but not quite) match the escalating challenge of the different patterned combinations to create an engaging experience. It is a strategy for entraining an audience by slowly introducing them to simple rhythmic patterns and then using repetition and combination to build complexity.

Connecting beginnings with the energy that progresses a work towards its final ending is another important observation made by Clare Grant. A beginning, she says, starts the logic of that something that "is going on and accumulating minute, by minute, by minute" in a work and, therefore, is the driver that shapes what its ending might become. Choreographer Jonathan Burrows describes something similar when he calls a good ending something that "elicits a noise" from the audience. This noise is "an accumulation of tiny exhalations from many people" and it is a noise that, he says, only arises if the ending is integrated with the logic of what has accumulated. That is, it only occurs if the ending doesn't "lose the plot" of what has been unfolding. The audience's satisfaction at the resolution of patterns within the work will produce a noise which has "notes of both celebration and relief, as well as a certain sadness" (Burrows 2010, p. 81). Where theatre and performance works usually have a single final ending, interactive applications such as games will involve many sub-endings as players complete levels or end a play session. An interaction design might also continue indefinitely without a single endpoint. However, even for endless works like these, their design will still involve rhythms that need to come to a point of resolution at times. Similarly, these points of resolution need to emerge out of the patterned logic that has been unfolding.

Game designers often struggle with how to resolve the frequently occurring rhythms of player fail and restart loops. These loops can act as endpoints within a play experience but usually you want to keep the flow of the game going and that, says Patrick Cook, means you want to very quickly bring players back to the game-play after they fail. How you do this depends on the frequency of the fails and the cognitive work the player needs to do to process them. In the game *Death Squared* (SMG Studios 2017), which had frequent fails, Patrick Cook kept the loop as short as he could to keep the game momentum flowing and still give the player "enough time to perceive the cause of the death". A shorter time would have meant that the player had no time to reflect and, without this pause, might lose the thread of the game. The game *Limbo* (Playdead 2010) also involves frequent fails but it takes a different approach to the rhythm of its failure loops. Here the death animations are quite drawn out, aesthetically beautiful and often delightfully surprising, with one reviewer describing how "each new tragedy becomes a perverse pleasure" (Edge

Magazine 2012). A death in *Limbo* creates a welcome entertaining moment of long reflective pause that punctuates the faster rhythm of the timed puzzles. This gives the player time to consider a new solution and often, the time needed to recognise something in the environment that will help solve the puzzle. As these examples show, in games and in other types of continuous interactive works with many ending points, points of resolution can take on the character of a rhythmic pause. A key design question for deciding the length of this pause is—what does the user need to have the space to think or feel?

There is one type of ending that interaction designers could perhaps pay more attention to and that is the "unhooking" of the audience, as referred to by Clare Grant and discussed in part in Chap. 4. Often, we are so focused on grabbing and holding our users' attention that we rarely consider letting them go. But, unless we want to risk our users shifting from play to addiction, thinking about rhythms that might unhook them, allow them to exit an application and return to the flow of their life, is imperative. Adam Alter's book *Irresistible* describes a woman whose game addiction harm reduction strategy involved not updating her gaming technology so that games will play slowly and occasionally crash, ejecting her from their loops (2017, pp. 178–179). For this player, it is a conscious harm reduction strategy but one that would be heartbreaking for any creative practitioner who has laboured over the works she is viewing. As designers, we could consider providing some of our own in-built harm reduction strategies: ones that would allow people to unhook their attention and release them back into their lives in a way that doesn't crush the creative spirit of our works. Like the woman's strategy above, doing this would involve providing rhythmic breaks, pauses or other strategies to rupture potentially addictive rhythmic absorption.

Rhythmic absorption is something video poker machine and casino designers actively seek to encourage. They want to create for their player "a continuous, rapid, responsive interaction with the machine, precluding pauses or spaces in which she might reflect or stop" (Schüll 2012, pp. 135, 168). This maximises the provider's monetary return because for problem gamblers, as Schüll's research reveals, this rhythmic absorption is what they eventually become addicted to, not the promise of winning (ibid., p. 97). A key component of creating this rhythmic absorption is the speed and patterning of small but frequent random rewards. Some of these rewards are real and some are created by disguising losses as wins and presenting the illusion that the player has almost won. Aside from generating positive feelings, the rhythm of illusory rewards works to obscure the actual patterns of a particular video poker machine, all the while maintaining the illusion that the rhythm of its rewards can be predicted. This maintains the flow of rhythmic absorption and the player continues to feed money into the machine. As a Gamasutra article on exploitative game design points out, similar rhythmic techniques are sometimes used unethically in non-gambling games in order to entice players to spend more money on in-app purchases or more time playing (McNeill 2013). The fault, McNeill argues, lies not with the rhythmic techniques themselves (because they could all be used in ethically) it lies in the exploitative way that they are used. Designing for an ethical playful rhythmic experience, as he suggests, is about avoiding the exploitation of a player's weakness or lack of understanding, and ensuring that the encounter between player and game benefits both sides equally.

Rhythm is a tool we can use to sweep our users both in and out of play, however, the beginning of a work must first captivate users before it can transport them anywhere. Beginnings need to set up rhythmic patterns of expectation and this involves thinking carefully about what users *need* to hear first. One common rhythmic design strategy for captivating users involves working with frequencies of human movement. Another involves building a rhythmic structure that moves from simple to complex through repetition and combination. During play, a rhythm of shared agency can exist even in situations where users feel a pleasurable sense of possession. The rhythm of shared agency is a valuable tool for designers of play experiences because of the energetic free movement of rhythm it creates. Rhythmic captivation can lead to the destructive possession of addiction and, if it does, it shifts users out of the world of play and often works against the creative aims of a design. The movement of rhythmic structures will eventually lead a playful design towards a point of resolution, a moment of letting go, or at the very least a moment of pause. Successfully designing different rhythmic endings involves, as Clare Grant says, answering accurately, ethically and early in the design process the question: what is it that you want to have had happen?

References

Alter A (2017) Irresistible: the rise of addictive technology and the business of keeping us hooked. Penguin Press, New York

Burrows J (2010) A choreographer's handbook. Routledge, London, New York

Costello B, Edmonds E (2009) A tool for characterizing the experience of play. Paper presented at the proceedings of the sixth Australasian conference on interactive entertainment, Sydney, Australia, Article 2, 10 pages. https://doi.org/10.1145/1746050.1746052

De Koven B (2013) The well-played game. MIT Press, Cambridge

Edge Magazine (2012) The Making of limbo. http://www.edge-online.com/features/the-making-of-limbo/. Accessed 9 July 2013

Emmerson S (2008) Pulse, meter, rhythm in electro-acoustic music. Paper presented at the electronic music studies conference 2008, Paris, France

Fitch WT (2013) Rhythmic cognition in humans and animals: distinguishing meter and pulse perception. Front Syst Neurosci 7(68). https://doi.org/10.3389/fnsys.2013.00068

Hall ET (1983) The dance of life: the other dimension of time. Anchor Books, New York

Hasty CF (1997) Meter as rhythm. Oxford University Press, New York

Hunicke R, LeBlanc M, Zubek R (2004) MDA: a formal approach to game design and game research. In: Fu D, Henke S, Orkin J (eds) AAAI'04: challenges in game artificial intelligence workshop, The AAAI Press, San Jose, 25–26 July 2004 pp 1–5

Iyer V (2002) Embodied mind, situated cognition, and expressive microtiming in African-American music. Music Percept 19(3):387–414

Jourdain R (1997) Music, the brain, and ecstasy: how music captures our imagination. Harper Collins, USA

Juul J (2005) Half real. MIT Press, Cambridge

Kanaga D (2012) Played meaning (concerning the spiritual in games) [blog post] 16 June 2012. http://wombflashforest.blogspot.com.au/2012/06/played-meaning-concerning-spiritual-in.html. Accessed 30 Sept 2017

Kaschak E (2011) The mattering map: multiplicity metaphor and morphing in contextual theory and practice. Women Ther 34(1–2):6–18

Konvalinka I, Vuust P, Roepstorff A, Frith CD (2010) Follow you, follow me: continuous mutual prediction and adaptation in joint tapping. Q J Exp Psychol 63(11):2220–2230. https://doi.org/10.1080/17470218.2010.497843

Levitin DJ (2006) This is your brain on music: the science of a human obsession. Dutton, New York

London J (2004) Hearing in time: psychological aspects of musical meter. Oxford University Press, New York

McGonigal J (2007) The puppet master problem: design for real-world, mission-based gaming. In: Wardrip-Fruin N, Harrigan P (eds) Second person: role-playing and story in games and playable media. MIT Press, Cambridge, pp 253–263

McNeill E (2013) Exploitative game design: beyond the F2P debate. https://www.gamasutra.com/blogs/EMcNeill/20130809/197958/Exploitative_Game_Design_Beyond_the_F2P_Debate.php. Accessed 26 Nov 2017

Nintendo (2007) Super Mario Galaxy. Video game. Wii. Nintendo, Japan

Playdead (2010) Limbo. Video game. PC, PlayStation, Xbox, IOS, Android. Playdead, Denmark; Microsoft Game Studios, USA

Ryan M, Costello B (2012) My friend scarlet. Game Cult 7(2):111–126. https://doi.org/10.1177/1555412012440314

Salen K, Zimmerman E (2004) Rules of play: game design fundamentals. MIT Press, Cambridge

Schüll ND (2012) Addiction by design: machine gambling in Las Vegas. Princeton University Press, Princeton

SMG Studio (2017) Death Squared. Video game. Xbox, PlayStation, Nintendo Switch. SMG Studio, Australia

Tale of Tales (2009) The Path. Video game. PC. Tale of Tales, Belgium

Team Meat (2010) Super Meat Boy. Video game. PC, Xbox, PlayStation, Wii U, Nintendo Switch. Team Meat, USA

Chapter 7
Sculpting Attention

> *No work of art can simply be; it always stirs and acts and forces the spectator to follow with his senses the many directions that it suggests.* (Sachs 1952, p. 386)

> *When we meet noise and fail to see a pattern in it, we get frustrated and give up … But once we see a pattern, we delight in tracing it and seeing it reoccur.* (Koster 2005, pp. 25–26)

Abstract Paying attention to a rhythm involves processes of pattern recognition and, depending on what we perceive, these processes can make an experience frustrating, delightful and everything in between. Attention can be played with. It can be focused, drawn in, sculpted and shaped during creative practice. In the moments of attending, our attention might be focused or unfocused, conscious or unconscious, pulled or pushed. We can attend to rhythms in many different ways and each will give a particular quality and colour to our experience. This diversity is something that we can use creatively within our interaction designs. In order to explore the process of sculpting attention, this chapter now focuses on two psychological models of paying attention. The first will help you to understand the relationship between attention and rhythmic structure. The second will help you to understand the relationship between attention and the pleasures of rhythmic experience. We will synthesise the lessons from each model and develop categories to describe some of the processes of playful attending that can be evoked in interaction design. We begin with interactive artist and designer George Khut whose biorhythm artworks interact with his participant's heartbeats or brainwaves. Audio-visual representations of these biorhythms are then fed back to participants to create a quality of slow, quiet, reflective attention. Khut's research often involves collaborations with doctors and hospitals, and during this research his artworks have been used as tools for helping to reduce pain and anxiety. Working in this way has given him a fine-tuned appreciation of the many different qualities of human attention. It has also produced design strategies for evoking specific modes of attending during interactive experiences.

© Springer International Publishing AG, part of Springer Nature 2018
B. M. Costello, *Rhythm, Play and Interaction Design*, Springer Series
on Cultural Computing, https://doi.org/10.1007/978-3-319-67850-4_7

7.1 Being as a Way of Doing: Interview with George Poonkhin Khut, Artist and Interaction Designer

George: For the last decade or so, my research has focused on what we can do artistically with the technology and method of biofeedback training. Biofeedback training is a process whereby changes taking place inside a person's body are measured, and translated in real-time so they can see or hear these changes taking place inside them and eventually control or influence the signals being measured. I've worked a lot with stress and relaxation responses using heart rate and breath. More recently I have been doing interactions based on alpha brainwave patterns, looking at how these can be influenced by alterations in the quality of our attention and mental focus. Through the analysis of these biological rhythms, I can start to show people the influence of different parts of the nervous system and, in particular, interactions between emotions, mental activity and physiology. For example, the stress response as the heart rate is speeding up and the relaxation response as it's slowing down. What I'm looking for is variations in these rhythms. Then I do mappings that help people see those different responses.

My recent interactive art project, *Behind Your Eyes, Between Your Ears*, incorporates an immersive audio-visual system that responds to changes in brainwave rhythms, recorded using a wireless brainwave sensor worn on the participant's forehead. In this work, I'm listening for one particular rhythm, the alpha rhythm: a rhythmic activity within the brain cells that occurs between eight and 12 times a second. These alpha rhythms are always there to some extent, but they get more intense as a rhythmic pattern when we quieten our mind. For example, when you close your eyes the alpha rhythms start to jump up immediately. Then, when you further quieten your mind by shifting towards an open-focussed form of attention, one where you are not focused on any specific thing, the amplitude of the alpha waves increases again. Working with alpha rhythms is a really interesting way to anchor an electronic artwork within a specific quality of attention, a way of being with ourselves and the world around us.

To begin this interaction in *Behind Your Eyes, Between Your Ears*, I do a short calibration test by asking participants to silently recall from memory, the names of five different kinds of fruit or cats or dogs. This lets me measure how much alpha wave on average they produce when they're thinking, in contrast to 'not thinking, just being'. This measurement then sets the baseline threshold for that person. Then they're introduced to a soundscape. I ask them to intentionally think of something in order to suppress the alpha wave and they will hear a crackle sound. That crackle is a metaphor for mental activity or mental noise. The participants are then told that when they can soften or quieten their attention, the crackle will get softer and more distant. Then the longer they can stay quiet, more layers of sound will be gradually revealed—for example gentle water dripping sounds, tinkling bells and similar gentle sounds. So, the interaction is about what can be revealed through being quiet.

A big part of my approach to helping people explore these quieter states is that it's much easier to do if you compare and contrast. This approach is also used in progressive relaxation where subjects are instructed to tense up a part of their body and then relax it and then tense it up again—to compare and contrast. Which is exactly what interactive systems can help people to do as well, to amplify small differences and help us to find ways to influence these changes.

Because these interactions and interfaces are really so novel and unfamiliar, I do rely on face-to-face facilitation a lot. Facilitation is generally what makes the experience more rewarding for people. This means there's someone to greet this person and say: "hello, this is a work where you can explore the connections between your body and mind, and different qualities of attention or emotion. Would you like to explore this? Take some time. Have a seat here. I'll attach these sensors." A lot of attention goes into that invitation process and during the process people determine the extent that they can trust and 'give themselves' to the work. We are establishing a connection and an understanding that the facilitator is somehow interested in what they're doing. This is distinct from the total indifference of an empty room with a computer where you sit down and poke things around.

Simultaneously to all that, in *Behind Your Eyes, Between Your Ears*, I'm also creating something for other people, spectators, to see. While the participant is sitting with their eyes closed, there is a screen where observers view the image of this person with their eyes closed in this very introspective state, overlaid with coloured patterns (Fig. 7.1). Those coloured patterns are changing as the quality of attention is changing. You can also hear sounds that the participant is hearing. For a spectator, it's like you're seeing into the quality of their attention—metaphorically being present to this inner state of someone and the dynamics of their inner state. The participant becomes a performer in a sense. People are present to whatever they're doing and imagining, or speculating on what they might be thinking about. They're present to this quality of consciousness. They're paying attention to one person's experience. Socially I find that really interesting as a space to create and hold.

The really beautiful provocation that biofeedback and psychophysiology provide us is that it's a different kind of control—sometimes described as 'being as a way of doing'. It's looking at that quality of being and observing how that influences your physiology. You can't just say "I'm going to speed up my heart rate now" or make it slower. It just doesn't work like that. And the challenge with this kind of interaction is that you're always looking back on a window of time. It's always retrospective and it can never really be immediate because you're having to compare this

Fig. 7.1 *Behind your eyes, between your ears*: Liveworks, 2015. George Khut with David Morris-Oliveros (visual effects programming). Alpha brainwave controlled interactive sounds and graphics. Documentation of participants interactive with the work, as shown at Liveworks 2015 festival of experimental art, performance space, Sydney, Australia

to what happened before. The other constraint is that you're trying to create feedback that is not going to be too jarring. You actually need to reduce the stimulus so it doesn't elicit a startle or stress response. It needs to be predictable enough and, I guess, soft enough to not call attention to itself too much. That's the challenge compositionally. And it's why I often smooth off the data so that it's not staccato. But in that smoothing, you're averaging and you're introducing a kind of latency. I try to tell people about that in terms of the idea of a drift—a gradual influencing, in contrast to the kind of direct manipulation we are accustomed to when interacting with regular tools and computer interfaces.

Another ongoing design challenge I have for myself is a dilemma around compositional form. When you work with pre-recorded music or performed music, rhythm and timing is central to that aesthetic. You're feeling different lengths of time, one phrase comes after another and all those timings, all those proportions, are really expressive. When you work in an interactive system, a lot of that goes away. You don't know what the user is going to do next. So, you have to find another aesthetic that's still to do with time but not in that proportional way. I respond to that challenge by focusing on texture and revealing layers, rather than emphasising phrases sonically. It's really more like looking at layers and then densities.

Scaling and mapping processes are also very important. For instance, how do you scale a very small change in heart rate or a very small change in

Fig. 7.2 *BrightHearts* app for iOS. Four screenshots of heart-rate controlled interactive artwork for Apple iOS devices, 2014–2017 (George Khut with developers Greg Turner, Jason McDermott and Trent Brooks). The colour and layering of the rings and circles is controlled by changes in heart rate

a brainwave rhythm? These are things we can't feel and so we scale it up sonically, visually or kinaesthetically into something that we can feel either through our hearing or through vision in a way that's effortless. So, it's like, "all right I can feel that. It's getting bigger, it's getting softer, it's getting further away." But there's always this idea of kinesthetics—feelings of physical movement—and how we experience that visually or sonically. For instance, in the heart rate work *BrightHearts*, every time you slow down it triggers a little note, and a bigger amount of deceleration may trigger a higher or lower note. For the visuals of these works I usually use fairly predictable intuitive mappings around the metaphor of heat (Fig. 7.2). Fast and intense things are red and hot. Slow, gentle cool things are blue or green. Then I plot colours between these two points. With the sounds, I'm looking for things like rough versus soft. Again, I'm using these as metaphors for calming, softening down, speeding up or getting more agitated.

A rhythm I work with a lot of the time is slow breath. That is a recurring frequency in a lot of my work, a ten second rhythm around six breaths per minute. I use that to entrain a slower breathing state, using the idea that when some very charismatic person starts breathing very slowly you automatically [he slows his speech] … start … to … drop … into … this … rhythm … that … they're … breathing … at [he laughs]. When I'm creating these sounds, they'll build or swell, and they'll reach a crescendo at timeframes of around ten seconds. With that I'm building in a bias towards slower tempos. I use this timeframe a lot sonically. Then visually I'll create things that have this push and pull at that slow rate as well.

But I often feel the works sonically at first then translate that into what sounds I can build and only then think about appropriate visual patterns. I'm always interested in a soft quality of seeing, in not looking too hard. I seek a kind of presence that sound gives me and that visuals don't necessarily have. And I guess that's about spatiality. When you're looking at things, generally you're looking at a particular thing. Whereas with sound, you experience it all around, even when it's localised. But you can soften the quality of how your eyes have to move around and register the signal or the image. Our brains are hard wired to respond to stimulus in different ways, so you can use things like repetition or the quality of the signal to make things soft, uni-focal or omni-focal. Generally, things that have a sense of softness and expansiveness work—things that have a kinaesthetic quality of expansion.

I tend to use facilitation to lead people in and lead people out, but then I also give them some unstructured time to spend in there. The tension is that it's an artwork and it has to have some mystery—you don't predetermine everything. But then, at the same time, for me it's failed if it's so mysterious that people actually don't know how to enter into it at all. So, you might facilitate the entry into it and the exit from it, and you might give them some suggestions for some things to do—some ways to play with work—and then the rest is always up to them. You can't work with a static idea about rhythm and compositional form because they're going to improvise with it. I do think it's really important to give people that space just to be there—to leave some space for people to go into their own experience. And providing space for that improvisational play is, for me, about layers. There is usually some layer that's quite easy to control that's not so ambiguous. In the brain wave work, it was that crackling sound and as soon as you start thinking hard or thinking about things, the crackle comes back. In the heart rate works like *BrightHearts*, it's your heartbeat. You're hearing the boom, boom, boom, boom and that's a consistent unambiguous reliable thing. Then within that there's all the other feedback layers relating to longer term changes—drifts in the heart rate patterning or the brainwaves. These are things that you're influencing but not necessarily controlling in the normal sense. They're much more ambiguous but they also keep people curious.

As a designer, you've got to find that edge between scripted and unscripted. Some people are just going to be lost—"no I couldn't control it at all, I didn't feel like I had any control over it whatsoever." Whereas other people will say, "yeah I could find some connections there." It's about giving them a structure but also giving them predictable and noticeably responsive feedback and combining that with things that are more ambiguous in terms of—"Is that me? Is that something else?"

7.2 Working with Qualities of Attention

George Khut intentionally strives to evoke an unfocused mode of attending in his work to see "what can be revealed by being quiet." In a similar vein, dancer Nalina Wait sometimes finds a dreamy unfocused state of attention useful because she feels it allows people to experience her dances in a more sensory, less cognitive way. Mobile game designer Patrick Cook takes the opposite approach, aiming for a focused mode of attention so that he can keep players "really actively involved in the game loop of play." Somewhere in the middle of these is the approach of composer and film maker Andrew Lancaster, who describes combining moments of focused excitement with moments of "tranquility and rest", so that he avoids exhausting the attentional energy of his audience. Each are working creatively with the range different qualities of focused and unfocused attention that are involved when we perceive a rhythm. The character that this attention has, depends on the capacities of the person attending. It depends on the rhythms that a particular user is able to perceive and thus pay attention to. It also depends on the nature of the rhythms within a design. One of our key tasks as interaction designers, then, is to accommodate the attentional capacities of our users as we simultaneously try to provoke different qualities of attention with our designs. The attentional character that results, influences and shapes the types of pleasures that the experience of our design might produce. To perform this design task well, we need a detailed understanding of the nature of attention and we begin this process here with an outline of two psychological models of attention.

The first model of attention comes out of the research of Mari Jones and Marilyn Boltz. Their research identifies two modes of attending, one "future-oriented" and the other "analytic" (1989). These modes each correspond to a rhythm of events with a particular degree of structural coherence. A rhythm of events that is highly coherent affords future-oriented attending because its structure is predictable. This means that a person attending is able to develop patterns of expectation about when future events might appear. Through this expectation and corresponding anticipation, their attention becomes focused on the macro structures of what will happen next. Conversely, a rhythm of events that has low coherence is less predictable and the person attending to these incoherent events will need to analyse "adjacent elements in an attempt to organize the unstructured information" (ibid., p. 461). A person attending to a rhythm with low coherence will, thus, focus on analysing the micro relations between events. Whether a rhythm is experienced as coherent or incoherent, and attended to in future-oriented or analytic mode, will also differ depending on the rhythmic schemas that a person is familiar with. Highly unstructured improvised Jazz will likely appear incoherent to those without musical training but will seem more coherent to a trained Jazz musician. Similarly, a person unfamiliar with computer games will probably begin a game experience in analytic mode focused on perceiving micro patterns between events. Their unfamiliarity with games will mean they are not yet able to see any coherence in its rhythmic patterns. Once they are more expert, their attention will become more future oriented, and as they begin to pay more attention to macro structures they will be able to develop strategic approaches to their performed rhythms of gameplay. Although each have their own character, both future oriented and analytic modes of attending can involve the full range of focused or unfocused attentional energy: someone can dreamily focus on predicting future events and be similarly dreamy when analysing relationships between events. Both modes of attending can also occur within a single creative work, the rhythmic oscillations between them contributing to the character of a work's rhythmic experience. The key distinction between the two modes is that one involves paying attention to micro relationships and the other involves paying attention to the unfolding of a macro structure.

This micro/macro structural distinction is one that several of my interviewees speak about, especially when they refer to moments in their design process when they focus on the audience experience of a rhythm. For instance, film maker Andrew Lancaster says that he thinks about the audience mainly in relation to the macro rhythms within a film. As he puts it, "the classic thing is the shifting in the seats—you always imagine they're getting bored." However, at the micro level when deciding the rhythm of an edit between two images, he thinks only of "how that works kinetically" and creatively. Lancaster focuses on both micro and macro structures during his design process but warns that, although both can impact the experience of the audience, it is possible to focus too much on the micro rhythmic relationships to the detriment of a film's macro structure. For him "none of that micro stuff actually means anything, if the whole rhythm of the pacing is wrong and people aren't engaging." In contrast, other creative practitioners describe putting more emphasis on the micro relations between events. For example, choreographer Rhiannon Newton focuses on evoking an analytic mode of attending during her dance performances. She actively works to make the audience pay attention to very micro changes in the dancer's rhythmic movement, wanting her audience to reflect on the relationship between rhythmic events and to notice "the difference between two things that you might assume are the same". Newton finds analytic attending useful because it encourages reflection. Lancaster finds future-oriented attending useful because it encourages audience engagement.

Jones and Boltz's research indicates that each mode of attending can have an interesting impact on the way a person will 'feel' temporal durations. Future-oriented attending generates expectations about when rhythmic events will occur and, when a rhythm might end. If a work contradicts these expectations by ending later than expected, it will feel longer. If it ends earlier than expected, it will feel shorter. Their research shows that this occurs even though the actual duration may be the same in both works. During analytic attending, there are processes of grouping and counting as a person tries to organise the rhythm into a pattern. In this case, works that have fewer events and less of this attentional grouping and counting work, will be judged as shorter. Similarly, works with a higher density of events will be judged as longer because they require more effort. Again, this is even though the two works may be of the exact same duration (Jones and Boltz 1989, p. 461). Different temporal qualities can, therefore, be created within a work by going with or against expectations and also by varying the density of rhythmic events.

Both of these creative strategies are used by George Khut in his creative practice. He describes working with density of events when he speaks of "focusing on texture" in his artwork. As he varies the density of events, he is producing different feelings of temporal duration for those who are attending analytically. Khut also describes working with predictability and expectation when he speaks of using both a layer that is predictably "easy to control" and a layer where the control is more "ambiguous." Here he is working with future-oriented attending and producing different feelings of temporal duration by layering ambiguous elements with unambiguous ones. Creatively playing around with expectations and density of events are, then, ways for designers to give a particular temporal feel to the rhythmic experience of a work.

Jones and Boltz (1989) also identify two types of time transformation that can make events more able to be predicted and a work more coherent. The first is called ratio time transformation and it involves hierarchies of nested durations that are multiples of each other in a regular ratio (e.g. 200, 400, 800, 1600). The second is called additive time transformation and it involves durations that increase by adding a consistent amount (e.g. 200, 250, 300, 350). Where ratio impact the rhythmic pattern of an event structure, additive time transformations impact the flow and velocity of a rhythm (ibid., pp. 462–465). The consistency and regularity of these transformations will influence the coherence of a rhythmic structure. Very consistent and regular time transformations create a coherent and predictable rhythmic structure and evoke future-oriented attending. Inconsistent and irregular time transformations are associated with low coherence and analytic attending. Ratio and additive time transformations will also give a rhythm it's unique character or style. To illustrate this, Jones and Boltz analyse the rhythm of a cat running and identify a signature style of movement arising from its "particular combinations of ratio and additive time invariants" (1989, p. 466). This rhythmic style is what allows us to hear someone we know approaching and guess who it is from the rhythm of their footsteps. Being able to perceive and understand both of these time transformations and any invariants, they argue, facilitates participation in many forms of synchronous interactive communication, including partner dancing, hunting and caring for babies. For instance, they might allow us to register a change in the duration that someone holds their smile and to understand something that they are communicating with this change in rhythm. This is why animators and robotics designers will pay close attention to rhythm when they are creating designs that will interact synchronously with humans. In order for successful synchronous communication to occur between a robot or computer character and a human, both sides need to be able to perceive, understand and communicate rhythmic time transformations.

Another model that provides a useful perspective on the processes of attention is that developed by psychologist David Huron and outlined in his 2006 book *Sweet Anticipation*. Huron's model focuses on the role of anticipation within attention and details the specific feelings this anticipation can evoke. He identifies five "feeling states" or responses that occur during the process of anticipating and then experiencing an event. Two of these responses occur before an event happens and three afterwards. The first response he calls the *imagination* response and this occurs when we anticipate an event by "imagining" or predicting different consequences that might result. Next is the "feeling of increasing tension" and increasing "physiological arousal" that can occur as an event approaches. This causes a *tension* response. Immediately after the event we feel a *prediction* response based on whether we correctly or incorrectly predicted the outcome. We will also have an instinctive *reaction* response "based on a very cursory and conservative assessment of the situation." Lastly, we reflect in more detail on what has happened and feel what Huron calls an *appraisal* response (2006, p. 17). The five responses occur in the order described, with the prediction and reaction responses occurring simultaneously in the microseconds after an event. Each response can activate positive or negative feelings, and the qualitative sense of the whole experience emerges from the way these five different feelings combine and interact together. As Huron explains, earlier responses are "susceptible to revision or augmentation" and, thus, an event that "we find initially exciting or startling may be completely transformed by further thought" (ibid., p. 14). We might, therefore, imagine something will hurt us, feel tension as the event approaches and recoil in reaction while simultaneously feeling pleasure that we correctly predicted the event. Finally, as we appraise the situation, we might feel an overall bitter-sweet sense of pleasure that we avoided any harm. The power of Huron's model lies in the way it breaks down the felt quality of an event into five stages each making its own contribution to the eventual feeling. This model provides a nuanced way of understanding how the eventual felt quality of a rhythm might arise.

Huron uses his model of five feeling states to explore the aesthetics of experiencing music and, in conclusion, proposes that the pleasure of anticipation in music results from two phenomena, both of which can be used by creative practitioners to choreograph expectations (2006, p. 366). The first of these phenomena is the pleasure we feel when we accurately predict an event. This pleasure arises from "the brain's tendency to reward itself for doing a good job of anticipating stimuli" (ibid., p. 197). This pleasure is about repetition because it results when the rhythm of events and their relations repeat an aesthetic pattern that the perceiver has already learnt. The perceiver is then able to feel the pleasure of accurate prediction. Huron argues that this pleasure from prediction is "typically misattributed to the sound itself" (ibid., p. 167). During this misattribution, he asserts, we associate our pleasure with the content of the event itself, for example, the notes within the melody or the sound of a particular drum. However, this pleasure is actually caused by our ability to correctly predict the what, when, how of the event's occurrence. Creative practitioners work with this pleasure when they set up easily learnable rhythmic patterns or motifs and then repeat them throughout a work. They also work with this pleasure when they, as online educational designer Simon McIntyre describes, design with "familiar rhythms" to which their audience is already habituated.

The second phenomena results from the heightened feeling of pleasure we will feel when an earlier negative response contrasts with a later positive one—as in the bitter-sweet escape from harm example (described earlier). This second pleasure of Huron's is about difference and occurs when the contrast between a negative and a positive response acts to increase a final feeling of pleasure. In the escape from harm example, our initial sense of danger lead to a heightened arousal that then increased the amount of pleasure we felt when we were not harmed. For example, imagine nearly tripping over and just catching yourself in time. Your gasp and increase in heart rate as you nearly fall will intensify your feeling of joyful relief when you have righted yourself. This pleasure of negative/positive contrast can also occur when a highly expected event is delayed and then delivered. The delay creates a negatively experienced tension that then contrasts with and increases the pleasure of prediction when the expected event finally arrives. This is a pleasure that dancer Nalina Wait describes occurring when a rewarding element that hasn't happened for a while finally appears. The moment it appears, she says, "will probably always feel like the right moment" and create a pleasurable feeling of "ah, yes" in the audience. Again, the initial suspense of waiting creates a heightened arousal that intensifies the pleasure when the event finally arrives.

Another way that this second pleasure of negative/positive contrast can occur is when something surprises by violating an expected pattern. Surprise within a real-world environment will cause a fight, flight or freeze response, however, within the safety of an aesthetic experience these can be experienced pleasurably as "frisson, laughter or awe" (ibid., pp. 367–368). A surprise creates an initial negative response that then contrasts with and increases the positive later response that might occur after we have assessed the aesthetic value of the surprise and responded with laughter, chills down our spine or a sense of awe at its beauty. The initial shock of the surprise again creates an arousal that intensifies the pleasure of the unexpected event. This pleasure of surprise is what dancer Nalina Wait is working with when she describes "setting up a rhythm and then shifting it in an unexpected way" in order to wake up her audience. It is also what Clare Grant is talking about in performances where she speaks about being aware of audience attention in terms of "allowing it be there and flicking it somewhere else just a little bit different." Both are speaking about choreographing expectations by working with rhythmic combinations of repetition and difference to evoke the possible pleasures of prediction and surprise.

These two psychological models of attention describe the ways that patterns are perceived in time, suggesting strategies that we, as creative practitioners, can use to design with and for attention. They portray our audience as perceivers who are actively and dynamically involved in finding, learning, predicting, completing and sharing patterns while they engage with the rhythms in our creative works. When we perceive a rhythm, we will actively seek to discover or find the patterns within it, and as we do so we will be learning patterns that we might then predict will reoccur. We will also chunk those patterns into groups and perceive patterns that have a beginning and an ending. In this sense, we will undergo processes of completing patterns. Lastly, in order to perceive a rhythm, we will draw on our shared cultural understandings and habituation to environmental rhythmic patterns. However, in our playful interactive works these patterns will not only be experienced, they will also be performed. Therefore, as our discussions in part one of this book suggest, we need to add a performative dimension to this list.

Our audiences are also perceivers who are actively and dynamically involved in repeating, expressing, combining, creating and breaking patterns. When we perform a rhythm, we might reproduce or repeat a pattern we have already learnt. We also

Table 7.1 The attentional processes involved in playful rhythmic experience are divided into those that relate more to perceiving or experiencing a rhythm, and those that relate more to actively performing a rhythm

Processes of playful attending	
Experience rhythm	Finding patterns
	Learning patterns
	Predicting patterns
	Completing patterns
	Sharing patterns
Perform rhythm	Repeating patterns
	Expressing patterns
	Combining patterns
	Creating patterns
	Breaking patterns

might choose also to add expressive variations to the way we perform a rhythm and in these patterned variations communicate something others can understand or feel. We might take multiple rhythms and combine them together or we might create something completely new. Finally, we might play with rhythmic patterns by breaking them down or actively subverting them. Table 7.1, combines both types of process, dividing them into those that relate to the experience of a rhythm and those that relate to the performance of a rhythm. This model of processes of playful attending is a conceptual tool that interaction designers can use during the design of rhythmic experiences. For instance, it could be used during concept development to help define the types of attentional processes we might want an interactive work to involve. It could be used during prototype evaluation to help reveal which attentional processes our design engages in its users. It could also be used to diagnose rhythmic issues as a design advances towards release. At all stages of a design process this model is a tool for thinking through the different modes of rhythmic attending that might occur within a playful design and also, perhaps more importantly, the possible pleasures that these modes might be working towards.

In this chapter, we have seen that as we attend to rhythms we can focus on predicting future events or on analysing the relations between events. One mode of attention engages us with the macro unfolding of predictable rhythmic structures. The other produces reflection about unpredictable micro relationships within a rhythm. The way in which the rhythmic patterns within a work might meet our expectations and the textural density of a rhythm's events will make a work feel longer or shorter to us. Also, our perception of invariants within a work's rhythmic time transformations will create a rhythm's particular style of pattern and flow. This style can be read, communicated and understood. These perceptions of rhythmic style can be essential for meaningful synchronous communication. As we attend to a rhythm, we are constantly anticipating. The process of anticipation produces five stages of response that combine together to give an aesthetic experience a particular felt quality and can evoke pleasure. The pleasures of rhythmic anticipation relate to the way a work choreographs expectation by working with predictability and with contrasting responses caused by tension and surprise. Within playful interactive experience the perceptual processes of attending to a rhythm will combine with performative processes. The experiential and performative processes of playful attending are a conceptual tool that we can use to design the rhythms within a playful interactive experience and to think through the ways that this experience might shape our user's attention.

References

Huron D (2006) Sweet anticipation: music and the psychology of expectation. MIT Press, Cambridge

Jones MR, Boltz M (1989) Dynamic attending and responses to time. Am Psychol Assoc 96(3):459–491

Koster R (2005) A theory of fun for game design. Paraglyph Press, Scottsdale

Sachs C (1952) Rhythm and tempo: an introduction. The Musical Quarterly 38(3):384–398

Chapter 8
Crafting Trajectories

> *Banal music raises common anticipations then immediately satisfies them with obvious resolutions...Well-written music takes its good time satisfying anticipations. It teases, repeatedly instigating an anticipation and hinting at its satisfaction, sometimes swooping toward a resolution only to hold back with a false cadence.* (Jourdain 1997, p. 319)

Abstract The overall rhythmic structure of an interactive experience creates a moving trajectory that through anticipation pulls our present and future attention ever onwards. It creates a journey over time, as composer Bree van Reyk puts it. Crafting the rhythmic structure of this journey is now our focus in this chapter. We look at the way rhythmic structures can work to unify an experience and outline practical techniques that creative practitioners can use to help map and conceptualise the overall rhythmic flow of a work. Then we focus on techniques for designing the structural dynamics of a rhythm. Many of these structural dynamics are also articulated by game designers Patrick Cook and Ilija Melentijevic, whose interview introduces this chapter. These two designers work for the Australian company SMG Studio where they have designed games for mobile, tablet, console and desktop. In their interview Patrick Cook and Ilija Melentijevic describe the structural rhythms of small-screen casual games and longer-form big-screen games. They speak about respecting players' investment of time in a game and staying true to the patterns of expectation that a game promises its players. As they point out, this respect is something that must also be given to the inherent momentum of the game form itself. Balancing out the dynamics of the trajectory of an interactive experience while providing multiple ways that rhythmic possibilities can combine and develop, is one of the fundamental design tasks we face as designers of interactive rhythmic structures.

© Springer International Publishing AG, part of Springer Nature 2018
B. M. Costello, *Rhythm, Play and Interaction Design*, Springer Series
on Cultural Computing, https://doi.org/10.1007/978-3-319-67850-4_8

8.1   Patterns of Rhythmic Possibilities: Interview with Patrick Cook and Ilija Melentijevic, Game Designers

Patrick: There are a lot of rhythms in games and in game design. You've got the rhythm of the game play loop. You've got the frequency of different points of interest. You've got how often a player in a game will need to do a certain action or stay conscious of timings of things.

Ilija: There's also the frequency of interaction. Whether it's pressing buttons or reacting to things. Then there's the rhythm of gameplay—if it's a racing game, you're driving a car; if it's a jumping game, you're jumping around collecting things. But quite often there is a larger, slower pattern that is commonly called the meta-game—a larger loop where some things will slowly unlock or happen, or change or modulate.

Patrick: It's all about the player's experience, which is true of all mediums. The rhythm is in the experience. But as the designer of the game, you can't predict the course that the game will take, because it's all driven by the player's input. So for a game designer, rhythm is more about curation. You don't lay the rhythm all out and then have it play out. You set up likely patterns and you craft something that might have one of many possible outcomes.

Ilija: Yes, rhythm in games relies on the player doing their part, so you can't really constrain it too much. Rather, you provide some context for it to develop.

Patrick: One rhythm could be the frequency of the player in a fail and restart loop in a very small reflex-based game. There's a lot of rhythm in trying to craft the approximate frequency of that taking place. Often, if the player has failed in some task, you want to very quickly bring them back so that they're straight back in again. For instance, in our game *Death Squared* (SMG Studio 2017), there are a lot of ways to fail or to stumble. Because failure is so frequent, it was very, very important to me to not send the player through a very drawn out, laborious loop. A loop where say, if something goes wrong, it takes five seconds or 10 s while an animation plays, then the player goes back to a menu and needs to press buttons to get back to where they were. In *Death Squared*, the loop is about 3.2 s, between dying and getting back to playing the game. I might have made the loop even faster in *Death Squared*, but the time I ended up with was actually about the player having enough time to perceive the cause of the death. Because if it was any quicker it was such a fleeting moment that the player couldn't really process what had happened.

Ilija: It's also so that death does not interrupt the pace of game play. That's a common strategy with mobile games. You fail, but you can quickly jump straight back in and continue doing what you want to be doing.

Patrick: Yes, in our mobile games, a lot of the timing and the rhythm, are really about attention span—about keeping people really actively involved in the game loop of play by holding their attention on a highly engaging, easily digestible task. That's not true of all mobile games. But certainly, a lot of the ones that we've made at SMG are about a very rapid loop and high engagement tasks that are enjoyable and easy.

Ilija: And you're trying to distil that—to encapsulate a small part of an enjoyable thing and provide just that—rather than trying to build an elaborate structure. Because there's not a lot of player commitment with free mobile games. There's a tendency for players to quickly discard them and go looking for the next game that immediately grabs them.

Ilija: In our games, we're also trying to make something that's interesting for us. We're trying to make our games different to what's already out there for the sake of creative fulfilment. But a game does need to be understandable. There needs to be a thread that people can grab onto, to get them to where you want them to be. People need new experiences but they will move towards familiar ones, so they will not make it easy for you to surprise them.

Patrick: Sometimes you break conventions on purpose and that's good fun, but other times it just makes a lot of sense to meet the players' anticipation about how they'll expect certain things to play out. A good example of an expected rhythm often used in game design is that new content, new ideas, and new mechanics are rolled out incrementally as you keep playing through a game.

Ilija: It is like a reward for engagement. You play and you're rewarded all the time with newer stuff.

Patrick: The way it's done well is usually; you introduce a new mechanic, you spend a little bit of time letting the player achieve a level of mastery with that new idea, and then you bring in another one. You repeat that cycle for a while and then sometimes you start blending them together by folding certain ideas into a new spin on another thing that's coming up. But it's like a staircase, you go up in shelves. You bring something in and you let people absorb that.

Ilija: It's a regular paced delivery, if you will. But it depends on the game or the context. Sometimes things will behave in a less linear, more logarithmic fashion.

Patrick: Although, you don't want to have the game progress at a certain rate and then all of a sudden there's just an extraordinary amount of learning before you can proceed. You want to not interfere with the tempo or the rhythm of that ascension through the complexity.

Ilija: It's all about making the player excited about things. Being a reward mechanic, you want it to be regular so that people can anticipate it and know that it's coming. You want to teach them that the time that they're investing will reap rewards. That there will be more fun stuff and, as soon as they master this, there will be new things to learn. You want to keep that promise constant. You want to deliver it consistently.

Patrick: And it's really important to convey the pattern that is in your game. Because if you were to put a bunch of new ideas and new mechanics only in the second half of your game, someone will play 50 of your 100 levels and they'll make an assumption about the rest of the 50 levels being the same as the first 50…

Ilija: …and most people will never see them.

Patrick: So, you do want to suggest and convey the rhythm of new material coming into your game to set up the correct expectation. One that also lines up with what they'll be hoping for as well.

Ilija: It's about guiding the player into the rhythm and teaching them what to expect.

Illija: In another one of our games, *One More Line* (SMG Studio 2014), we changed some of the standard rhythms of the learning curve. Usually a game will start slow and then get faster, faster, and harder, harder. What we did was we immediately threw the player into a very fast-paced game.

Patrick: The game starts and stays at maximum.

Ilija: It's like dropping someone into a pool to learn how to swim. There's no introduction. You're just there. You need to figure it out. Our idea was that people are going to figure it out fairly quickly. Once they get the hang of it, they won't have to sit through the slow and boring bits until the fun, exciting, challenging part comes up. And that seems to have worked. That game was quite popular.

Patrick: But often an ascending difficulty makes the most sense in a game, because you try to pair the difficulty rising with the player's competency rising. If you can match that well, then it works.

Patrick: The player's physical gestures can have an interesting effect on their experience of rhythm. For instance, the games in our mobile *One More* series have a binary input. You are either touching the screen or not. You are tapping. In those games, because of this tapping gesture, I think the rhythm of the game is more obvious. But in our mobile game *Thumb Drift* (SMG Studio 2016a) you've got a non-binary, very organic sense of steering.

Illija: It's one thing to click with one finger or even tap with your thumb, but if it's a more analogue thing like in *Thumb Drift*, keeping your thumb on the screen and then swaying or pulling, it's more organic. It's more like a flow.

Patrick: I think a rhythm is there in *Thumb Drift*, but you kind of melt into it a bit more—it's more of a subconscious feeling. The main rhythm in *Thumb Drift* comes from the frequency of the turns—you'll have a very brief moment where you can go straight and then you really need to yank into a hard turn again and then back the other way. Then you've just got a really momentary reprieve.

Ilija: These kinds of rhythmical patterns are not always obvious, but I think if you are physically engaged then it's easier for people to feel them. For example, in another mobile game of ours, *One More Bounce* (SMG Studio

2016b), the tactile element was disconnected from the music. You're a ball that's bouncing around and you need to guide the ball, but you do that indirectly by drawing a line that it will bounce off. You draw the line and then the ball bounces, so the action is decoupled from the gesture. We tried to bridge that gap in physical engagement by making all the sounds that the interaction causes part of the music. Every time you hit a wall there is a sound, but on lots of different frequencies—like notes in a scale. It's a slower-paced game, and we wanted to make that slower pace, and the game's slower music, more engaging by making the music a consequence of what the player does.

Patrick: In terms of the overall rhythm of a game, you want to keep a good even flow. Then you can bring peaks into that. At the same time, you don't want to give people a non-stop peak experience, because they'll just burn out on sensory overload. You want to keep a good, even keel of regular engagement, regular thought, regular input.

Ilija: But it needs to have some fluctuation. Quite often this fluctuation sort of exists already and we just cultivate that so it feels good.

Patrick: It really depends on the game, though. The design solution will be different for different genres of games. As a game designer, what I try to avoid comes from what I really dislike as a game player—I hate to feel lost or stuck, because then I'm out of the rhythm of the game and it's frustrating. I like to be able to keep things moving along. It's fine if the game lets you go off somewhere—you could spend half an hour looking at a tree because it's interesting. But you don't want to halt the momentum that is naturally inherent in the game (whether by force or accidentally) because it's not designed well, or it's not clear, or you're making the player wait for something, or you're making the player do something very menial for a very long time. I always think that's something to avoid.

Ilija: In some of our games, even though we do let the player modify their movement and interact with it, the player is constantly moving and they can't stop. This imposes a certain pace or momentum and that affects the intended rhythm of the game. I think it helps to convey the rhythm of interaction that is expected from the player. But I do think it's also really good to leave it open to the player to choose their own pace. So, in the game *One More Line*, the game moves at a fast speed and you can't stop, but you can latch onto these pegs and move around them…

Patrick: …you can let the peg go when you're ready.

Ilija: But while you are rotating around the peg you're sort of stationary. You can look ahead, choose exactly when to try and make the jump, et cetera. Interestingly, a lot of players, (including us when we were testing the game), were trying to play it safe. We would grab the next peg, wait and then do the jump. Then, at an exhibition in Boston, this guy showed up who had obviously played the game a lot. The way he played it was the best thing I ever saw. He was so fluid. We realised that the game is actually much more enjoyable if you have a rhythm that is continuous, like skipping stones

across water. You get more enjoyment out of playing like that, even though
it's riskier. The only reward is the feeling that you get out of it, and that
feeling is a sense of rhythm really.

8.2 Rhythm as a Unifying Force

Patrick Cook and Ilija Melentijevic suggest that there is a rhythmic momentum
inherent to every interactive work, one that a designer can intentionally create or
amplify but also unintentionally destroy or stifle. Many of my interviewees speak
about rhythm in a similar way. Rhythm has a momentum that drives a work as it
is experienced, and also drives their decision-making process as they design. For
instance, performer and director Clare Grant calls rhythm a "diagnostic spot" and
the part of a work "where you can most clearly tell what's happening." Similarly,
composer Andrew Schultz describes rhythm as something that you can use "to test
whether something actually belongs in a piece or not." He calls rhythm part of the
overall expressive language of a work and he uses it to evaluate whether a new idea
is speaking the same language as the rest of the work. Language is also the word
interaction designer Andrew Johnston uses to describe rhythm. For him, it is a "useful
language" for noticing things within a design that are often overlooked and a way of
breaking out of habitual patterns of creative practice. One way, then, that structural
rhythm is a unifying force within creative practice is as an evaluative tool that allows
practitioners to test out the how, why and when of placing new elements within a
design. Structural rhythm also unifies a design by acting as a diagnostic tool for
revealing points where a design might be heading in the wrong direction.

A second way that my interviewees describe rhythm unifying a creative work is
as a means for thinking about what is essential at any given moment. When teaching
improvisational dance to young dancers, Nalina Wait found that her students would
often begin well, but as time progressed their improvisation would lose its tone. She
attributes this to them feeling the freedom of "realising that anything is possible"
but not understanding that "just anything isn't interesting after a certain point." She
had to teach them to focus in on what was essential to the moment and they had to
be led by the rhythmic momentum of their prior accumulated decisions. Someone
who also works with improvisation, choreographer Rhiannon Newton, describes this
progressive accumulation as a relational "feeling that this is needed because I've been
doing that." These relations have a force that pushes her dance towards a future that
"is going to be like this because we're already on this trajectory." This, for her, creates
a unified unfolding structure that then gives meaning to a work's eventual ending.

In a different area of creative practice, the process of defining what is essential
is described by film maker and composer Andrew Lancaster as being about giving
priority to the thing that is most needed to do "the work" in a scene. The example
he gives is of making decisions about the blend of music and sound effects on a film
soundtrack. The mix of the two can sometimes create competing rhythms that clash

and confuse the audience, so a director needs to be clear about which takes priority. He says:

> ...you pick your areas that you want to do the work. If there's a big explosion, as a composer you won't be putting a big orchestral note on the explosion. Because probably nine out of ten times the explosion will be the better way of aurally explaining this huge fireball on the screen. It's a way of helping define what's doing the work - whether it's sound or music - and making sure that they're not fighting against each other.

As these examples show, regardless of the type of creative practice, the decisions a designer makes about what is essential to a given moment combine to create the rhythmic trajectory of a work. This trajectory creates an accumulating sense of rhythmic progression that then acts to define what can come next.

A common way that creative practitioners will use rhythm as a diagnostic tool involves creating scores or maps to chart the different types of rhythm that might occur within a work. Representations of this kind can also support conceptual development. One composer of electronic music describes the visual representation he draws of his tracks as "a map for the inside of my head" without which he would "get lost" and could not compose (aciddose 2007). A visual score "freezes time in a concrete form," revealing aspects of structural rhythms that may not be noticed during in-the-moment experience (Burrows 2010, p. 142). In game design, these might be visual scores created to chart the rhythms of rising and falling player interest (Schell 2008, p. 253). They might be heatmaps created of various game events and, in tandem with player interviews, these could then be used to diagnose issues with overall pacing (Mirza-Babaei and Nacke 2013). Level maps could also represent long-term and short-term goals creating tartan-like two-dimensional charts (Fig. 8.1) that track the density of layered events across their sequencing in time. The thickness of these lines highlight the rhythmic frequency of major and minor events (Totten 2014, pp. 376–378). For more functional forms of interaction design, you could create visualisations that map the rhythms of the user's emotional journey through an interactive experience (Souza 2011). Each representation reveals a different type of rhythmic pattern within an interaction design.

Rhythmic representations are used in a similar way by film maker Andrew Lancaster to support the concept development phase of his films. He describes creating a mock edit of his visual storyboards to get a feeling for the rhythm of film shots, and a better sense of what he needs to shoot when he is on set. Once edited, his visualisations can be played back and, thus, also represent temporal rhythmic movement. Similarly, other creative practitioners find less fixed visual forms of representation useful for diagnosing structural rhythmic issues. Composer Andrew Schultz mentally visualises each composition as a room with a particular character and feel, creating an internal embodied representation. The body is also involved in film editor Karen Pearlman's representation of the rhythm of her edits. She describes singing the movements and rhythmic phrases within the shots of a film. While she sings she is "listening to breath, intensities, tensions, and releases of the flow of energy, time, space, and movement", using these to detect whether there is a "false note" in her edited sequence (2009, p. 97). Pearlman has observed other editors doing something

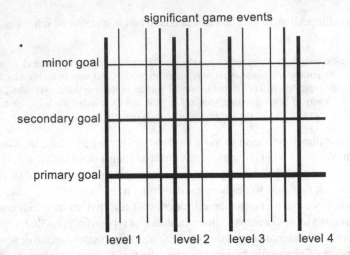

Fig. 8.1 An example of the kind of tartan-like pattern used to map the rhythmic density of major and minor events across a game, its goals and levels (as suggested by Christopher Totten). Significant events and goals have the thickest lines

similar but using sympathetic body movements instead of voice. The editors would mark the rhythms of their edits with the nod of the head, lift of an eyebrow or blink of an eye. The diversity of approaches here echoes our discussion of methods for analysing rhythm in Sect. 3.4 of Chap. 3. They add weight to our recommendation that researchers of rhythmic experience should experiment with multiple representational forms, including those that foreground temporal relationships, maintain the complexity of rhythmic flow and involve embodied performance. Such representational practices help designers grasp the unfolding rhythms in a work, diagnose issues and develop unified rhythmic structures.

8.3   Structural Dynamics

The unfolding trajectory of a rhythmic experience needs to have a dynamic structure of changing pace. If it consists purely of peak experience, it will, as Patrick Cook points out, cause users to "burn out on sensory overload." To avoid this burnout, a designer will often focus on varying the rhythmic speed and number of events within a work. As with all design, doing this well is a matter of balance. If everything moves quickly and/or there is a constant high density of events, it will sap the energy of an audience. Moving too slowly and/or having sparse events will have the same effect. Both tempos, composer Andrew Schultz says, can cause the audience to "put down the shutters" and retreat into their own thoughts. Schultz and musician Roger Mills advocate thinking through the overall structural dynamics of a work at the very beginning of a creative process. There may be circumstances, for example spontaneous improvisation, where you won't map out these dynamics precisely, but you will nevertheless still begin, Mills explains, with "a conceptual scaffold" of the overall dynamics and a sense of "what you would like to achieve by the end." Through that scaffold, you can then use varying layered rhythms of "tempo or attack" to create a "sense of movement" across a work.

When Roger Mills speaks of creating movement with attack, he is referring to the amount of energy that musicians use to produce sound from their instruments. Attack refers, for instance, to the energy that drummers put into the strike of their sticks on the surface of a drum. It also refers to the energy that trumpeters put into the breath they blow into their trumpet. The attack involves a transfer of energy from musician to instrument, and it influences both the duration and intensity of the sound that is then produced (Levitin 2006, p. 53). Within playful interaction design, the idea of attack corresponds to the amount of energy that a player puts into the interactive system at each moment. It could also correspond to the amount of energy a system gives back to the player. Translating tempo and attack into a playful interaction design, therefore, involves considering the elements within a design that might impact energy, intensity, duration, density and speed. We can see all five of these occurring within digital games, for instance, in this description of the gameplay in *Viewtiful Joe* (Capcom 2003) where "easy monsters give the player a feeling of accomplishment and the game pace a 'faster' feeling" because the player progresses through the game "relatively quickly" (Squire 2005, p. 80). Here the players are expending *energy* as they fight monsters. They are also experiencing the *intensity* of accomplishment, feeling the short *duration* of each fight, noticing the *density* of how often the fights occur and sensing the *speed* of movement through a sequence of fights. Like musicians, interaction designers can use such variations in energy, intensity, duration, density and speed to create rhythmic movement across a user experience.

Roger Mills describes another strategy for creating structural dynamics—one whose impact relies on extreme contrasts of energy and intensity. Early in his career, as a member of the UK band *Statik Sound System*, Mills wrote and performed dance music and used a common technique known as "the drop." In this technique, a rhythm would become ever faster then suddenly drop out before coming back in again. The drop builds intensity, releases it and then re-engages it. It is a cycle of tension and release that drummer Simon Barker calls a method for ensuring that dancers will "move in a certain way." It is, thus, a method for producing a specific rhythmic experience for an audience. To build something up and then release it is "a very satisfying rhythm", as dancer Nalina Wait says, and one that can be used to engage audiences in all manners and contexts. For instance, we can see the drop being used as a design strategy in an aspect of the game *Death Squared* (2017). Patrick Cook describes the strategy:

> …[there are] a large number of levels where it's rigged up so that if you move just a little bit you'll instantly destroy either one person or everybody. It was rigged up that way to create these really explosive moments of exclamation. To have people affect other people and for that to then spark a conversation…

The explosive moments in *Death Squared* punctuate the tension of cooperative play, resulting in the sudden release of laughter and exclamation. These moments are associated with difficult puzzles and, thus, there is a building tension before they occur. The intensity of the explosive release of this moment of failure, which will eject the players from the rhythm of the game, is similar to the intense release of the drop. There is also a similar moment of re-engagement when the game restarts and it feels as though the previous rhythm has begun again. The emotional intensity of this sudden explosive release adds a vitality to the cycle of failure and restart, and potentially masks any sense of a break in rhythmic flow that such moments of failure can cause when it halts game momentum. Patrick Cook and Ilija Melentijevic propose another strategy for dealing with the rhythmic interruption that can be caused by cycles of failure and restart, which is to reduce the time spent before play resumes. This smooths out the potentially staccato feel that failure can create. Game designers will also often work with randomness and variation to make each restart after failure feel like a renewal rather than a repeat (Juul 2010, p. 90). This strategy reduces the sense of repetitiveness that restarts can create and, thus, potentially reduce any feeling that progress and momentum are stalled. These techniques all work to feed and maintain the energy and flow of a rhythmic trajectory.

Within many entertaining rhythmic experiences, it is common to have a moment of peak intensity somewhere towards the end of a work that creates a climax. Leading up to that climax, there will be an ascending rhythm of peaks and troughs. This type of dynamic structure is described by game designer Jesse Schell as a way of maintaining player interest and something game designers should map during their design process (2008, p. 253). Schell advocates an ideal shape for the mapped line of player interest, based on advice he was given when he was working as a street performer (Fig. 8.2). A fellow performer told him he needed to begin his act with "a bang" in order to grab audience attention and to follow this with "something a little smaller" that would let the audience "relax." The rest of the performance would then gradually build to each peak before giving the audience "a grand finale that exceeds their expectations" (ibid., p. 247). The resulting shape of this interest curve charts, from the audience's perspective, their rhythms of engagement. Schell proposes that creating a game experience that roughly follows this path will produce an entertaining experience.

Shifting rhythmic patterns of peaks, troughs and climaxes can operate across all kinds of levels within a design. While at one level a game's structural rhythmic pattern might be working well, at another it may not. An example of this occurs in the game *Limbo* (Playdead 2010). The game is very successful in many ways, but there was one rhythm that both players and reviewers felt did not work so well—the rhythm of living things within the work. The player character in *Limbo* is a small boy who moves through a mostly empty back and white world (Fig. 8.3). As the game progresses, players will encounter other boys and eventually the sister they are searching for. Players will also come across various creatures, including a particularly scary spider and a slug that attaches itself to their head. The chart in Fig. 8.4 shows the distribution all these living (and in some cases dead) things throughout the game, with those that result in the most intense experiences in darker colours. It reveals

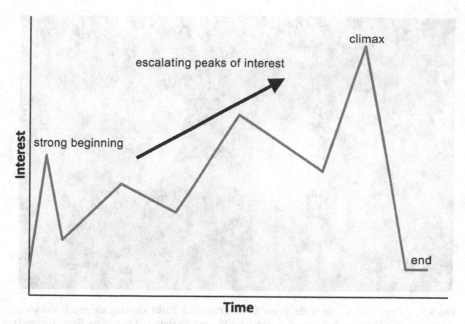

Fig. 8.2 An example of the rhythms within the interest curve that game designer Jesse Schell proposes will create an entertaining experience

how the living things tail off after chapter 20 to create what one reviewer referred to as the "lonely and puzzle-centric second half of the game" (Thomsen 2010). In terms of player engagement, the elements that create the most intensity (the spider and the nasty boys) are mostly clustered in chapters 5–15. The only intense engagements with living things in the second half are two meetings with the sister. Limbo's game director Arnt Jenson wanted the last section of the game to feel lonely so that "when you meet the little sister…the impact will be so much bigger" (Nutt 2012). However, the two moments of intensity around the sister come so late, and are so far from the intense early section and each other, that they are unable to keep the momentum of this early intensity going. They form a separate rhythm, disconnected from the other rhythms of this aspect of the game. In this rhythm of living things, the game has that sense of "the drop" after chapter 15, but it fails to re-engage the player afterwards and, therefore, what should feel like climaxes, when the player meets the sister in chapters 29 and 39, end up feeling less intense than they could.

Within all my interviews, when creative practitioners speak about the trajectories and structures of rhythms, they describe alternating between two contrasting states that are often grouped in structures of threes. These two states might relate to tempo, for example, film maker Andrew Lancaster speaks about working with the symphonic structure of "fast, slow, fast." This is a structure, similar to Schell's interest curve, that he says first "gets you in," then in the middle "there's some breathing points" and then it "builds up to a climax towards the end." Lancaster likes to flip this structure to "slow, fast, slow" when he wants to challenge his audience's expected rhythms.

Fig. 8.3 An example screen of the game *Limbo* (Playdead 2010) showing the black and white colour scheme. The main little boy character is on the middle right and two of the living (or dead) things in the game are on the left—a bird and a dead boy

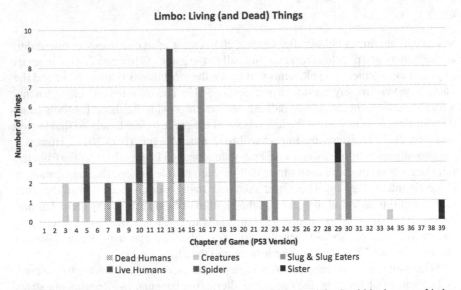

Fig. 8.4 A chart representing the rhythm of other things (living and dead) within the game *Limbo* (Playdead 2010). The horizontal axis shows the chapter number of the game in the PS3 version. The vertical axis shows the total number of things in each chapter. The different shades show the different categories of things. Those that cause the most intense engagement are in darker shades

For director and dramaturg Clare Grant, the two states she describes are knowing and not knowing. During a performance, she says, the audience will "get to know a certain amount and then suddenly... [they are] flying, not knowing." Something similar to this is described by interaction designer Andrew Johnston. Right at the beginning of a work, Johnston often makes the connection between the performer and his interactive system quite obvious to the audience, so that the audience knows immediately that there is a creative interaction going on. In the middle, he might then "go into states where the connection perhaps isn't quite as obvious." At the end, in what he describes as a "traditional arc," he will return to the obvious state. There are also pairs of alternating states in interaction designer Simon McIntyre's description of the way we "consume technology in rhythms." As we experience an interactive application there is, he says, "the calm, the action, the pause, the refresh, the rebuilding, the strengthening, [and] the new challenge." These cycles of contrasting elements create the linear rhythmic journey through time that is the user experience. Whether the contrast is in terms of speed, awareness or activity, there is a sense of tension and release within each that will lead to corresponding feelings of high or low intensity. As we discovered in Chap. 7, these contrasts can work to heighten affective peaks of intensity. However, as with the *Limbo* living things example, we also saw how contrasting states will only work effectively if they are read as a related pair within the same moving rhythmic structure.

Across the span of a whole experience, rhythm has an energy that unifies the elements of a design. It produces a momentum that propels an experience onwards and reveals what needs to happen next. Thus, rhythm is a useful tool for diagnosing structural weaknesses within a design and this diagnosis involves creating a variety of representations of rhythmic structures. To build a structural rhythm, designers will create patterns of energy, intensity, duration, density and speed across all kinds of layered elements within an interactive experience. These patterns will often build in intensity and move towards a climactic peak. The patterns within a work might also involve contrasting states that will create cycles of tension and release in ways that could add vitality or disguise cyclic repetition with the cloak of a new beginning. Much of the affective power of a rhythmic structure lies in the perceived relationships between events as they are experienced across time. Therefore, for these patterns to do this work, a continuous unfolding momentum of a rhythm across time is important, so that the rhythm will be perceived as a single related structure.

References

aciddose (2007) Nonstandard notation systems [Online forum comment]. https://www.kvraudio. com/forum/viewtopic.php?f=99&t=167600. Accessed 16 Oct 2017

Burrows J (2010) A choreographer's Handbook. Routledge, London; New York

Capcom (2003) Viewtiful Joe. Video game. GameCube, PlayStation. Capcom, Japan

Jourdain R (1997) Music, the brain, and ecstasy: how music captures our imagination. Harper Collins, USA

Juul J (2010) In search of lost time: on game goals and failure costs. In: Fifth international conference on the foundations of digital games, pp 86–91. https://doi.org/10.1145/1822348.1822360

Levitin DJ (2006) This is your brain on music: the science of a human obsession. Dutton, New York

Mirza-Babaei P, Nacke L (2013) Storyboarding for games user research. Gamasutra. https://www.gamasutra.com/view/feature/186514/storyboardin. Accessed 11 Apr 2013

Nutt C (2012) Hanging in Limbo. Gamasutra. http://gamasutra.com/view/feature/162457/hanging_in_limbo.php. Accessed 9 July 2013

Pearlman K (2009) Cutting rhythms: shaping the film edit. Focal Press, Elsevier, Burlington

Playdead (2010) Limbo. Video game. PC, Playstation, Xbox, IOS, Android. Playdead, Denmark; Microsoft Game Studios, USA

Schell J (2008) The art of game design: a book of lenses. Morgan Kaufmann; Oxford; Elsevier Science, San Francisco

SMG Studio (2014) One More Line. Video game. PC, IOS, Android. SMG Studio, Australia

SMG Studio (2016a) Thumb Drift. Video game. IOS, Android. SMG Studio, Australia

SMG Studio (2016b) One More Bounce. Video game. IOS, Android. SMG Studio, Australia

SMG Studio (2017) Death Squared. Video game. Xbox, PlayStation, Nintendo Switch. SMG Studio, Australia

Squire KD (2005) Educating the fighter: buttonmashing, seeing, being. On the Horizon 13(2):75–88. https://doi.org/10.1108/10748120510608106

Souza L (2011) How to transform the minds of clients. Smashing Magazine. https://www.smashingmagazine.com/2011/12/effective-user-research-transforming-minds-of-clients/. Accessed 11 Apr 2013

Thomsen M (2010) How Limbo Came To Life: behind the scenes with the breakout Xbox Live Arcade game that took six years to make. IGN Australia. http://au.ign.com/articles/2010/09/14/how-limbo-came-to-life. Accessed 9 July 2013

Totten C (2014) An architectural approach to level design. CRC Press, Taylor and Francis, New York

Chapter 9
Textures and Transitions

> *...a drop of water hanging off the end of a faucet; you know it is going to drop, but you don't know when. The drop of water is imminently watchable because you know something is going to happen... When the drop falls, there is a moment of relief. Then another drop of water forms and you watch and wait....* (Lanki 2013)

> *Rhythm is the setting up of new tensions by the resolution of former ones.* (Langer 1953, p. 127)

Abstract All rhythms involve patterns of change and the way they transition between (or resolve the tensions between) the changing states has a felt quality. That felt quality will also emerge out of the rhythmic textures of densities, layers and accents within a work. Both textures and transitions contribute to the overall affective tone of a work and this makes them an essential component of the processes of designing for rhythmic experience. In order to create textures, designers will go through processes of addition, subtraction, sequencing, and layering. To create transitions, they will shape the ebb and flow of the dynamics of rhythm and, in particular, shape that moment when two rhythmic energies connect. Within interaction design, these two processes allow designers to create expressive rhythmic possibilities that can then be brought to life by the unfolding of a work and the playful interactions of its users. To begin our discussion of textures and transitions, we have an interview with classical composer Andrew Schultz. For Schultz, transitions are about creating movement between ideas. Shaping this movement is part of the process he goes through to develop and build textures within his compositions. Schultz has composed a broad range of award-winning chamber, orchestral and vocal works, including several large symphonies and operas. In common with interaction designers, he often designs for an audience who will be experiencing something unfamiliar when they first listen to one of his compositions. He shares many of the same concerns we interaction designers might have about engaging an audience and shaping their affective experience.

© Springer International Publishing AG, part of Springer Nature 2018
B. M. Costello, *Rhythm, Play and Interaction Design*, Springer Series on Cultural Computing, https://doi.org/10.1007/978-3-319-67850-4_9

9.1   The Speed an Idea Needs to Happen: Interview
with Andrew Schultz, Composer

Andrew: I see rhythm in terms of patterns of temporal durations - how the whole
time element of a piece of music is organised. That can be looked at in
terms of the passage of time over the full duration of a composition or
you can talk about it in terms of note by note. Then in between there's all
sorts of levels going from that very large macro level, down to the tiny
micro level.

I think the experience of rhythm is tied into a lot of other things in music.
The experience of pitch, the experience of dynamics, the experience of
tone—they are all interconnected. Rhythm is very important, but it's integrated with other elements. A melodic idea, for example a tune, will tend
to have its own rhythmic language, its own rhythmic shape. On the larger
level—say a whole movement will also have a rhythmic character that
determines much of its mood. I'd say rhythm functions as part of a larger
expressive language.

My attitude to rhythm is to not actually think about it terribly much as
a separate entity. Rhythm is just one of the elements that I'm dealing
with. It's part of the construction when I compose. That said, with nearly
every aspect of music, as you're learning it you need to separate it into
its individual elements to try and analyse each one. Because to get them
all right at once is too challenging. So, it's like taking baby steps. When
you are learning, you have to break the task down into its components.
For example, you have to spend some time just really thinking about the
rhythms of a piece. You have to spend some time just thinking about
the sound, the pitch of a piece, making sure every note's in tune, the
volume, the tone colour. Those things are actually quite difficult for an
inexperienced performer to achieve all at once.

But when I think about rhythm, I'm thinking about a particular idea, a
musical idea, which needs to have a certain rhythmic character to function
really well. That's because I'm trying to find all of the things I can put
into that idea that will make it as effective and powerful as possible. It
could actually be very simple rhythms in some cases, or in others it could
be very complicated. There may be pieces in which you want things to
happen really quickly. You want the experience to be sped up, almost like
it's a hyper state, but there are other times when you want the opposite,
when you want really for everything to be stretched. Rhythm is one of
the tools you use to achieve that.

Perhaps at the start, when I'm composing, I may think in terms of, is
there a rhythmic unity about the ideas of the piece? Are there motivic,
rhythmic ideas? In other words, things which are going to be germinal to
the piece and repetitious, like a motif. So, I'd be thinking about that in the
background. Also, I suppose thinking about rhythm is one of those things

you can use to test whether something actually belongs in a piece or not. Sometimes you have ideas and they're a nice idea, but they don't really belong in the same piece. It's like a character has wandered in from the wrong play. And the rhythmic language can be a way of assessing that. There is this comment that Stravinsky is meant to have made, which is that he couldn't write a piece until he knew the tempo of the piece. This is something I admire in his music—and in Beethoven. Even though you can be fast and slow, there needs to be an underlying sense of pulse about how events happen. So, I start by thinking more about that question. Do these ideas actually belong together in terms of pulse? Do they have a common lifestyle rhythmically? Do they belong together, or are they incompatible characters? I would say that's actually also about tempo, the speed at which an idea needs to happen, but also the actual structure down to the micro level of the idea.

I tend to think about the audience experience in terms of the passage of time and how the audience might relate to moments—for example, moments where something is going to happen that is dramatic or exciting or a shock. There are also situations where you take risks and slow things down as much as possible. I'm always fascinated to see how audiences deal with that. Do they fidget? Are they interested? Are they engaged?

The key thing is actually the speed at which an audience can hear and process and move with an idea and I think that has changed over time. People are able to listen more quickly in some ways now, than they might have been at an earlier period. I think it's because of the constant exposure to a bigger range of sounds, than would have happened say 200 or 300 years ago. Then on the other hand, people seem to crave now, very, very slow things, with very little happening and I think that's partly a response to that overload.

When you are watching your work with an audience for the first time, the pacing of it changes completely—you're experiencing as an outsider for the first time, what someone as an audience member is experiencing. You become acutely aware of little fidgets, how people move, when they look completely absorbed and when they're not. Those are actually about the large scale, the macro level of rhythm. They're about how much you've engaged the attention of an audience. Are they with you or are they someplace else? That's actually the experience that in the end you're trying to create, one where you completely absorb people. Even in the slow, uneventful sections, you want them to still be caught up in what you're putting before them.

So, I suppose there has to be some kind of empathy for what an audience experiences, without going to the extent of trying to manipulate a reaction all the time, stepping into that real Hollywood, deliberate playing, with the experience of the audience member as a way of controlling them almost. I think there has to be a level of people being able to consciously engage. To say: "yes, I want to engage with this." For a good piece of art,

I think that always happens. There's always another step beyond that just instinctual level, another step where you get drawn in.

And that's about the passage of time, because it's a completely relative experience of time, in film and in music. It speeds up. It slows down. Five minutes can feel like an hour. An hour can feel like five minutes. So, I think there needs to be an interest threshold. People need to be interested. There needs to be enough stress and interest in it for them to stay with it. But there can't be so much that they switch off because they've lost it. Ironically, if it's too slow or if there's too much density or activity, the audience reaction is the same, which is to put down the shutters and just go off into their own happy place, or unhappy place—whatever it is.

That passage of time and the level of interest is incredibly important to me, which doesn't necessarily mean that I expect the audience to be engaged or interested all the time. But I do want to feel that there is a level of connection with an audience. I don't like the idea of presenting something which people just have no connection to. It doesn't mean the audience has to like everything. It doesn't mean they must have a particular reaction to it. It just means there needs to be a level of engagement.

I'm just starting a piece at the moment. It's probably around 30 min long. It's a three-movement piece and I have a very clear idea of what the different movements are going to do in terms of the journey—the creative journey. I'd probably use that as a phrase more than rhythm. I'd say it's more about where is this going to take someone? Where will they be at each point in the piece? Not right down to every second, but maybe over a two or three-minute chunk of time.

When you are mapping the rhythm at that macro level of a composition, you need to have a fairly good, clear sense of the shape of where you're going in a piece. In the sense of: where are the highs? Where are the lows? How do you get from the lows to the highs, the highs to lows? All those things. That experience of the design is really important and something which I try and imagine in a fair amount of detail before I start.

Getting from one thing to another, getting from one idea to another idea, or continuing an idea—those transitions in music are probably the trickiest thing. Once it's reached its exhaustion, how do you go with an idea after that? So, I spend a lot of time on those passages and a lot of time thinking first of all about what the bigger structure is going to be. In other words, just in starting a piece, what do people need to hear before the piece starts? Or when the piece is started, is there something they needed to hear before it started? That sounds funny, but I quite often find that I will start something with a sketch and then realise that actually there was something that had to be done before that.

I like to build things from fairly small ideas and just try to accumulate material from that. To start, I need to have a sense of where the overall structure is and where the bit that I'm beginning with is going to be in the overall character of the piece. I don't particularly think about that in terms of rhythm. If I had to use a creative analogy for that process of imagining the creative landscape of a piece, I'd actually describe it as like imagining building a room. In other words, by the time I'm ready to the start the piece, I need to be able to walk into a mental room. That is the piece.

And they're never the same room. Until I can walk into that room creatively, then I can't really start. Because it's like, well what's this note doing here? Why that note rather than any other note? Why begin like that, rather than this? I need an overall feeling for the experience. Of course things happen as you go along. That's part of the pleasure of doing it—that it takes its own way as well. But then there's always a way of standing back and saying—hang on, what is that doing there? Perhaps it didn't really belong to what you were imagining.

I think the single biggest challenge is the unfamiliarity of the thing that you're putting in front of an audience, because they don't know what to expect and they might be nervous and so forth. The experience has to be controlled by a composer. But you can over control it—so that every time you go to hear a particular composer's work, it's always the same thing. I don't agree with the idea of becoming a purveyor of the same thing over and over and over. I think that's sterile—you may as well not bother. I think that there has to be an artistic integrity to what you're doing.

9.2 Turning a Corner

Moving from one idea to another and the transition between them is, Andrew Schultz says, one of the "trickiest" aspects of composition. These transitions play an important role in the rhythmic flow of a work. So much so, that interaction designer Andrew Johnston considers transitions to be the major cause of a design's eventual success or failure. Johnston uses the phrase "turning a corner" to portray the way an orchestra conductor might successfully transition between two tempos. This success, he emphasises, is not about creating an imperceptibly smooth transition. It is about finding the exact right quality of transition for a particular meeting point of two rhythms. The process of creating transitions, then, asks designers to really focus on the specific quality of any moments of energetic change within a work. These moments of transition could involve a slow process of transformation or they could involve a fast metamorphosis. They could meet in a way that feels smooth or abrupt. A transition might involve an enormous or a minuscule change in direction. It might have the intense contrast of stillness meeting movement or the mild contrast of a slow deceleration. Individual transitions will have a particular texture of felt quality that is determined by how the energies, dynamics and speeds that are meeting together match or collide (Pearlman 2009, p. 55). Then at the macro scale, across a whole work, there will also be a diverse range of transition qualities. Shaping the patterns of these qualities, as drummer Simon Barker points out, will allow you to produce "certain kinds of feelings" that then combine and contribute to creating the particular experience of a work.

It is the dynamic felt qualities of transitions that are described by psychologist Daniel Stern's term vitality forms. Stern defines vitality forms as "process waves" that give the content of an experience its dynamic form and describe the "how" of the way that this content will arrive, depart, or move through time (2010, p. 93). For instance, does something explode, swell, crest, rush, flutter, tense, glide, surge or disappear? These words all describe the dynamics of the way something might move, and it is this movement that Stern associates with the vitality of aliveness (ibid., p. 25). Vitality forms describe a movement's "felt experience of force," its felt "temporal contour" and also its "sense of aliveness, of going somewhere" (ibid., p. 8). Vitality forms are not the 'what' or 'why' of an experience but are solely the 'how' and are thus content independent. As Stern explains, the same content, for example anger, "can appear on the scene explosively, or build progressively, or arrive sneakily, or coldly" (ibid., p. 23). Equally, different content can appear in the same range of ways. Thus, a smile could also appear explosively, progressively, sneakily or coldly. Additionally, someone can develop understandings about the person, creature or thing that is moving, based on the felt quality of these vitality forms, such as whether a smile is fake or genuine. Stern associates vitality forms with the excitement, stirring up and animation of arousal, and argues that they play a primary role in life and in artistic creations.

Vitality forms are what allow creative practitioners to exquisitely fine-tune their works by modulating and shifting their audience's "orbit of arousal" (Stern 2010, p. 83). When choreographer Sue Healey describes playing with the transition between how long "to leave a certain idea or rhythm before I mix it up, introduce a new idea or have a dialogue with that last idea", she is working with vitality forms. These forms are also in play when Rhiannon Newton focuses her choreography on the transition process of "a rhythm becoming another rhythm…so that there's these small, little steps or slow transformation." Both practitioners are working with the 'how' of the way the ideas in their work arrive, depart or move through time. They are working with the vitality of evolving form. Stern's theory echoes the importance my interviewees attach to the moments of transition within a work and the qualitative impact they describe these moments having on its rhythmic experience.

Similar creative ways of shaping transitions will also occur within playful interaction design. For instance, Patrick Cook and Ilija Melentijevic speak about designing a form of failure loop into their games that they call "tempa-death." This describes a moment of failure that does not eject players completely from the game rhythm nor impact their game progress permanently. Instead it uses timers to stop players from performing an action, or actions, for a defined period of time. A tempa-death like this creates a particular felt quality of failure transition, one that, unlike a game restart, maintains most of the momentum of game play and provides the added tension of waiting for a timer to end. Cook and Melentijevic used this technique in the tower defence game *OTTTD* (SMG Studio 2014). They describe how they were able to create a truly satisfying rhythm with a very "full" tempo by combining different durations of timers across the game's three characters and their various skills. Where one action might take 60 s to begin again, another more tactical action might take 20 s. This means, Cook explains, that players need to think about how to balance their actions and consider "Yes, this is useful now, but when will I need it next?" With a skilfully crafted mix of multiple timers and different durations, the strategy creates an experience with very little stillness or inactivity, and one that has many transitioning cycles of tension and release. It is this that creates what Cook describes as the very "full" tempo.

Another example of shaping transitions within playful interaction design, is the procedural architecture for interactive dialogue that Michael Mateus and Daniel Stern created for their game *Façade* (Procedural Arts 2005). The game is a first-person narrative and its primary interaction revolves around conversations between the player and a married New York couple, Trip and Grace, who the player is visiting for evening drinks. Mateus and Stern developed a procedural system for sequencing the narrative that divided its possible paths into a granular structure of 27 narrative beats, each with its own goal (2007, pp. 191–2). A beat contained 10–100 short sequences of dialogue that could be selected and sequenced based on player input and the progression of the narrative so far. The order and sequencing of these beats was then controlled by a higher-level drama manager. Mateus and Stern paid a lot of attention to the way the drama manager transitioned between each narrative beat, to make sure that the tone of the beat that was ending matched the tone of the beat that was beginning. This match in tone meant that players would "often perceive them as causally related" and, thus, a coherent rhythm of dramatic flow was maintained even though the beats were being sequenced and transitioned in real-time based on player interactions (ibid., p. 193).

Something similar occurs in the procedural sound system of the game *Inside* (Playdead 2016). Like Matteus and Stern, the game's audio team developed a granular structure of sounds, where each grain was able to be filtered, adjusted, mixed and sequenced in real-time based on player interactions. This was a strategy to create what they call "unbreaking immersion" (Andersen and Schmid 2016). In one case, these granular sounds were used to create naturally uneven rhythms of breathing for the main boy character: rhythms that could move across a continuum from relaxed to panicked. This rhythm of breath would in turn drive "the rhythm of the boy's interactive movements", for instance, the rise and fall of his chest (Broomhall 2015). In this way, they were able to procedurally match the intensity, action and emotion of the boy's physical exertion and to transition in a way that maintained player immersion as the boy moved from standing still to walking, running, jumping or climbing.

The audio team also used this approach to design the sound transitions across the many death/respawn loops within *Inside*. In a video presentation, composer Martin Stig Andersen explains the importance of these transitions using an example scene from the game (Audiokinetic 2016). The scene involves a puzzle with a six-second loop that the player needs to be in sync with in order to survive. Because the sound in the game helps you to keep this sync, Andersen needed to create a transition across death and respawn in a way that maintained the player's entrainment with the aural rhythm, otherwise, the player would die, get out of sync with the rhythm and frustratingly, quickly die again. Andersen and audio programmer Jacob Schmid say that this way of transitioning the sound allows the game to "create the illusion of no time passing" during scene transitions (Andersen and Schmid 2016). The team also created different aural transitions depending on whether a player was respawning or returning to the game after a break in play. Andersen explains, that they did this to accommodate the difference between a respawning player who would be annoyed at "hearing the same line or music cue over again" and someone reloading after a pause who probably does want to hear the same sound so that they can quickly re-engage with the game (Broomhall 2015). The focus on audio transitions at each of these different levels within *Inside* create a unified rhythm that contributes to the overall felt quality of the game.

The *Inside*, *Façade* and *OTTTD* examples are just three approaches for creating transitions within procedural rhythmic structures in playful interaction design. What they make clear is that, as Daniel Stern observes, the vitality of their forms communicates a felt quality that contributes to the overall experience of an interactive work. In the three examples, that felt quality is primarily about maintaining a flow in which multiple transitions between fluctuating rhythms form a coherent, unified and immersive structure.

9.3 Building Textural Layers

Like Andrew Schultz, many of my interviewees create rhythmic textures using processes of building and layering. Both Schultz and choreographer Rhiannon Newton will start small and then build onto this beginning, to create what Newton calls "small accumulations of complexity." The complexity emerges out of densities created by layering and ordering events. It is also produced by the repetition and fluctuating combinations of these events as they are added or deleted across a work. The way an event arrives, transitions and then returns in differently ordered ways also works to create a texture and coherence that, as dancer Nalina Wait points out, involves a satisfying "coming together, like a picture that starts to make sense." The shaping of textures, like transitions, therefore contributes to the overall affective quality of a design. The affective power of textures that are created by working with layers, and the densities and changes within them, allows interactive artist George Khut to expressively shape time within non-linear interactive structures. This is what game level designer Neil Alphonso is also doing when he uses density of objects, movement or interactivity to direct players to the things in a level to which they need to pay attention. This strategy, Alphonso finds, is a subtle way to let players know when they are in an "important" place without overly directing them there (Seifert 2013). For both of these interaction designers the use of texture is particularly important for creating the rhythms within interaction design because it compensates for the lack of expressive control a designer has over the rhythmic duration and sequencing of events in interactive contexts.

To build densities a designer will work with processes of addition, deletion and substitution. They might, for instance, build up a sequence by slowly adding new events one by one. This is a technique drummer Simon Barker uses to create "more complex rhythms" out of an increasing density of events. Such rhythmic complexity is something that can create coherence and, paradoxically, can also make a rhythm feel less dense because of the way that one rhythm can reveal another. As Chernoff points out in a description of African music:

> One drum played alone gives an impression of a rhythm tripping along clumsily or senselessly accented; however a second rhythm can make sense of the first. (1979, p. 52)

Two predictably coherent rhythms can feel less 'noisy' and dense than a single unpredictable and incoherent one. In African drumming, any conflicts within such densely textured rhythms are also seen as a way of creating tension and dynamic power. A master drummer will play with these tensions by accenting different rhythms within the overall pattern (ibid., p. 53). Game designer Patrick Cook identifies a similar strategy of playing with textural accents and tensions within the game *Don't Starve* (Klei Entertainment 2013). Cook praises the way *Don't Starve* has many different rhythmic layers, for example, the rhythm of hound attacks every seven days and rhythms of things that replenish and respawn. These combine with the rhythms of hunger, and the durability of the tools the player builds, across the game's cycles of day and night. This dense rhythmic complexity creates, he says, a "beautifully" structured texture of shifting tensions and accents. A texture that provides momentum for current and future player actions. So much so, that you could say, as Cook does, that "the whole game lives on rhythms."

The speed and complexity of a rhythm will also impact the perceived density and texture of a work. As Andrew Schultz points out, there is a "speed at which an audience can hear and process and move with an idea." Extremes in both the number of overlapping events and the speed they occur will produce too much information for an audience to process in detail. The result will be, like the blurring of windows on a fast train, as "objects cease to be observed in their parts and begin to be perceived as textures" (Jourdain 1997, p. 142). Thus, excess speed and the number of events can paradoxically create a work that feels less dense. The presentation of events speeds up but audience perception slows down as they stop focusing on detail and turn to larger structural groupings (ibid, p. 143). For a design whose experience relies on the perception of detail, this effect might be a disaster. In other design contexts, it might be a useful technique for shifting perception towards larger structures and form, or for placing an emphasis on texture. This is a strategy that composer Bree van Reyk describes using in works that have "multiple layers of people making events in time." Although there are rhythmic events occurring, the audience does not perceive them as a rhythm "because it drifts around too much for you to perceive it." With this strategy van Reyk is intentionally producing "a texture of sounds" by creating a level of rhythmic density that is beyond her audience's perceptual capabilities.

Once a rhythmic pattern has been developed through addition, a designer might create texture by then deleting an event from the rhythm or substituting a new or existing event in its place. This process is involved in another strategy common across many of the creative practitioners I interviewed. For instance, musician Roger Mills describes how, when writing recorded dance music with the band *Statik Sound System,* the band would often start composing a track by creating a looping rhythm from a drum sample. They would then build the rest of the track on top of that and at the end of the process:

> we might take the rhythm out again - just right at the beginning - and we'd be left with some of the other textures that we'd built up around that rhythm…and then suddenly, bang the rhythm comes in and off you go.

Just like "the drop" technique discussed in Chap. 8, this is something that dance audiences appreciated and expected. Similarly, composer Bree van Reyk describes starting a composition with a rhythmic layer and then removing "the bottom layers so that the top layers actually never know what started it off." The resulting composition becomes "all just response and not the original." However, there is usually a trace of the rhythmic original that will be perceived by an audience and, in this way, deletion can not only reduce textural density but also subtly increase it. Both addition and subtraction, then, can create an expansion or contraction of density within a work.

Texture is also created through the way events within a rhythm might be grouped together, interlaced with each other, and then reordered in different permutations. This process of ordering rhythm can be approached in very structured way. For instance, choreographer Rhiannon Newton has a "mathematical approach" where she will "do things slowly" then "halve duration" and keep on dividing by two, until division is no longer humanly possible. Then she will often reverse this process. It is an approach that allows her to produce novel and "unusual durations" and thus is a creative strategy that can reveal and rupture habitual rhythmic patterns. Methods for creating and exploring new forms of rhythm are also a particular focus of percussionist Greg Sheehan. To do this he has devised a structural approach where rhythms are expressed using numbers to denote accented groupings of beats. These numbers and their different permutations are then represented in a pattern that he calls a rhythm diamond (Fig. 9.1). The left side of Fig. 9.1 shows a rhythm diamond made up of eight beats that are grouped into accents of three, three, two. Using this diamond, a player can move in any direction to play its combined 24 beats in all their permutations and the right side of Fig. 9.1 shows two possible ways the diamond could be played. During improvised performances, Sheehan and fellow band members will sometimes begin by playing a diamond in unison and then split up and each choose their own way through it. As Sheehan says, "there's a thousand different ways" that you can travel through each one of the rhythm diamonds. He finds that some of the groupings create better rhythms than others and no matter how you combine them, they "always sound really good…because they interact so well." To compose with his rhythm diamonds, Sheehan might play with just a single diamond or any combination of them. His rhythm diamond structure is a way of expressing a rhythm as cycles of multiple possibilities for moving through and combining rhythmic patterns. As such, it is a creative approach that aligns well with the challenges of designing for the variability of user interaction and multiplayer

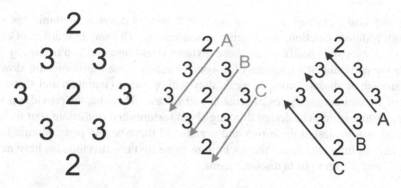

Fig. 9.1 Left is a rhythm diamond based on 8 beats grouped in a 3, 3, 2 pattern. In the centre and right are two example ways of playing through the 24 beats in this diamond. The rhythms of both ways of playing will align because they involve the same number of beats

structures. Both Greg Sheehan and Rhiannon Newton's creative strategies are also ways for designers to open themselves up to new rhythmic possibilities.

Another way of approaching the creation of rhythmic textures is to play with combinations of repetition and delay. In one of Bree van Reyk's compositions she used this to create a "really dense harmonic, melodic and rhythmic structure." The composition had multiple musicians playing the same 21 bar melodic phrase but each musician started to play at different times. As she explains:

> ...the first person starts the phrase and then eight bars later someone else starts playing the exact same thing but from the beginning. Then seven bars after that the next person starts and then six bars and then five. It's not a perfect spiral but it starts from being eight bars apart to being one apart and then three beats, two beats, one beat and then it breaks down the beat as well.

The resulting pattern has what she calls "a trance like effect" that audiences appreciate. A similar technique is used by choreographer Anne Teresa De Keersmaeker as a way of superimposing and creating "overlapping imitations." Like van Reyk she might get dancers to perform the same movements at different times or she might do the opposite and get dancers to perform different movements at the same times. In another related approach called "video-scratching," dancers will perform a short sequence of movement in loops. These loops can then be run backwards and forwards, either with the same or different durations, and be combined in layers. Occasionally, De Keersmaeker will also get two dancers to perform identical loops and will make these phase-shift with each other, by accelerating one dancer until he or she again syncs up with the other (De Keersmaeker and Cvejić 2015, pp. 192–3). These approaches could easily translate into interaction design contexts and, in particular, could inspire the sequencing of the type of layered timers that Patrick Cook describes above, and used in his game *OTTTD* (SMG Studios 2014).

Through the shaping of textures and transitions, interaction designers are able to develop rhythmic expressiveness within a work and also provide structures of rhythmic possibility that might allow users to play expressively with rhythm. Therefore, both designers and the interactions of users can develop rhythmic textures through addition, deletion, substitution or sequencing. The way that different energies, dynamics and speeds within these textures might intersect and transition will create the particular felt qualities of a work. Whether these transitions are slow or fast, smooth or abrupt, strong or weak, they will operate to maintain and shape the flow of rhythm across cycles of tension and release. This chapter provides a few strategies to inspire your design thinking about textures and transitions, but there is no fixed way to design these two and nor should there be. As percussionist Greg Sheehan gleefully exclaims, "there's billions more rhythms that humans have never played" and it's up to us to discover them.

References

Andersen MS, Schmid J (2016) Unbreaking immersion: audio implementation for INSIDE. Wwise Tour 2016 Presentation [PowerPoint Slides]. http://schmid.dk/talks/2016-06-16-wwise/schmid-Wwise_2016-INSIDE_Audio.pdf. Accessed 14 Aug 2016

Audiokinetic (2016) Wwise Tour 2016—Playdead INSIDE (3 of 3)—scene change. [YouTube Video file]. https://youtu.be/TcSuVzUjmLw. Accessed 20 Oct 2017

Broomhall J (2015) Heard about: how Playdead used a real human skull for Inside's audio. Develop. http://www.develop-online.net/interview/heard-about-how-playdead-used-a-real-human-skull-for-inside-s-audio/0209170. Accessed 14 Aug 2016

Chernoff JM (1979) African rhythm and African sensibility: aesthetics and social action in African musical idioms. The University of Chicago Press, USA

De Keersmaeker AT, Cvejić B (2015) Drumming and Rain a choreographer's score. Rosas, Mercatorfonds, Belgium

Jourdain R (1997) Music, the brain, and ecstasy: how music captures our imagination. Harper Collins, USA

Klei Entertainment (2013) Don't Starve. Video game. PC, IOS, Android, Xbox, Playstation, Wii U. Klei Entertainment, Canada

Langer SK (1953) Feeling and form: a theory of art. Charles Scribner's Sons, New York

Lanki C (2013) 間: an aesthetic of space-time. Ricepaper Magazine, vol 14, 2 [online]. https://ricepapermagazine.ca/2013/02/間-an-aesthetic-of-space-time/, Asian Canadian Writers' Workshop Society, Vancouver, Canada

Mateus M, Stern A (2007) Writing Façade: a case study in procedural authorship. In: Wardrip-Fruin N, Harrigan P (eds) Second Person: role-playing and story in games and playable media. MIT Press, USA, pp 183–207

Pearlman K (2009) Cutting rhythms: shaping the film edit. Focal Press, Elsevier, Burlington

Procedural Arts (2005) Façade. Video game. PC. Procedural Arts, USA

Playdead (2016) Inside. Video game. Windows, Xbox, PlayStation, Nintendo Switch, IOS. Playdead, Denmark

Seifert C (2013) Level design in a day: your questions, answered. Gamasutra. https://www.gamasutra.com/view/feature/188740/level_design. Accessed 11 Apr 2013

SMG Studio (2014) OTTTD. Video game. PC, IOS, Android. SMG Studio, Australia

Stern D (2010) Forms of vitality: exploring dynamic experience in psychology, the arts, psychotherapy, and development. Oxford University Press, Oxford, New York

Chapter 10
Predictability

> *The audience wants to see something they haven't seen before, but they want to recognise it when they see it.* (Burrows 2010, p. 65)

Abstract To design a rhythm with a focus on predictability involves creating patterns of repetition and change. Although they can be closely intertwined, each will tug at an audience's attention in different ways. Where repetition can create a soothing predictability that might lull or mesmerise, change can bring an unpredictable energetic vitality that arouses. Repetition draws attention close. Change pushes attention outwards towards an openness of patterned possibilities. These two can occur synchronously across multiple layers of a rhythm, creating a change that is repetitious or a repetition that changes. Patterned layers of repetition and change create complexity within rhythmic experience. How repetition and change pull the audience's attention produces a flow of fluctuating highs and lows that transport the audience along together with a rhythm; one instant soothing with predictability, the next arousing with unpredictability. Both are valuable within playful interaction design and help to produce the to and fro rhythm of the free movement within a play experience. Repetition is something that choreographer and dancer Rhiannon Newton uses to create a form of permanency within the transient art form of live dance. Her performances often involve nuanced changes within a field of repetition, changes that draw her audience into a particular state of very focused attention. Newton also works with rhythm at many different temporal scales and provides inspiration for thinking about rhythmic possibilities within interaction design. Following Rhiannon Newton's interview, this chapter looks first at the satisfactions of repetition and then explores creative strategies for breaking habits and creating uncertainty. In both, predictability and unpredictability interact together and against each other, creating tension, shifting focus and producing intensities.

© Springer International Publishing AG, part of Springer Nature 2018
B. M. Costello, *Rhythm, Play and Interaction Design*, Springer Series
on Cultural Computing, https://doi.org/10.1007/978-3-319-67850-4_10

10.1 If You Rock the Baby It Will Go to Sleep: Interview with Rhiannon Newton, Choreographer

Rhiannon: What I talk about in regard to rhythm is timings, durations, intensities, speeds and accents—in order to craft trajectories and to feel the way a rhythm tells you that something is changing or that we're somewhere else compared to where we were. That's something that you see, something that you perhaps hear, but also something you feel within the body.

One of the things that I'm more and more aware of is that a person is a good dancer because of their rhythm. You can watch certain dancers that just land the extension of the movement, or the shift of weight, in the centre of the beat. It means that often it's a quality of ease of going through the pathway and knowing that they just need to get there. As opposed to the dancer beside them that is going: "I know the movement ends there, I know the end of the beat is coming, oh no, I was there early." When you watch a dancer who has that feeling for timing, they have this sense of being incredibly grounded, but also floating.

A lot of my work to date is based on simple accelerations and de-accelerations, small accumulations of complexity. And durations and timing are definitely one of the main tools my work uses to connect to the audience. It's a focus on what is changing, what is happening, and what is intensifying.

In relation to the audience, the intensities that you can create with rhythm ideally do something also to their bodies. At least I know with myself, when something has a longer duration and slower time it can actually make me quite on edge. As soon as something falls into a more natural rhythm, I can relax. Also the opposite, when something is going really fast, it does something to the watching body and the attention as well.

In most of my works I also try to create some sort of tension between the essence of dance that comes from dance's live quality and processes of repeating or writing dance. My first solo work was about improvising and then repeating improvised movement, with the durations getting shorter so that a single movement became like a concrete object in the space. Then in my more recent work, I'm still working with improvised scenarios, but using repetition more as a base to transform or to notice the growth or development of things. Dance is this thing that you do and then you can't see it anymore—because it has already happened. But you can repeat something and it starts to be like the formation of a language—I've done it, you've seen it, I do it again. When I do something different you notice that it's not that thing that I was doing before.

When I'm improvising, rather than going straight to the thing that I've thought something could become, I always try to slow down the very initial thing and notice all of the things that could potentially happen along the way of that pathway and maybe allow it to transform, or change or take on something. There's something in that holding off in the first instance that really wakes up the whole system. This kind of approach produces a bubbling quality of having many things to pick up and play with, and a kind of aliveness—a state of alertness or rushing around the body—that naturally swells.

In improvisation work, there are certain things that we do that are really about encouraging difference. For instance, going from a big part of your body and staying with that thing leading you for a long time and then changing your attention to a small part of your body and moving that quickly. As Rosalind Crisp [the Australian choreographer] says, "if you rock the baby, it will go to sleep". If you make that rhythm asymmetrical or change it, then it will wake it up. This is in a dancing situation, where you're trying to keep your own attention engaged, so it's actually for yourself as a dancer. That changing of speed is a useful thing to wake up your own attention to possibilities.

That comes from a different place to me choosing to work with repetition. In staying with a constant repetition, you start to see the lack of precision in the ability of the body to actually repeat. In one solo that I did there was an actual beat that would keep these durations. When I got to the very tight beat, you would really see me fail and slow down and miss the beat and then have to speed up. For the audience, the repetition does really put them to sleep. But then there's something else that happens beyond that. Where the audience goes: "wow the dancers are still doing that thing, why are they doing it? Oh, it has changed or are they getting really exhausted? Gosh, they're sweating a lot." So, there are rhythms to watching as well.

Another thing I have played with is mechanical and non-mechanical movement rhythms because we often improvise and then catch a little part of it and repeat that. We've tried this quality of doing that very mechanically. So you take the form and that initial rhythm but you are really prioritising image and form over timing. There's that quality of precision and clarity of direction and functionality. Then another approach, which is a bit more like an animal, where you are kind of like: "oh, there's a thing there, a movement, I'm interested in that. What was that?" To approach it with a quality of curiosity—to prioritise the feel of the rhythm, but not worry too much about the formal edges of the anatomy of the body. There's some sort of tension in those two approaches between a formulaic based re-execution of a movement and something that is feeling the heart of the rhythm—something from the inside that has messy edges, but really catches the little sequence of accents or qualities.

In my recent work *Bodied Assemblies*, I'm working with lots of different scales of time.[1] The first one is the speed of minerals, earth, or rock and is about noticing that it is in movement constantly. It is not stationary. It's acting in relation to its own particles, in relation to gravity all the time. The dancer's body can't be that still or that slow, but it can attempt to be. The next scale of time is plants and, of course, we're speeding that up too. In that section, we are focusing on the quality of growth, on an upward trajectory that is not a real speed but it is a different temporal experience for the body than the human sense of time. The next one is the animal and begins from sight, ears, and sound. Straight away these senses connect the dancers to the speeds of the environment around them and also to more to visceral body feelings like blood pumping. Then the next section is based on language. It is very much connected to naming things around the dancers and, therefore, the rhythm comes in the words and the repetition of words. Then there's the machine section. In that part, we weren't working with something in particular, but thinking about more asymmetrical timings or cause/effect rhythms, thinking of things that have different weight or different material qualities to them. And the final section is the speed of the dancer. With that section, I am proposing (a little ironically) that the dancer is more radical in movement than any of these other things: they can go faster, can turn around and go upside down. There's something about spending a moment on that disciplined body and its rhythms that are particular to the size of the body and the length of limbs and the pathways of the muscles.

At the moment, I've spent a lot of time on how each of the sections in *Bodied Assemblies* begin. Ideally, this thing is logically producing the next thing, which again, is logically producing the next thing. And that is reflected in the rhythms, where there's a build up or push in order to go into that new territory, but then there's also a quality of a wave of arrival into something that has a certain breath, or suspense… or perhaps not suspense but a [she exhales loudly] breath out or something.

By starting *Bodied Assemblies* with the very slow speed of minerals, earth or rock, I'm interested in introducing this way of watching that is not watching the whole body on a scale relative to the space, but asking you to think: "ahh, there's nothing to watch other than the movement of two centimetres." So, the scale of attention is shifted from the outset. The first thing that you see is really slow movement and the difference between slow movement and stillness. In order to set up that scale, it feels important that it is at the beginning, even though I know it's hard for the audience. But it's the difference between really slow and still. It's not the difference between still and move as much as you can. It's about noticing the difference between two things that you might assume

---

[1] Video documentation of Bodied Assemblies can be viewed here: https://vimeo.com/206345086.

are the same, inviting that closer attention to movement. So, it's about increasing attention to what is changing.

In terms of audience attention, rather than the place that we're getting to, I'm trying to emphasise the middle of sections or ideas. To pull out the process of that—of a rhythm becoming another rhythm or of a movement quality becoming a different movement quality, so that there are these small, little steps or slow transformations between things. There is a tension in the process of change, rather than a collage of things. I don't really make works that have separate sections that I can montage. I'm interested in works that have a unifying formula or one structure that unfolds, so that there's a reason for the end.

If I think about rhythmic progressions in my work and how I work with those, it's almost like a mathematical approach. I will often do things slowly, then I will halve the duration and halve them again, and halve them again and halve them again, and also reverse that. That's the basic math that my first solo was based on. In that work, I started from dancing for 60 s and down to 30 and down to 15. I felt like I created really unusual durations that were quite unnatural for the body. I think it's to do with creating these bounds for durations and then that becoming a beat that wasn't a normal beat.

So, I would say I work in two ways. First, that external mathematical approach to rhythms. And the second (more recently), starts from very small repetitions that are connected to breath, where the actual in breath and out breath creates some movement that's already happening, that then either becomes enlarged with voice or with movement. Then I work with a group and find group rhythms from that more organic beginning place, noticing accelerations or a group trajectory towards: we're getting tired, we need to slow down; this is getting boring, we need to speed up, or change something. Feeling those thrusts of "the future is going to be like this because we're already on this trajectory." It's about diversity, difference and the relationships between things. This thing being needed because of that thing being there. It's about listening to your instinct for feeling that something is needed because you've been doing that. Or this is an acceleration and therefore I'm going to follow it… [laughs] I'd say that philosophically I'm aligned to letting the reality of the present and the force of the past produce the future.

10.2   The Satisfactions of Repetition

Repetition draws us into music, and repetition draws music into us. (Margulis 2014, p. 180)

When Rhiannon Newton reminds us that "if you rock the baby, it will go to sleep" she is speaking about the soothing effects of repetitive rhythms. For babies, a rocking movement mimics the familiar ambulatory and other bodily rhythms that a baby senses and becomes habituated to as they grow in their mother's womb. Once they are born, the repetition of these familiar rhythms soothes a baby and makes them feel safe. As they get older, a child might be soothed by the repetitive rhythms of familiar stories or by games with repetitive movements and sounds. Then, as an adult, the jiggling of a leg, twirl of a piece of hair, or fiddling with coins in a pocket might similarly soothe. In common with the rhythms of train travel, these familiar repetitious movements create "a state of kinaesthetic and tactile relaxation" (Edensor 2012, p. 6). When people repeat an action, they know how to do it, what it means, and what will most likely happen when it is done. Thus, repetition also produces a state of "cognitive ease" that feels "comforting" (Kahneman 2011, p. 66). Interaction designers, like Simon McIntyre, work with these soothing effects of repetition when they set up repeating rhythmic patterns of "where to find new information" in educational applications. These patterns engender comforting familiarity and avoid the unease of confusion. Percussionist Greg Sheehan describes something similar when he explains why the 4/4 rhythm is so common in Western music:

> I think 4/4 is very safe and obvious and maybe in our music we need that safety and obviousness… A lot of people turn to music for solace, for joy, or for letting out their emotions and feelings. If they've got that 4/4 rhythm, they can understand how it's all working. People can look very confused if you go out there and play something in thirteen and a half. They don't look very relaxed, [laughs] especially if they are trying to dance.

Unfamiliar rhythms confuse or arouse because they require cognitive effort. In contrast, familiar rhythms relax the audience because they require little cognitive effort. Familiar rhythms also provide that satisfying pleasure of accurate prediction that we discussed in Chap. 7.

Within a rhythmic experience, such familiar and satisfying moments of repetition can also provide a stability that then makes it possible to create a layer of instability. This is a strategy composer Bree van Reyk uses when she grounds a composition with an easily understandable beat structure like 4/4—a structure where an audience can clearly perceive the downbeat. As she says:

> you can get away with a lot if that downbeat is really clear - you can create a lot of mess and a lot of noise and other things around it. If it comes back to that point, that heartbeat, that regular thing occurring, it's still got that kind of satisfying primal response.

The familiar and repetitive downbeat in her example, provides a point of stability for the audience that then allows them to take on board the instability of other rhythms within the composition. Game designer Ilija Melentijevic describes something similar when he talks about needing to design "a thread that people can grab onto to get to where you want them to be." This thread allows him to get around the way that although players "need new experiences…they will move towards familiar ones." He uses the attractive power of familiar experiences to draw players into more unfamiliar moments of change and surprise. Repetition creates a stable field against which the difference of change can emerge and, through contrast, be more easily perceived. It is by playing with the scale of the contrast between the two, as Rhiannon Newton does, that a design is able to provoke differently focused qualities of attention.

Attention during moments of repetition becomes less focused on the relations and meanings of rhythmic events, and more intensely focused on the nuance of each performed repetition. In this way, repetition can cause a focusing inward of attention that becomes mesmerising and even hypnotic (Emmerson 2007, p. 68). This quality is what leads choreographer Jonathan Burrows to describe repetitive movement as "something that hovers between marching and abandon" (2010, p. 17). An example of this occurs when the controlled machine-like repetitive rhythms in a dance-club environment tilt the dancer towards abandon and, as musician Roger Mills observes, create an entrancing ecstatic "transcendental experience." The trance state is precarious and when a DJ mixing beats gets the rhythm wrong by not putting enough "emphasis on repetition" you will, he says, "see the energy just sap out of the dancing audience." Audience energy is fed by repetition and it builds its ecstatic intensity through the dancers' collective, interlocked synchronous movement. Although there may not be much ecstasy involved in performing repetitive tasks in functional computer applications, these too can be associated with the mesmerising pleasure of repetition. People often choose to do repetitive computer tasks manually even if automation is possible, and in so doing, Jonas Löwgren suggests, seek the "hypnotic" rhythmic pleasure of performing repetitive movement (2009, p. 8).

To watch repetitive movement can be similarly mesmerising. Composer and film director Andrew Lancaster tells a story where he becomes mesmerised by the repetitive rhythms of car windscreen wipers:

> I'd be waiting in a queue at a traffic light to do a right-hand turn with music on and the rhythm of the indicator flashing. It would be raining and there would be the rhythms of the windscreen wipers going across. I'd look through the line of windscreens and wipers of the other cars ahead, and at one point there would be rhythms that would all be in sync. It was a moment of randomness that becomes controlled and repetitive, stays there for a while and then turns into another thing. That synchronicity was fascinating.

An interesting aspect of Lancaster's description is its emphasis on the impact of the moment of transformation from one rhythmic state to another. There is a connection here to Rhiannon Newton's emphasis in her work on extending moments of transformation, and on the value of increasing attention to "what is changing" and "what is intensifying." Repetition can create an intensity of attentional focus on change. It can engender expectations, predictions and anticipations around the probability that change will or won't happen. There is an inherent tension in this that will then bring a satisfyingly pleasurable sense of release when change finally comes. It is a tension that fascinates. As Elizabeth Margulis argues in relation to music, the transcendent potential of this fascination lies in the way repetition keeps us "endlessly listening ahead" so that when the predicted repetition or change appears it seems "almost to execute our volition" (2014, p. 12). We feel as if we are "inhabiting" the rhythm and our sense of self expands (ibid., p. 14). The boundary between our self and the rhythm dissolves.

Repetition is often negatively associated with an absence of creativity and with performances or designs that lack innovation or expressiveness. However, repetition also has the potential to create or result in novelty. Both negative and positive repetitions can occur during game play, where repetitive actions might be experienced as pleasurable or grindingly tedious to perform. The difference between the two, Ara Shirinian argues, lies in whether performing a repetitive action requires non-trivial time and effort to master (2012). A task that requires repetition to master its skill, will have a range of performance outcomes over time and these add a sense of creative variety to each repetition. Also, the conscious effort involved in learning the task adds a pleasurable sense of ownership to the performance that tedious tasks will not have (ibid.). Even when a repetitive action has been mastered, as any musician or dancer will tell you, there is always an effort and a contingency involved in maintaining consistency in its performance. Novelty and unpredictability are produced during repetitive performances by the way that "each iteration may reinforce precedents or subtly alter them" (Miller 2012, p. 226). Novelty also emerges because every performance of a repetitive physical action will involve subtle, unpredictable differences.

Novelty can similarly be involved in the process of perceiving repetition. This is because perceiving the same rhythm multiple times, no matter how repetitive, can develop different understandings and potentially different experiences (Margulis 2014, p. 180). The perception of layered repetitive rhythmic structures can also create a loosening of predictive focus that then allows a perceiver to "inventively connect different time points" and "generate novel, changing experiences" (ibid., p. 50). During this process, a perceiver will construct an individual rhythmic pattern that is related to what they are perceiving but differently organised. This type of creative process is what Rhiannon Newton talks about when she points out that although repetition can put an audience to sleep, "there's something else that happens beyond that." In all of the above examples of positive repetition, we see repetition simultaneously providing both the rigid structure and the free movement that is essential for a play experience. Repetition that imprisons and creates a negative experience, is all rigid structure and allows no free movement. It has no play and it is not play. In contrast, create a context where repetition can produce variety and expand a player's sense of self, and you will have a playful rhythmic experience.

10.3 Breaking Habits and Creating Uncertainty

Play is associated with a safety that disconnects it from real-world consequences. For Grodel, this is what makes repetition so central to a play experience "...because somehow repetitive (reversible) activities are felt as less serious, less 'real' than activities...that represent irreversible processes" (Grodal 2003, p. 140). This safety is also what makes the unpredictability and novelty that in the real-world would be seen as threatening, feel pleasurable. There is a frame of safety in games and other aesthetic experiences that allows us to enjoy unpredictability and novelty without feeling in danger (Koster 2005, p. 116). This sense of safety is not a fixed quantity that can be designed or attributed to a particular experience. Our ability to take on board the cognitive challenge of unpredictable or novel rhythms is personal and contextual. We all have, as Daniel Levitin puts it, a personal "adventuresomeness" quotient and this can vary day by day. To accommodate this variability, he recommends that interaction designers let users have some control over the mix between familiar and new in a design (2006, p. 245). However, Levitin's suggestion does need to be used with caution. Let users control the mix too much and you risk removing the cognitive challenge of unpredictability and causing boredom. Repeating any rhythm, no matter how "beautiful", will eventually bore or tire an audience and, as choreographer Sue Healey observes, you will need to introduce a change "to keep awareness".

Introducing rhythmic change is also about making an audience "care what happens next" by making it harder to predict the future flow of events (Burrows 2010, p. 108). It's about keeping the audience in the loop, that Clare Grant described in Chap. 6, of knowing, not knowing and then knowing again. It's also about waking up the audience and, as composer Andrew Schultz says, keeping the performer "alive" by introducing "things which are unsettling." Unpredictability, novelty and the cognitive challenge they present, produce an energetic vitality in both performers and perceivers of a rhythm.

One strategy that my interviewees use to unsettle an audience is to challenge them with unfamiliar rhythms. For example, choreographer Sue Healey wants her audience to "think about rhythm and timing in a different way." To do this she will use "odd durations and rhythms", particularly those that are not the familiar western 4/4 rhythm, to "upset the balance a little." Others challenge their audience's rhythmic habits by using a familiar repetitive rhythm and layering unfamiliar rhythms on top of that. For instance, percussionist Greg Sheehan describes how he will play in 4/4 and then introduce "odd times" to it. He still wants his audience to dance, so someone in the band will be playing "the pulse" of 4/4 for dancers to lock into. On top of this, the rest of the band will be playing less danceable and unfamiliar rhythms like "four sevens and a four, or three nines and a five." A similar layering strategy is used by architect Joe Agius in a building based on a potentially lifeless repetitive rhythm of a 6.6 m grid due to client requirements. To create a sense of contrasting rhythmic "exuberance," Agius deliberately introduced a free rhythmic randomness to the outside façade that broke away from the repetitive grid of the building's inside. His strategy involved layering and contrasting predictable repetition with unpredictable randomness.

Another way of working with contrast is to set up a particular rhythm, familiar or unfamiliar, and once established, deliberately subvert its patterns to challenge and unsettle the audience. Game designer Ilija Melentijevic describes doing this on the game *Death Squared* (SMG Studio 2017). The game, he says:

> …teaches you things and then it changes what you've been taught. Sort of like, "okay, now you have to spin it all around." And "don't trust us that this will always behave like that."

As Melentijevic describes it, this is a process of building trust and then undermining it. It's a process of creating a secure feeling that a rhythmic pattern has been mastered and then introducing uncertainty. Each of these strategies for challenging the rhythmic habits of an audience will have a different rhythmic feel and create a different rhythmic experience. To introduce unfamiliarity right from the beginning, like Sue Healey does, will create an immediate sense of unease and challenge. To interweave the familiar with the unfamiliar will provide a comforting and enlivening blend of predictability and unpredictability. To build familiarity and then undercut it will create a sense of tension and, at the moment of change, may provoke laughter and excitement.

Other interviewees describe strategies for challenging rhythmic habits or introducing uncertainty that work in more subtle ways. Composer and film director Andrew Lancaster deliberately avoids composing music for films that mimics the predictable pop music rhythm of the "snare hitting the two and four." If you have that beat, he says, the music "draws your attention" away from the meanings and experience that is being set up by the film because of the audience's existing familiarity with pop music. The two rhythms of music and film become separate entities and the music dominates. To avoid this he does not, as you might expect, create two rhythms that match each other. His approach instead is to create two rhythms that can play productively off each other. Another example of this that Lancaster describes, is the process of adding sound effects over a visual film sequence. Often, sound designers will create sounds for every element in a sequence, from the breath of the character to the rustle of a jacket or the clink of a coin. This is sound that for the audience "is just hearing what you see." To Lancaster this type of sound design is a "big mistake" because it is too predictable and creates multiple clashing rhythms in a film. Lancaster takes a more selective compositional approach, adding sound effects sparingly in his films while always considering the way they might rhythmically intersect with and play off other elements in the film. Dancer Nalina Wait has a similar aversion to any "mickey mouse" alignment between music and dance in her performances. If the two are aligned, she finds, they collapse too much into each other. When they are not aligned there is a "tension that's held in the space between the music and dance" and she finds that tension creatively useful. In these examples, habits and expectations are challenged by working with rhythms that align in unexpected ways to produce tension but also to amplify the coherence of the rhythmic flow in a work.

Working with extremes of slowness, like Rhiannon Newton does, is another technique for challenging an audience's habitual rhythms. In video game design, any type of slowness is rare and, therefore, often unpredictable and challenging. One example of a game that works with this strategy, is *Vesper.5* (Brough 2012), a small experimental game that was created in one night. The game is a navigable maze that only lets the player take one step per day. With around 100 possible steps it takes over three months to complete the game. This slowness was a deliberate strategy by the game's creator Michael Brough to get players to incorporate the game as a ritual within their daily life. Similar to Rhiannon Newton, his design aimed to focus attention on the nuances of rhythmic change. As Brough puts it, "even the smallest decisions have their consequences amplified when you can only move daily" (2012). Another example, the game *Sailor's Dream* (Simogo 2014), also works with slowness but across a few different scales. In this game, there are some elements that you can always experience, some that only appear on certain days of the week and others that only appear at a particular hour in the day. Arrive at the Transmission Horologe (Fig. 10.1) at the wrong time of day and you will hear nothing but static on the radio. Arrive and be waiting when the hour strikes and you will hear one of twelve radio

Fig. 10.1 Screen shot of the clock radio that can be found on the Transmission Horologe island in the iPad version of the game *Sailor's Dream* (Simogo 2014). The time on the clock matches the time on the players iPad. If the player is in front of the clock when the hour strikes, they will hear that hour's radio transmission. At any other time, they will only hear static

transmissions. Like *Vesper.5*, this binds *Sailor's Dream* to the player's daily rhythms in a way that focuses attention and amplifies the intensity of particular actions in the game. Writing about games that also use slowness like *Everybody Dies* (Jim Monroe 2008) and *Knytt Underground* (Ripstone 2012), Chris Dahlen describes the pleasure he gets from the breathing space they can create:

> …games are just locks and keys; you find the one and it opens the other, and that goes on until the end. But when a game finds a way to make you linger over a key, to wait before you find the lock, to stop and feel what it's like to open the tumblers – that's sublime. (2013)

In his description, we see a similar connection made between slowness, focused attention and an intensity of experience. As we saw in the previous examples, this strategy of rhythmic design requires a degree of contrast or extreme of scale for it to challenge habits and have this kind of deep impact.

For drummer Simon Barker, uncertainty is what creates a sense of mystery within a rhythm and is an essential component of really interesting music. He describes how in shamanic music the musicians are consciously "trying not to give you all the information in a way that you can understand." That lack of understanding, or sense that you are "just not sure what's going on", creates an uncertainty and an aura of mystery. In the shaman rituals of Korean hand gong playing, this mystery is created through a combination of predictability and unpredictability that they describe as being like "sailing smoothly down a trickling stream but occasionally bumping into rocks" (Mills 2010, pp. 154–155). A hand gong player like Kim Junghee will move unpredictably between rhythms that develop linearly, rhythms that repetitively cycle and rhythms of constant variation (ibid., p. 164). By avoiding repetition of accents and patterns across the transitions between the three modes, Kim Junghee teases expectations and maintains a state of uncertainty. Listen to a Korean hand gong ensemble play together, with each player taking a different rhythmic line, and you will hear "their lines intertwine to create a truly bewildering overall effect: a wall of shimmering metallic sound, out of which fragments emerge and then disappear" (ibid., p. 146). For listeners, these fragments might emerge and disappear at different points so that each experiences a different rhythmic composition. Therefore, this rhythmic experience of layered uncertainty will, in a similar way to the repetitive layers we discussed earlier, produce novel and changing experiences.

The uncertainty of ambiguity is also associated with open-ended rhythmic experiences in Daniel Levitin's description of the music of Joni Mitchell. He says that Mitchell sometimes tunes her guitar with ambiguous chords that "could have two or more different roots" (Levitin 2006, p. 214). This ambiguity unsettles a perceiver's ability to predict what might come next but also creates an openness of interpretation. Those listening attentively are able to "write and rewrite in their minds a multitude of musical interpretations as the piece unfolds" (ibid., p. 215). As they listen to the ambiguous chords, their attention turns towards an openness of patterned possibilities. Levitin describes how Joni Mitchell's ambiguous tuning also created a kind of "possibility space" during performance that brilliant fellow band members, like the bass player Jaco, could "wander around…reinforcing the different chord interpretations with equal emphasis, sublimely holding the ambiguity in a delicate, suspended balance" (ibid.). This possibility space was not easy to hold and Mitchell was often frustrated by the way other bass players would try to tie the chords down to a single interpretation, reducing the openness of the music. As this suggests, ambiguity can be challenging for both perceivers and performers because it involves conceptualising the past, present, and future of a flow of multiple possibilities. It requires a lot more effort to hold this multiplicity in balance than it does to follow a single rhythmic thread. However, this example also suggests that ambiguity can be enlivening because of the openness and variety it produces.

Games can also be described as possibility spaces (Salen and Zimmerman 2004, p. 67) and here ambiguity can be similarly challenging. The danger for a play experience is that ambiguity will make a rhythmic pattern so difficult to decipher that it is read as noise or judged to be illegible. If this happens, it will lead to a level of frustration that could deflate a play experience (Koster 2005, p. 44). The openness and variety that ambiguity brings can be useful but perhaps, like some of the compositional strategies we have already explored, needs to be tempered in play with a rhythmic layer that is easily mastered. In earlier research, I observed that layering ambiguity with a more legible pattern produced the feeling of safety required for play (Costello and Edmonds 2009). Mastering the legible pattern created a level of trust in the work and a willingness to explore. Players who had this sense of safety were able to be more open and playful in their reactions to the ambiguous elements. They trusted there was a pattern to find and then usually found one or more possible ways of resolving it. For these players, the ambiguous elements also added a layer of unpredictable vitality that kept them caring about what happened next and engaged in play. This aspect of rhythmic ambiguity makes it very valuable for designing playful experiences. To benefit from it, a design needs to use ambiguity within a context that maintains the protective frame of play.

Predictability and unpredictability can be said to define each other in the mind of the perceiver, because of the way each creates a field against which the other can emerge. Designing with these two rhythmic qualities, therefore, is always about contrast and about the tensions, intensities and qualities of attention that this contrast can create. For designers, this involves working with strategies for modulating the scale and character of juxtapositions between familiar and unfamiliar rhythms across a design. The familiar soothes with the comforting ease of comprehension. The unfamiliar arouses with the unsettling vitality of challenge. The familiar also has a fascinating quality that can be used to draw users towards more challenging moments of unfamiliarity. Predictability often acts to focus attention inwards towards greater levels of subtlety, while unpredictability often creates an opening of attention towards a space of possibilities. A play experience needs to build and disrupt both rhythms to create that to and fro of free movement within a more rigid structure. Thus, the most playful forms of repetition are those that produce novelty. Correspondingly, the most playful forms of change are those that combine instability with stability.

References

Brough M (2012) Vesper.5. Video Game. PC

Burrows J (2010) A choreographer's handbook. Routledge, London, New York

Costello B, Edmonds E (2009) Directed and emergent play. Paper presented at the creativity and cognition 2009, Berkley, CA, USA, 27–30 October

Dahlen C (2013) The special pleasure of a slow game. Polygon. https://www.polygon.com/2013/8/29/4667610/opinion-the-special-pleasure-of-a-slow-game. Accessed 22 Sept 2014

Edensor T (ed) (2012) Geographies of rhythm: nature, place, mobilities and bodies. Ashgate Publishing, Farnham

Emmerson S (2007) Living electronic music. Ashgate, Great Britain

Grodal T (2003) Stories for eye, ear and muscles: video games, media and embodied experiences. In: Wolf MJP, Perron B (eds) The video game theory reader. Routledge, New York, pp 129–156

Kahneman D (2011) Thinking fast and slow. Farrar, Straus and Giroux, New York

Koster R (2005) A theory of fun for game design. Paraglyph Press, Scottsdale

Levitin DJ (2006) This is your brain on music: the science of a human obsession. Dutton, New York

Löwgren J (2009) Toward an articulation of interaction esthetics. New Rev Hypermedia Multimedia 15(2):129–146. https://doi.org/10.1080/13614560903117822

Margulis EH (2014) On repeat: how music plays the mind. [Kindle iOS version] edn. Oxford University Press, New York

Miller K (2012) Playing along: digital games, YouTube and virtual performance. Oxford University Press, New York

Mills SRS (2010) Playful patterns of freedom: Hand Gong performance in Korean shaman ritual. In: Mills SRS (ed) Musiké 4—analysing East Asian music: patterns of rhythm and melody. Semar, The Hague, pp 145–170

Monroe J (2008) Everybody Dies. Video game. PC

Ripstone (2012) Knytt Underground. Video game. PC, PlayStation, Wii U, IOS. Ripstone, UK

Salen K, Zimmerman E (2004) Rules of play: game design fundamentals. MIT Press, Cambridge

Shirinian A (2012) The value of repetition. Gamasutra. https://www.gamasutra.com/view/feature/174974/the_value_of_repetition.php. Accessed 11 Apr 2013

Simogo (2014) Sailors Dream. Video game. IOS. Simogo, Sweden

SMG Studio (2017) Death Squared. Video game. Xbox, PlayStation, Nintendo Switch. SMG Studio, Australia

Chapter 11
Vitality

Even if you start off feeling tired or lonely or bored. It doesn't matter, because you're willing to play and you know that any game will do, that any game will get you there. You know that because you know the energy resides not in the game but in playing with people. (De Koven 2013, p. 14)

To be aroused is 'to be put in motion' or 'stirred up' or 'excited into activity', physically, mentally, emotionally. It is synonymous with 'to animate'. (Stern 2010, p. 58)

Abstract In this chapter, we now explore the concept of vitality and focus on the way that a playful rhythm can produce vitality, animating both people and interactive systems. Vitality emerges through a process of energy exchange. Energy will travel both into and out from an interactive system during a rhythmic experience and it is the play of intensities, contrasts and durations within this flow of energy that produces rhythmic vitality. We begin with Andrew Johnston, a digital artist, musician and Research Director at the Animal Logic Academy at the University of Technology Sydney. Johnston researches and practices across the disciplines of live performance, digital art and human-computer-interaction. This gives him a unique perspective on rhythm and the role it plays within interactive experience. His collaborations with dancers and musicians to create interactive systems for live performance have given him particular insight into the design of rhythms that generate expressive vitality. As he explains in his interview, doing this is about creating a type of interactive control that has an energy of give and take, and a fluidity that feels conversational. This leads us to explore the questions: what distinguishes a lively rhythm from a mechanical one? How do we create a design whose interactions might allow a user to be rhythmically expressive? And, how do we create dynamic rhythmic vitality? These discussions make connections with several of the previous chapters, bringing together many of the concepts we have developed so far about playful rhythmic vitality and expressiveness.

© Springer International Publishing AG, part of Springer Nature 2018
B. M. Costello, *Rhythm, Play and Interaction Design*, Springer Series on Cultural Computing, https://doi.org/10.1007/978-3-319-67850-4_11

11.1   It's like Blowing a Feather: Interview with Andrew Johnston, Interaction and Software Designer

Andrew: Rhythm is a word that is used in so many different ways but I guess at a higher level, rhythm is structuring flows of things. Then there's smaller rhythms, like moving your hand and moving your body in a constant tempo. And there's bigger rhythms, which might be the structure of a composition or the way a composition opens with a particular theme, goes into some other theme and then comes back to the original one. Rhythm is about changing things over time: if you can perceive those changes, and you can perceive the time, then that's what rhythm is.

My most recent interactive system for musical performance was the inter-active system, *Blue Space*, that I worked on with Andrew Bluff and oboist Linda Walsh. We had Linda playing behind a scrim—a semi-transparent screen—which we were projecting onto from the front. There was a microphone on her oboe and an infrared light on the end of her oboe so we could track the movement of her instrument, through the scrim. When she played, streams of particles and other graphic shapes would flow out of the end of her instrument based on what she was playing (Fig. 11.1). The colour and the speed of those particles would be influ-enced by the timbre and the volume of what she was playing. There was also a dance element to it, because when she moved, it wasn't just the sounds that made the particles come out. When she moved, she could stir the particles.[1] So, the concept was to blur the boundaries between dance and music a little bit.

Rhythm came into that project at different levels. At the micro level, the note level, depending on what the oboe player was doing, the rhythm of the particles would either be relaxed, loose and flowing or much jerkier, computer-y and harsh. We used a fluid simulation for the particles in the relaxed state and they really are literally flowing in slow rhythmic tempos. There was a more up-tempo feel to the harsher particle movement state or at least a different feel to the rhythm. So, in the harsh state, rhythms were not shaped like a sine wave but were more like a square wave. They had a more angular rhythm.

At a macro level, there was also the rhythm created by the shifts between these different states in the piece. There were 10 or 11 different states, or something like that, and we would transition live between them. The composition was improvised and we would look for certain cues from the performer, Linda Walsh. So, although it didn't always exactly change at the same point, it was more or less cued. Sometimes the transitions would change straight away and sometimes they would take a while. So

---

[1] See video documentation of *Blue Space* here: https://vimeo.com/157974674.

even though you might cue it, it doesn't just go snap, boom, next state. It would actually take 20 s to morph from one to the other.

That process of morphing is another tempo change in a slightly more metaphorical sense. It's turning a corner—as good conductors can do. They get those transitions between tempos just right. When it's done well, it's super powerful. It feels like it's a natural flow from one to the other. But the quality a tempo change has depends on the kinds of rhythms and the styles of the music that are involved, for instance, the change might be floating or it might be abrupt. With really good conductors and musicians, somehow the relationship between the first tempo and the second tempo and how they have transitioned makes it build the energy or sustain interest in a good way. With a bad conductor, the tempo changes in a way that is somehow inappropriate, and you notice it.

I really think transitions are a big part of what makes a piece succeed or fail. Working with computer design tools I find I have a tendency to fade from one thing to another—to ramp or transition smoothly. Maybe that's because digital material has a tendency to change abruptly and it's relatively easy to do that. So, making it change more gradually is part of showing that you've mastered the craft. Or maybe it's a way of surprising people—that you can do smooth transitions with digital. So, we tend to have a lot of smooth transitions. But I don't have rules about it. I try to remain open to any possibilities. There are definitely times when I think a sudden transition is the way to go. You just have to try things out: some things work and some things don't.

Fig. 11.1 Image of oboist Linda Walsh performing in *Blue Space* in September 2015 at the Creativity and Cognition Studios, UTS, Australia

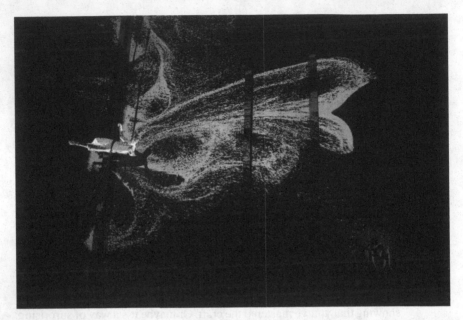

Fig. 11.2 Image from a performance of the Stalker Theatre Company work *Encoded* first presented at Carriageworks in Sydney in November 2012. This image shows the type of fluid simulation that Andrew Johnston describes as relaxed loose and flowing

Another thing you can play with in terms of rhythm is the link between the performer and the system. You might start off a piece with a very clear link for the audience between what the performer does and what the system does. But then you can mess with it—shift to a different interaction style where the link is no longer as clear or possibly even completely unclear for a little while. And that can work. If I've got certain interaction styles or states where the link is more apparent, I tend to put that at the beginning as way of establishing that connection with the audience, and saying "Yeah, this is happening live. There is a connection going on here."

Another project I have been working on recently is the large scale interactive dance work *Encoded*, involving four performers and three main interactive systems. My team worked on one of these three interactive systems. Our system used motion tracking combined with big projections on the wall behind the performers. The projections were all based on a fluid simulation and when the dancers moved they could stir the fluid with their movements. We could also visualise the fluid in lots of different ways and change the viscosity of the fluid (Figs. 11.2 and 11.3).

Many of my interactive systems amplify the effect of certain gestures and in *Encoded,* if a dancer goes like this [he waves his arm], then the fluid

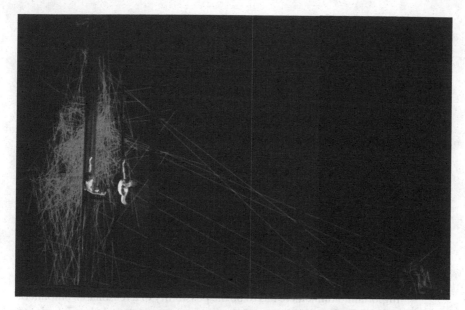

Fig. 11.3 Image from a performance of the Stalker Theatre Company work *Encoded* first presented at Carriageworks in Sydney in November 2012. This image shows the type of fluid simulation that Andrew Johnston describes as jerky and harsh

flies off.[2] So, that gesture is now not just this scale, but it's scaled up by a 100% or something. I see that as a resonance or an amplification. Dampening is the opposite of that, where some gestures are not seen by the system. Whether ignored deliberately or not, those gestures are dampened in a way. One way of thinking about these interactive systems, then, is to think of them as systems that resonate and dampen—a bit like an amplifier.

For me, the most interesting thing is when the performer is really connected with the system, shaping it, and being shaped by it—in conversation with it. And I think that the key to creating that conversational relationship is having a balance between the performer being in control and the system being in control. That real dialogue of the performer shaping the projections and the projections shaping the performer—a continuous dialogue going on. I don't mean a dialogue where someone says something and then someone, the system, says something back. But a much more embodied fast, to and fro conversation. Where one or the other takes the initiative for a while and does something and then the other one will respond. Of course, that can happen in that turn taking way, but more often in a much more fluid and quick acting way.

---

[2] See video documentation of *Encoded* here: https://youtu.be/hopxlmyVp7A.

Generally, if you pick the right kind of physical system and the right settings for it, then it will also have enough complexity so that there's a lot for the performer to explore, get more out of, and still be surprised by. Even though they can predict more or less what it would do if they did something, they can't predict it completely. That's where the conversation comes in, I think. Just like if you're playing with a feather or something like that. You might throw the feather in the air or you might blow it. You can see that your air is directly having an effect on it. You can see that the way it responds is as you'd expect. But you couldn't necessarily predict exactly where it would go because it's got that complexity to it. It's like the way a musical instrument brings a level of un-control, even if you are the most virtuosic virtuoso. There's something about the struggle even to master it that makes it interesting. So, it's the combination of intuitiveness and complexity that makes you want to keep playing with those things.

It seems to me that there's no point to an interactive system if you're fully in control of all aspects of it. It doesn't bring anything. But there is a trap, an artistic creative trap, that you could fall into if you think control is not important. I think there has to be the possibility of a reasonable amount of control. Because if it's just all about complete un-control, then I don't see the interactive system actually adding much. It's just a computer doing random stuff in the background—I've seen plenty of that. Or where it might as well be random stuff in the background because somehow the actions of the performer don't really seem to be linked in any way that's perceivable to what the computer is doing. Even though as a performer it can be fun sometimes to have random things thrown at you, I think complete randomness, or too much randomness without the possibility of the control coming back a little bit to the performer, doesn't work. But that's an aesthetic choice, it's not a rule.

One of the early things I made was an interactive object that span around more or less with its own rhythm. A musician would poke and prod it with their sounds, then it would spin faster or slower and repeat their sound back to them. I always felt that work wasn't really very successful. It had too much of its own energy somehow and it was very easy for it to become dominating. Since then, a strategy I use often is that the system itself doesn't bring too much extra energy beyond what the performer injects into it. It might resonate, but it doesn't do stuff on its own too much. It doesn't start moving without some energy being injected by the performer. And that feels important for my aesthetic. If the system does too much stuff, the system tends to dominate because energy is essentially unlimited with digital systems. You can make energy with no actual physical effort. If you do too much of that, then it can cause the interaction to become too dominated by the computer and that can swamp that conversational relationship.

I think that rhythm within interaction design is something that's often implicit and perhaps should be made more explicit. It is a useful language to make some things more visible than they otherwise might be. It's useful for getting out of the habits of making things the same as always.

11.2 Mechanical Repetition and the Automaton

As Andrew Johnston points out, digital rhythms have a "tendency to change abruptly" and this is one of the characteristics that can lead to mechanical rhythms. To call a rhythm mechanical is to link it, often in a negative way, to the differences in movement qualities between living beings and machines. Machines don't have a muscular need for relaxation after tension and so can move with a rhythm that has none of the organic balance of "recuperation in movement" that occurs with living things (Lange 1975, p. 31). Due to this need for muscular recuperation, living things like human beings will move in rhythms that speed up and slow down as each movement arrives and departs from a point of rest or stasis. In contrast, machines can shift from still to moving and back again with an abrupt speed that is beyond human muscular capabilities. If someone mimics this abruptness, they will create a movement rhythm that might then be described as mechanical. Another cause of the speeding up and slowing down that occurs during human movement is the fluctuating level of effort and precision required to negotiate different environments or contexts of action. Effort can add an energy that will speed up a movement but, equally, a movement that requires a lot of effort or careful precision will slow a movement down. These rhythmic variations will occur constantly throughout your daily life. For instance, when you move around inside a house as:

> …you cross a room and exit, your pace increases and then slows as you pass through the door, perhaps with a moment's hesitation before regaining velocity along the hallway. You pick up speed as you approach a flight of stairs, pumping out higher energy as you strain harder toward the top, then discretely relax a bit before resuming your stride across the landing above. (Jourdain 1997, p. 145)

If you didn't move with this varying tempo and tried to match the constant beat of a metronome, you would trip over, bang into things and end up with "plenty of bruises" (ibid.). Organic movement rhythms have the vitality of form that we discussed in Chap. 9 and this gives texture to their rhythms of arrival and departure. Mechanical movements either have none of this nuance or move with a rhythm that exceeds the capabilities of living things.

An absence of nuance in the rhythms of electronic music can also lead to it being described as mechanical and lacking in vitality. Such mechanical rhythms are described by musician Roger Mills as having "no perceivable movement outside of the strict measurements that only a computer can create." Percussionist Greg Sheehan echoes this, saying that the rhythms of the electronic music he would describe as mechanical have "no movement in the tempo." In some circumstances, he finds this precision useful and will play along to a drum machine because he can "rely on the accuracy" and "totally pinpoint the beat." In other circumstances, he prefers the creativity of playing with fellow musicians where there can be more "push and pull" and "emotion" in the beat. A similar connection is made between creativity and the movement of live performance by drummer Simon Barker. He has tried using electronic beat-makers as part of his composition process but finds the rhythms they produce too "literal" with no "sense of shape…or inner microtiming." Without this, they cannot express the nuances of rhythmic movement he is trying to compose. Some rhythmic movement can, of course, be deliberately added to an electronic beat. For instance, you can, as composer Andrew Lancaster describes, shift precise electronic beats "off the grid" to create a sense of "life" and a feel or groove that precise beats won't have. The liveness that he describes coming from the way this added imprecision often mimics the rhythms of human performance (Iyer 2002, p. 403). Even electronic beats that have "superhuman hit rates" can have an expressive impact that is linked to their association with human movement and will be perceived with the "same energy generation and excitement" as a live virtuoso human performance (Emmerson 2007, p. 85). A common aspect to all these descriptions is the way that vitality and expressiveness are linked to the variety produced by the shifting tempos of perceived human performance, whether solo, collective or computer generated.

While movement is associated with liveness and expressivity, a lack of movement is associated with death and lifelessness, devoid of expressivity. Lack of movement, Stern says, is what makes seeing a dead person "immediately shocking because they do not move, nothing moves, and even the most subliminal vibrations of tonicity stop" (2010, p. 9). We need these subtle movements to perceive "mental activity", "thoughts" or "emotions." Without any of this sense of animation or arousal there is a shocking lack of expressive presence (ibid., p. 10). A similar association between lack of movement and lack of expressive life also appears in unfavourable descriptions of live performance. A musical performance with no expressive variety might be described, for example, as "deadpan or computer generated" (London 2004, p. 163). In this case, it is the rhythms of the performance that appear dead. They move along, but with such precision that they do not communicate anything beyond the form of the composition and this lack of expressive movement associates them with the lifelessness of the mechanical. A focus on precision of form is also involved in choreographer Rhiannon Newton's description of the contrast between dancing mechanically and organically. For her, mechanical rhythms involve "prioritising image and form over timing," which gives them a "quality of precision." In contrast, dancing organic rhythms involves a questioning curiosity of approach that allows her to feel "the heart of the rhythm." This heart lies not in the form of the rhythm but comes "from the inside" and this means it creates a rhythm that has "messy edges" and "really catches that little series of accents." The rhythm of the organic movement she describes is embodied within its expressive accents and nuance, not within its external form. Similarly, in music, a performance that focuses on the perfection of external form will often be criticised as mechanical in its virtuosity. Such performances draw attention to the skill of the performer rather than the music being performed so that the skill is "in the work but not of it" (Dewey 2005 [1934], p. 146). The skill of virtuosity is, thus, experienced as separate from and unrelated to the expressive workings of the rhythm being performed and this lack of embodied relationship is what will deaden the performance's expressive movement.

The vitality of expressivity is something that is also associated with agency and creative control. Paul Souriau makes this connection when he describes a conductor of an orchestra who keeps time without being constrained by the strict tempo of a metronome. The freedom of movement in his tempo creates a feeling that the conductor "has mastery over it" and if she or he is strict with the meter, it then feels like this strictness arises out of free will. It feels as if the conductor wishes it to happen. As a result, the music will then lose its "mechanical character," a character that would only be felt if there was a perceived lack of free control and self-determination in the performed rhythm (Souriau 1983 [1889], p. 89). This association between the mechanical and a lack of control is quite common and it can mean that mechanical rhythms will produce fear or feelings of discomfort. For example, these feelings arise in Elizabeth Margulis' description of the way that extremes of spoken repetition can be perceived as "inhuman and sinister." With such repetition, she says, it will feel as if the utterances are "products of some invisible, subconscious script" and, thus, are an expression of a non-spontaneous "automaticity" (2014, p. 84). Margulis is linking the fear that such rhythms are able to possess or take over someone against their will to the mechanical repetitive rhythms of the automaton. In both examples, free control, or at least an audience's perception of it, seems to be an essential component of performed rhythmic vitality. They also suggest that this freedom is not just about having control over a rhythm. It is about having the power of mind to choose whether and when to exercise that control. The liveliness of freedom of thought, that sense that there is a being with agency performing the rhythm, contributes to the creation of vitality within rhythmic experience.

Rhythmic vitality, then, is associated with movement and particularly with subtle deviations, imprecisions and nuances that mimic the rhythms performed by organic living things. A rhythmic performance that has vitality will prioritise the expression of these accents over the external form of a performance. However, it will do this in a way that preserves an integral relationship to the work that is being performed. Such a performance will then usually be described as rhythmically expressive and will be perceived to have a vitality that speaks of a playful liveliness of free will and of animate thought.

11.3 Expressive Rhythms of Control

The expressive conversational relationship that Andrew Johnston tries to create in his interactive designs relies on a particular quality of control, one that he describes as embodied, fluid and fast. A similar focus on embodiment and speed occurs in the design of real-time control within video games. This control relies on a tight micro-timed coupling between physical human input and video game output. The microsecond speed and rhythmic nuance of the coupling will impact the feel of this control, with response times of 50–100 ms needed to create a pleasurable sense of real-time control and avoid a feeling of sluggish unresponsiveness (Swink 2009, p. 45). Within the simulated space of a video-game these rhythms of real-time control can combine with the other audio-visual and haptic elements of a game to create that embodied "tactile, kinesthetic sense of manipulating a virtual object" that is known as game feel (Swink 2009, p. xiii). This type of embodied control is also needed in musical video games for players to be able to perform with rhythmic expressiveness. As Marczak et al. argue, "time must never be completely delegated to [the] computer" because this would make the performer's gestures "precipitated and not felt" (2009, p. 5 of 6). The lack of felt connection between gestural input and game output would then disconnect the performer from their embodied internal rhythm and impede expressive temporal performance. Designers of electronic instruments have a similar need to create this kind of embodied intimacy. Without it, performers will not experience the "consistent and clearly perceivable 'cause-effect' relationship" required for instrumental control (Emmerson 2007, p. 94). In addition, they will not be able to sense and vary the temporal nuances of their played rhythm and this type of subtle control is needed to play an instrument expressively. In electronic instrument design, achieving this subtle control often rests on the type of mappings created between performer gestures and system response. As drummer Alon Ilsar points out when he describes the gestural mappings he created for his electronic instrument *AirSticks*, a design needs to map several scales and speeds of gesture to achieve expressive control:

> Within drumming, there's three ways of really playing a stroke. You either use the arm, the wrist or the fingers. Good drummers can combine all those in really interesting ways. The speed comes from the fingers and the power comes from the arm or the wrist. So, I think it's a similar metaphor for me with the gestural mappings in *AirSticks*. There are big strokes that are obvious. Then there are ghost strokes so to speak, the ones where I use the button and the fingers, that might be more hidden but they're really important in creating the expression.

It was this combination of large powerful and small subtle nuanced gestures that allowed Ilsar to produce rhythms of varying tempos across a spectrum of heavily to delicately accented. Through this he was able to expressively control "the feeling" of the rhythms he performed with his electronic instrument. Expressive control, as these examples all suggest, requires both the power and the delicacy of a rhythm to be tangibly felt and embodied during performance.

Composer and percussionist Bree van Reyk created two interactive musical installations for contexts where such embodied control needs to be developed quickly. The first, *Melody Fence*, was created with designer Elliat Rich and is installed at Ross Park Primary School in Alice Springs, Australia. *Melody Fence* takes its inspiration from a common rhythmic practice of children: to walk along a row of fence palings and drag a stick so that it creates a rhythm as it hits everything in its path. In this work, the fence is constructed from different metal tubes placed, like fence palings, the same width apart. The width controls the meter of the melody the tubes will play when a stick is dragged along, each tube playing a different note when hit. The fun thing for children, van Reyk says, is to "try and see how fast they can run along and make the sound happen." In this musical design, the notes and order of notes is controlled by the interactive system, while the children can play with the speed and direction of the notes performed.

The second installation, *Arbour Sonata* (created with Chloe Goldsmith), is also designed for children. In this case, it is a temporary installation set up during outdoor events. *Arbour Sonata* is a tree like sculpture that is hung with various household objects that children can hit to create sound. Bree van Reyk found these objects in supermarkets and selected them based on whether their pitches were in tune, for instance, choosing "rice bowls that were all in C major." This tuning creates a visual percussion instrument with "no wrong notes" and it is this aspect of both these designs that, for van Reyk, makes them able to be played with expressively. Liberated from the need to worry about which notes might work together, the children could focus on playfully making up patterns. She was astonished by the way little groups working together would all "take a different point of inspiration" and come up with a musical pattern that was "completely unique." As we saw in our discussion of improvisation in Chap. 5, a well-chosen restricted palette increases creative expression because it pushes the performer towards investigative exploration. These two designs also quickly develop the type of embodied control that allows a performer to play expressively by creating an easily learnable, perceivable and performable rhythmic structure.

Unless an interaction design is specifically musical we might not think so carefully about developing the possibility for this type of expressive rhythmic performance. However, even in non-musical contexts these same strategies can be used to encourage expressive play. A comparative study I conducted into the rhythmic experience of the games *Minecraft* (Mojang 2011) and *Don't Starve* (Klei Entertainment 2013) discovered that there were similar strategies involved in creating an environment for rhythmic expressiveness (Costello 2016). The study looked at just thirty seconds of play in each game, which in both cases involved chopping down a tree to collect wood. It found that rhythmic expressiveness was possible in *Minecraft* because the Lego-like block structure of its world created a rhythm of tree chopping that was repeatable, easily learned and easily performed. The game's audio-visual responses to player actions not only created that sense of real-time control discussed above, but they also actively helped the player to perceive the timings and rhythms of their actions. Once learned, the tempos of the different tools and methods that could be used to chop a tree gave the player control over ways to vary and repeat these rhythms and, thus, the ability to play *Minecraft* with rhythmic expressiveness.

In contrast, the tree chopping in *Don't Starve* had a rhythmic groove where the player felt held up or pulled back by the game. This was caused by a lack of real-time control and the generally opaque and inaccessible rhythmic structure that the chopping responses had. The player would often trigger rhythms in *Don't Starve's* tree chopping sequence, rather than perform them in an embodied way. Those rhythms that the player did perform were obscured by audio-visual randomness or variety, and thus their patterns could not be clearly perceived across sequences of actions. These factors combined meant that there was little room for expressive performance while a player was chopping down a tree in *Don't Starve*. Although in both games the action of tree chopping is a relatively insignificant part of game play, it is an action that would be performed repeatedly by a player. The possibility for rhythmic expressiveness in *Minecraft* makes this repetitive action feel less laborious than it does in

Don't Starve and this contributes to the overall vitality of the feel of its gameplay. Designing interactions that allow a user to perform in rhythmically expressive ways can, therefore, be a way to make repetitive actions more pleasurable. This rhythmic expressiveness is also something that will produce a feeling of system vitality and encourage playfully creative interactions.

11.4 The Push and Pull of Dynamic Vitality

...a rhythm is interesting in terms of its potential to be affected by other rhythms. (Chernoff 1979, p. 60)

Collaborative musical improvisation is a process that can have a conversational cyclic rhythm of "call and response," explains musician Roger Mills, with each cycle adding depth and levels of expression. This conversational rhythm is also something Andrew Johnston aims for when he creates his interactive systems for live performance. If Johnston can create a connection between a performer and his system where the performer is "shaping it, and being shaped by it," this, he says, gives the experience a creative rhythm that is similar to the conversation of musical improvisation. When this is working well in an interactive performance, the musician will be "seizing the initiative for a time to steer the conversation in a particular direction, then relinquishing control and allowing the virtual instrument to talk back" (Johnston and Clarkson 2011, p. 14). In his description, this is a rhythm whose push and pull involves a to and fro of control and, thus, also an exchange of energy between performer and system. It is this two-way relationship of energy transfer, Emmerson suggests, that allows an interactive system to become "animate", the exchanged energy creating a sense of vitality in the system (Emmerson 2007, p. 53). Such oscillating movements of control and energy will also create that essential feeling of having something to play off that needs to occur when two musicians improvise creatively together. Thus, designing for a conversational rhythm of improvisation between a human and a computer will involve composing potential paths for rhythms of control and energy to be exchanged. As the quote above suggests, it is the potential transformations that can occur during these rhythmic exchanges that will then make a rhythmic experience truly interesting.

Designing for conversational rhythmic exchanges requires a lightness of touch, explains educational designer Simon McIntyre. This is because the rhythms of a conversation can't be forced and, as an example, he describes how forcing students to make posts in a discussion forum failed to create any genuine discussion. Rather than mandating forum contributions, he recommends designers take a less controlled approach, one that allows students to freely congregate and set up their own threads. This, he finds, creates a more "legitimate social construction" where the students feel like they "own" the forum. It also gives the rhythms of discussion a vital energy that then builds and sustains conversational momentum. In another example, McIntyre describes how the conversational rhythms of a videoed exchange between himself and another lecturer were ruined when a video producer made them sit on stools at an unnatural angle and distance. This meant that on camera they "weren't even paying attention to each other." Their exchanges were consequently stilted and lacked a responsive energy. The conversation was reshot with both standing and, with the freedom of movement they now had, they were able to create a "rapport" with a more natural conversational rhythm. This rapport would have been readable from all kinds of physical rhythms right down to the way they blinked their eyes: another rhythm that can easily be disrupted and cause a breakdown in conversational energy. This type of rhythmic breakdown, film editor Walter Murch observes, might lead someone to think we are not telling the truth during a conversation:

> It's a perennial problem for politicians, because they're up there giving a speech and, most often, they're not really in the moment. They're reading a text, and they're thinking about ten thousand different things. Their mouth is in motor mode. As a result, their blinks are off, especially with the ones that don't get elected. We don't trust them. We say there's something funny about this guy, and we don't know what it is. A good percentage of that is the fact that he's not blinking at the right place. (Melnick 2012)

As these examples show, we are very attuned to the nuances of all kinds of rhythm within conversation and might mistrust or not participate in any exchange where these feel wrong, forced or fake. They also reveal how conversational rhythms rely on an in-the-moment freedom of action that can be easily disrupted by distraction or constraint of movement. For designers of interactive conversational rhythms, this suggests a need to pay attention to the free flow and nuance of rhythmic exchanges and also to the potential for system responses to feel phoney or forced. Here is where a strategy we discussed in Chap. 6 is useful: to design with rhythms that mimic human movement. Also useful is the related strategy of Andrew Johnston's, to work with rhythms that mimic real-world physical relations, like fluid simulations, springs or rubber bands. With these physical mappings, he finds that performers can walk straight up to an interface and go "right I see how that works." They are able to immediately start to play with the system and this speeds up the creation of a conversational rapport. Simulated real-world rhythms that users are already familiar with are less likely to feel phoney or forced and, thus, less likely to impede the development of conversational rhythms.

False, forced or stilted rhythms will deflate conversational energy because they make it difficult for somebody to perceive and anticipate the rhythms of their conversational partner. This an issue that arose for drummer Alon Ilsar when he was improvising with another musician while playing his electronic instrument *AirSticks*. At the beginning of the collaboration, the other musician did not understand the gestural mapping of the digital controllers and as a result could not grasp the relationship between the gestures and the rhythms Ilsar was playing. This musician was used to being able to see "when the drummer is playing the toms…[or] hitting a cymbal" and with a physical drum kit that ability to anticipate the rhythm allowed for a successfully responsive improvisation. It gave the musician that something to play off that we discussed earlier. Once the musician was more familiar with the mapping of gesture to sound in *AirSticks* they liked the way the gestures provided a similar kind of "cue" and how the "intensity of…movements reflect the sound." The ability to predict and anticipate Ilsar's rhythms of playing made it feel as if "I am playing with someone" and that created a collaboration that was less "one sided" and more "inspiring for the improvisation" (Ilsar et al. 2014, p. 341). As this suggests, in order for a conversational rhythm of improvisation to develop, both sides of the conversation need to be able to read and understand the rhythms of the other. In an interaction design, this will involve making the system and the user's rhythmic performance perceivable not just in terms of when an event will happen but also in terms of its intensity.

The conversational rhythms of improvisation also need what Andrew Johnston calls "a level of un-control." This is because an unpredictability of control brings an enlivening "struggle" of mastery into the exchange between a performer and an interactive system. Without this struggle, the system will have a lifeless responsiveness and not contribute anything to the exchange. The word "struggle" is also used by choreographer Rhiannon Newton in her description of the conversational rhythms of improvisation in dancing. In her world, this struggle is about controlling the direction of movement of the different rhythms the dancers are performing. Sometimes the improvisation hinges on finding "an average with the people around you." Sometimes there is a "symbiotic coming together" or a "vibing off each other." And sometimes there are the struggles of "I'm not coming towards you, you can come towards me." Within the variation of these responses lies the "psychological buzz" improvisors will get from the possibility that something could go rhythmically wrong (Emmerson 2007, p. 26). The buzz gets its energy from the unpredictability of control that comes either from the instrument, the musical structure or a fellow improvisor.

A similar, energetic unpredictability is what leads Kaffe Matthews, who performs live electronic music on a laptop, to see the computer as both a collaborator and a fellow improvisor. She describes how:

> One of the big attractions about working with a computer was that the machine…would do things and make sounds I would never have imagined on my own, which were often the most interesting things. And these were not sounds that I owned or that were a product of my toil, but simply material I could use, more like in a collaboration…It was about collaborating with this instrument that could produce stuff…I started putting the machine in situations where it was going to produce sounds that I wasn't thinking of. (Emmerson 2007, p. 113)

There is a relationship of exploration and discovery in this description, similar to the one that Andrew Johnston ascribes to finding that right balance between predictable and unpredictable control. The balance creates a conversational blend of intuitiveness and complexity that, he says, "makes you want to keep playing." It is an interactive experience that Johnston compares to the experience of blowing a falling feather. Such a feather with its "indirect or sinuous movement" has a freedom of purpose and this connects it to that liveliness of self-determination and thought that we spoke of in the previous section (Souriau 1983 [1889], p. 91). Designing an interactive mix of intuitiveness and complexity is, therefore, something that can provide a vitality that animates an interactive system and positions it as an active playmate within an interactive exchange. The system here becomes both an instrument that can be played and a collaborator that can be played with.

The energy that is exchanged during a conversational improvisation is another element that needs to be balanced in a design that aims to achieve this type of vital rhythmic dynamic. Digital systems, as Andrew Johnston observes, have an "unlimited energy" and that can mean that they will "dominate" and potentially "swamp" a conversation during improvisation. Digital systems can also easily exceed human physical capabilities and this can create rhythms that are difficult for humans to interact with expressively. The dancer China Laudisio describes how the rhythms of the choreography of Merce Cunningham changed in this way for her, once Cunningham started using choreography software:

> Before the computer, the movement - for me - was heavenly. I loved it. Lots of play with throwing the weight around, yet at the same time being in control…[After the computer] the work became somehow painful…my mind and emotions rebelled against it, and physically it went against how I wanted to move…we had to jump and within the jump change our back 'x' many times…painful because things were dissected and compartmentalized and there was no freedom of flow. (Reynolds 2007, pp. 215–216)

To avoid this mismatch in energy and corresponding disruption of expressive rhythmic potential, Andrew Johnston advocates creating a system that "doesn't bring too much extra energy beyond what the performer injects into it." This keeps the energetic balance of rhythms at a human scale and also at the particular human scale of the person performing with it. It can, therefore, create a vitality that feels human in character and that character will help create a conversational playful rapport.

In my own interaction designs, I have also observed how interfaces that respond to an injection of a user's energy can produce a vitality that then encourages play. The work *Just a Bit of Spin* had a large disc as the interface and users rotated it backwards and forwards to control, mix and animate images and sounds (Fig. 11.4). Rotating things like this disc, have a sense of vitality because of the way they continue to move after you have provided the original energy boost to start them off. It feels as if you have breathed life into something. A lot of work in *Just a Bit of Spin* went into getting the weight, balance and mechanical motion of the disc just right, so that it had a pleasurable tactile and vital motion that encouraged a playful rhythm of energy exchange. A spinning disc, however, without any further injection of energy will eventually slow, and this decay could deflate any sense that the system has vitality. What this suggests is that a system like this might also need an element to give it that sense of unpredictable control that we discussed above. Such unpredictability might then allow the system to maintain both its energy and the perception that it is an active partner within the play of rhythmic improvisation. In this case, this might mean that the system also needs to produce some energy on its own or, at least, to be more like the example of the falling feather and respond complexly to multiple rhythms within its environment.

Film maker Andrew Lancaster has a lovely memory of a playful rhythmic experience that has a similar mix of complexity and intuitiveness to the example of the falling feather. He describes how as a small child he would drum on his single bed:

> The big bit of wood at the end of the bed base was kind of like a percussion box and I used to play rhythms constantly. I actually learned about frequencies and rhythm by tapping on that

Fig. 11.4 Images of the artwork *Just a Bit of Spin* by Brigid Costello exhibited at the Powerhouse Museum, Sydney Australia in 2007. Similar to early animation devices, the black disc had slits that the participant looked through to see audio-visual material that animated in response to the spinning of the disc

bed and hearing the mattress springs resonate. Then I would hum with the mattress springs. It's a wonderful thing of old mattresses - if you're speaking on a bed, some frequencies will just suddenly make the springs rattle and hum. Because it had so many rattling and weird springs…it became this whole wonderful world of the bed being this percussion piece that I could play with.

In Lancaster's story, we can see the playful pleasure of being a cause that Karl Groos maintains is the "psychological foundation for all play" (1898, p. 295). This pleasure was sustained by the way the bed provided both the direct control of hitting the wooden base to create sound and the less predictable control of creating resonances with its metal springs. The multiple springs could be set in motion in a way that felt like they were producing sounds out of their own vitality and this created a conversational exchange of energy that lead to expressive play. It was the movement and intersection of the rhythms of the differently resonant springs that provided that vital sense of unpredictability needed for playful collaboration.

Interestingly, resonance is also something that Andrew Johnston finds useful for playful interaction design. He thinks of his interactive works as "systems that resonate and dampen." These two processes allow him to balance the energies exchanged during an interactive performance in a way that will evoke the conversational rhythms of improvisation. Johnston might, for example, amplify the impact of a performer's gesture so that its energy matches that of the system, producing an exaggeration that expands their sense of self and enlivens them (Johnston 2015, p. 64). Sometimes he might also have the system deliberately ignore a gesture, to reduce rhythmic noise, create unpredictability and quieten the level of energy being exchanged. Amplification is also used in a similar way by interaction designer George Khut. In his case, it is a way of making the small changes in the heart rate or brainwaves of his participants perceivable "sonically, visually or kinesthetically." Scaling these up allows him to turn the energy of a rhythm "we can't feel" into something we can and he does this in a way that produces a slowly resonant type of control that feels like "a gradual influencing." Educational designer Simon McIntyre describes an opposite need for scaling down to make rhythmic energy more readable in online forums, with "1000 different threads" and discussion posts that "speed past" too rapidly for a conversation to develop. Each of these strategies for amplifying or dampening the rhythmic energies of the user or system work to create a balance within an interactive experience. That balance prevents one side from dominating and the other from not being 'heard'. In using them, however, a designer can, as Johnston cautions, modulate the energy of an interactive experience in a way that involves no possibility for creative transformation to emerge. Doing so, he says, would create an "echo" box that might "merely amplify movements" but would not resonate in a way that might "provoke audiences and/or performers to discover nuances and unexpected details" (Johnston 2015, p. 65). This type of productive resonance is what I think makes Andrew Lancaster's percussive bed story such a beautiful example of interactive play. Lancaster's memory involves a relationship of energy exchange that is creatively transformative and expressive.

In this chapter, we have seen that a patterned flow that has rhythmic vitality will have a range of timing variations and nuances related to the movements made by humans and other living beings. These rhythmic nuances and variations will, similarly, play a major role within the vitality of expressive performance. Vitality in performance is something that will often be read as an expression of freedom of thought and agency. In this way, the energy of a rhythm can produce vitality whether in the mind of a perceiver or the body of a performer, and by association also animate an interactive system. Rhythmic vitality within human computer interaction can be designed to produce a similar conversational push and pull to that of collaborative improvisation in musical performance. Creating this relationship is about balancing energies using processes of amplification or dampening, so that one or other side does not dominate the exchange. It also involves creating a balance of predictable and unpredictable control. If both are well balanced, the interactive system will have a dynamic energy that makes it feel like a vital and active collaborator within this process of improvisation. In order to create the type of control that will allow performed actions to be vital and rhythmically expressive, a designer needs to focus on making a design's rhythm able to be controlled in an embodied way. This involves combining real-time control with a learnable, perceivable and performable rhythmic structure. Most importantly, it involves giving the user ways to control the variety and timings of these rhythms at multiple scales and intensities. Do this and you will create a design whose responses won't have the false vitality of an echo. They will have a vitality that resonates, transforms and creates.

References

Chernoff JM (1979) African rhythm and African sensibility: aesthetics and social action in African musical idioms. The University of Chicago Press, USA

Costello BM (2016) The rhythm of game interactions: player experience and rhythm in minecraft and don't starve. Games Cult. https://doi.org/10.1177/1555412016646668

De Koven B (2013) The well-played game. MIT Press, Cambridge

Dewey J (2005) Art as experience. [Original publication 1934] Perigee edn. Penguin, New York

Emmerson S (2007) Living electronic music. Ashgate, Great Britain

Groos K (1898) The play of animals (trans: Baldwin EL). D. Appleton and Company, New York

Ilsar A, Havryliv M, Johnston A (2014) Evaluating the performance of a new gestural instrument within an ensemble. Paper presented at the international conference on new interfaces for musical expression, Goldsmiths, London, UK

Iyer V (2002) Embodied mind, situated cognition, and expressive microtiming in African-American music. Music Percept 19(3):387–414

Johnston A (2015) Conceptualising interaction in live performance: reflections on 'encoded'. Paper presented at the proceedings of the 2nd international workshop on movement and computing, Vancouver, British Columbia, Canada

Johnston A, Clarkson D (2011) Designing for conversational interaction with interactive dance works. Paper presented at the OZCHI 2011 workshop the body in design, Canberra, Australia

Jourdain R (1997) Music, the brain, and ecstasy: how music captures our imagination. Harper Collins, USA

Klei Entertainment (2013) Don't Starve. Video game. PC, IOS, Android, Xbox, Playstation, Wii U. Klei Entertainment, Canada

Lange R (1975) The nature of dance: an anthropological perspective. Macdonald and Evans, London

London J (2004) Hearing in time: psychological aspects of musical meter. Oxford University Press, New York

Marczak R, Robine M, Desainte-Catherine M, Allombert A, Hanna P, Kurtag G (2009) Enhancing expressive and technical performance in musical video games. Paper presented at the SMC 2009, Porto, Portugal, 23–25 July

Margulis EH (2014) On repeat: how music plays the mind. [Kindle iOS version] edn. Oxford University Press, New York

Melnick J (2012) Josh Melnick and Walter Murch in Conversation. Paris Rev. https://www.theparisreview.org/blog/2012/02/07/josh-melnick-and-walter-murch-in-conversation/. Accessed 26 Aug 2015

Mojang (2011) Minecraft. Video game. PC, IOS, Android, Xbox, Playstation, Wii U, Nintendo. Mojang, Sweden; Microsoft, USA; Sony Interactive Entertainment, USA

Reynolds D (2007) Rhythmic subjects. Dance Books Ltd., Hampshire

Souriau P (1983) The aesthetics of movement (trans: Souriau M) [Original publication 1889]. The University of Massachusetts Press, Amherst

Stern D (2010) Forms of vitality: exploring dynamic experience in psychology, the arts, psychotherapy, and development. Oxford University Press, Oxford, New York

Swink S (2009) Game feel: a game designer's guide to virtual sensation. CRC Press Taylor & Francis, London

Chapter 12
Architectures of Rhythm

> Periodicity. Every game has it.
> Solitaire. Hopscotch. Roshambo. Quake. Myst. Grand
> Theft Auto.
> Periodicity in time, and in space.
> An architecture of rhythm.
> These games and all others can be described as
> entrainment engines.
> Systems designed to coax the behavior of participants into
> mutually satisfying rhythms and patterns.
> As a game designer, you are an entrainment engineer.
> (Moriarty 2002)

Abstract Our journey into rhythm, play and interaction design has taken us along many interesting paths, each inspired by one of the eighteen creative practitioners interviewed for this book. Through the ideas of these creative practitioners, we have understood rhythm as something that shapes societies, cultures, thoughts, bodies, meanings and perceptions. We have also uncovered strategies for designing rhythms across all its dimensions and gained insights into the feelings rhythm can evoke when it is performed and perceived. Before finishing, we now have a short summary of the many rhythmic design strategies that have been uncovered. This summary cannot possibly express the full nuance of all that we have discussed nor the true vitality of each strategy, but it will act as a reminder of the detail covered in the previous chapters. The summary is divided into sections that address the three major themes of the book—strategies for creating dynamics, designing for expressive control and the pleasures of playful experience.

12.1 Strategies for Creating Dynamics

Throughout the book, many chapters have revealed strategies for creating dynamic movement within the flow of a rhythm. Some strategies involved working with rhythmic contrasts. For instance, we saw how intensity of affect can be increased by working with contrasting extremes of speed, energy, duration and density of events.

© Springer International Publishing AG, part of Springer Nature 2018
B. M. Costello, *Rhythm, Play and Interaction Design*, Springer Series
on Cultural Computing, https://doi.org/10.1007/978-3-319-67850-4_12

For such contrasts to work, however, it is important that the two things being contrasted are read as part of the one continuing rhythm and not as separate elements. Another common rhythmic strategy involves creating contrasts between linear and cyclic rhythms. Doing this produces both stability and clarity because one rhythm works to define its contrasting other. In the same way, repetition can be used to create a satisfying stability that will then through contrast make the uneasy instability of change work. Fluctuating contrasts between repetition and change can also work to create a dynamic contrasting flow of expectations being met and then surprised. An example of this is the musical technique of 'the drop,' where a fast rhythm will suddenly drop away, pause and then restart. Versions of this technique can be used within all kinds of rhythmic experiences to create an exciting contrast of intensity and to produce rhythms of tension and release. Contrasts of tension and release can also be layered, transitioned and overlapped to create a multiplicity of rhythms that will then have a constant, vital fluctuating intensity.

Other strategies that involved working with layers and density of rhythmic events were about creating texture within the flow of a rhythm. Creating these textures involved processes of addition, deletion and substitution, whether of single events or of layers within a rhythm. We saw how, depending on the way they are used, both adding and subtracting can expand or contract rhythmic density. Although adding elements to a rhythm would usually expand its density, a rhythm can sometimes feel less dense because either the layers create more coherence or because they create so much noise that the events blur and perception moves to larger simpler structures. Similarly, a rhythm can sometimes feel more dense if there is a trace of a removed rhythm that lives on in perception despite the fact that subtracting elements would usually contract a rhythm's density. These strategies for working with texture can also compensate for the lack of expressive control interaction designers often have over the duration and sequencing of rhythm within non-linear interactions.

To create movement in a rhythm involves designing variations in energy, intensity, duration and speed. If this movement has similar deviations, imprecisions and nuances of rhythm as those within the movement of organic living things then it will feel like it has an expressive vitality. There may also be a sense that there is a living being with a vitality of mind behind the rhythmic movement. This vitality of movement will have a particular felt quality that depends on the rhythms of its arrival and departure. When a design moves or transitions between two rhythmic tempos it creates a dynamic groove, whose character develops in the way the two temporal energies and speeds match or collide. Another rhythmic movement that interaction designers need to consider is the rhythms of stop, pause or rest within an experience. Strategies for designing these were about resolving patterns and maintaining rhythmic flow so that the experience felt like one continuing rhythm. There were strategies for carefully timing the duration of pauses, masking a pause with a feeling of explosive release and using randomness and variation to hide a cyclic restart. Another technique for maintaining the flow of rhythm across temporal changes involved sensitively matching various layers of rhythm with user interactions. For use in multiuser contexts, there was also the strategy of creating modular rhythms that can be moved through in different ways by different players to create new rhythms while maintaining rhythmic flow. In contrast, there were the strategies of collective participatory performance, which instead of novelty relied on rhythmic repetition and predictability to encourage multiuser participation and sustain the flow of performance.

We also saw how repetition could be used to produce novelty. For instance, the way that creating overlapping repetitive structures with a delay between each, produces a new form from repetition. A repetitive performance might also create novelty out of the instability of muscular performance. Additionally, someone experiencing this repetition might perceive something different each time the repeated event is experienced and, thus, novelty can also be produced during perception. Another strategy for breaking the monotony of repetition involved layering the linearity of repetition within cyclic return. The rhythm's potential monotony will then be broken by the vital spark of each renewal. Each of these strategies can help overcome the laborious grind of repetitive performance by producing the vitality of free movement that is needed for a play experience. Although play needs a level of predictable control, it also needs the vitality that unpredictable control brings. The rhythm between these two wakes up perceivers and performers by introducing the struggle of mastery. The art of designing playful rhythmic dynamics lies in getting the balance right, so that play does not collapse from boredom or frustration and so that there is enough emergent complexity to keep giving the player rhythms that can be played with and against.

12.2 Designing for Expressive Control

A strong theme throughout all our discussions has been how to give the player expressive control over the rhythms they perform within an interaction design. Such expressive control will create an engaging feeling of vitality within the free movement of a play experience. However, a player will not be able to perform expressively unless a design has a rhythmic structure that is perceivable, understandable and performable. In previous chapters, we saw how this ability to perceive, understand and perform a rhythm can be impacted by many factors. For example, it can be impacted by cultural perspectives, socio-cultural experience, gender and general life experience. It can also be impacted by the rhythmic knowledges and understandings that are developed as we move our bodies.

Players' ability to perceive, perform and understand a rhythm might also be influenced by the way the rhythms of a design intersect with the other rhythms in their everyday life. These external rhythms can disrupt, confuse and distract a design but equally a design can generate rhythms that might have a similar adverse effect on users' lives. This means that rhythms need to be considered at multiple scales, temporal dimensions and perspectives to fully understand how they might intersect with the user's own rhythms. It also means that we might need to develop strategies that allow our designs to intersect flexibly with the multiplicity of everyday rhythms. There is an ethical dimension to the design of these rhythmic intersections. Interaction designers need to consider rhythms as expressions of social and political structures and think about how these might impact a player's agency. They also need to consider the potential power of addictive rhythmic absorption and design ways to unhook users. The rhythms of interactive technology could cause problems in user's lives, but a clever and playful design can also be part of the solution. Particularly, if it gives users the power to orchestrate these rhythms and those within their everyday lives.

To have the potential for expressive play, a design needs to work with rhythms in ways that mesh well with the scale, habits and capabilities of the moving, breathing, sensing human body. A design also needs to facilitate the development of a player's bodily memory of a rhythm and give players the flexibility to choose a particular participation intensity. Expressive performance is possible when a design gives players embodied real-time control over their rhythmic actions and provides an interface that allows them to sense and control rhythmic nuance. There is a whole palette of bodily motion that interaction designers can tap into in order to create the variety of movement needed for an expressively dynamic performance. However, before a player can play expressively they need first to learn the palette of rhythmic possibilities within a design. One strategy to speed up this learning process is to work with rhythmic frequencies familiar to the user. Another is to introduce a rhythmic palette in slow stages and use repetition to reinforce it. This strategy often involves combining simple structures so that a design can quickly create an easily graspable rhythmic complexity. The interactive system or another player can also speed up the learning process by acting as a rhythmic leader. Like the drummer in a band, this leadership not only makes rhythm perceptible, it also creates an energy that drives rhythmic momentum and provides a structure that can be played against. The energetic flow of a rhythm involves a to and fro oscillating exchange between player and system. This energy is something that needs to be fed and balanced to maintain momentum, and the possibility of expressive control. Let the computer become too energetically dominant or merely echo the energy of the player and the vitality of expressive performance will dissipate.

Many of the strategies for creating a design that gives players the ability to be expressive with the rhythms of their performance emerged from the practice of those who improvise with music or dance. Their practice revealed how constraints and a restricted palette will provide a rhythmic structure within which improvisational play can then occur. Constraints such as these allow players to quickly finish exploring what it is they have to play with and begin investigating instead how they can improvise playfully. The constraint of a restricted palette also provides that balance between open and closed possibilities from which rhythmic novelty and complexity can emerge.

One strategy for producing novelty and complexity during an improvisation is to work with multiple layers of uncertainty, creating a structure so complex that each person will perceive a different rhythm. Another is to use the unsettling power of an ambiguous rhythm, which, with its multiple ways of being resolved, produces a space of possibility for perceivers and performers. To create the conversation of a collaborative improvisation both sides need to perceive, communicate and understand each other in order for their energies to be exchanged in an expressive way.

A design that aims to create this relationship needs, therefore, to create an ecology where rhythms can be exchanged between component parts. This exchange might involve allowing energies to combine and grow. It also might involve blocking or containing energies to shelter and support the process of exchange. All are processes of amplification and dampening that allow an interaction design to balance the scales of energies involved in expressive rhythmic play. The important thing is that both sides bring something expressive to the relationship. There needs to be a productive oscillation between leading and following during collaborative improvisation. This is a relationship of mutual adaptability and shared agency that will produce the vitality needed for expressive rhythmic performance.

12.3 The Pleasures of Playful Experience

Another theme throughout the book has been the affective dimension of rhythmic experience and the pleasure or displeasure it can evoke. Our discussion has revealed ways that physical rhythmic movement is enjoyed and showed how this involves balancing effort with pleasure. It has also revealed that we enjoy and are engaged by rhythmic dynamics that have an escalating intensity. We have seen how repetitive movements (whether performed or perceived) might lead to a pleasurable mesmerising sense of being possessed or controlled by something. And how we can feel a sense of an expanded existence and new understandings can emerge, so long as there is an element of free play within this rhythmic repetition. Repetition can also feel like something we are in control of, especially during that moment when we feel the pleasure of predicting a rhythmic event and getting it right. This kind of predictability in a rhythm will focus attention on its larger structure and lead us to be engaged with the possibilities of what might happen next. In contrast, unpredictability in a rhythm will cause us to compare rhythmic events and to then reflect on, and analyse, the relationships between them. Both modes of attending to a rhythm can be pleasurable. The pleasurable familiarity of the predictable will attract us, even though we also find the unfamiliar and the unpredictable pleasurably challenging. This is why combining predictability with unpredictability by delaying an expected event and then delivering it in a surprising way is a rhythm that is particularly enjoyable. A similarly pleasurable mix of contrasts occurs when we predict a negative experience but then something positive happens. The contrast acts to heighten and intensify any resulting pleasurable feelings.

Our discussion has also revealed ways that a rhythmic experience might fail and result in less pleasurable feelings. There can be a failure caused by a clash of rhythmic cultures, leading to a lack of synchrony, miscommunication and misunderstanding. A rhythmic experience can be masked, clouded, disrupted or adversely complicated by the rhythms of daily life. Rhythms within an experience might operate at a scale that makes it difficult for users to synchronise with or perform them, and this can also cause injury or perceptual illness. Additionally, such mismatched scales can disrupt or block the flow of a rhythm and reduce its expressive potential. Both the perception and the performance of a rhythm can also be adversely impacted by things that distract, constrain freedom of movement or are very unfamiliar. A playful rhythmic pattern that fails to entrain its performers and perceivers will often be described as boring, but this boredom can be tinged with either frustration or triumph. We will feel boredom and triumph if we guess a pattern immediately, thinking there is no more to unravel, or by mastering a pattern completely. We will feel boredom and frustration if we perceive only noise, dismiss a pattern as repetitive or decide a pattern is not something we want to bother figuring out (Koster 2005, pp. 44–46). As a rhythmic performer we will feel bored if we cannot control rhythmic events and create or break patterns. We will also feel bored if we are not able to combine rhythmic layers and vary the range, density, timing and intensity of a rhythm in interesting ways. All these different forms of failure can create a rhythmic experience that is not pleasurable.

In previous research I developed a framework of the pleasures of play. One key focus of this book was to think about how these pleasures might operate in relation to rhythm and rhythmic experience. The seven categories within my framework are: mastering and competing; making and building; imagining and acting out; exploring and discovering; leading, following and collaborating; feeling and sensing; and acting up and taking risks. They are possible categories of pleasure that a player might feel during a play experience and they emerged out of a study synthesising the ideas of six theorists: Karl Groos, Roger Callois, Mihaly Csikszentmihalyi, Michael Apter, Pierre Garneau and Marc LeBlanc (see Costello 2007; Costello and Edmonds 2007, 2009). In earlier versions of the pleasure framework there were thirteen categories, here they have been combined and renamed to reflect the way that in practice many playful pleasures are interdependent or intertwined. The seven categories describe pleasures that might be experienced across the whole spectrum of play, from free-form to rule-based. These pleasures can occur in all types of playful interactive works, such as games, interactive artworks, functional applications or creative tools. As you read the description of each category below, you may recognise that we have discussed many of them in various ways over the course of the book. At the end of each description, there is an outline of the relationship between the pleasure and the rhythmic processes of playful attention that we discussed in Chap. 7. These relationships, also summarised in Table 12.1, map only the major and most common possible pleasures that might be experienced during each mode of attending. The specific character of an interactive experience, the particular players involved, and the socio-cultural context of play will, of course, shape which pleasures are actually felt while a rhythm is perceived and performed. Any of them might occur within any of the modes of attending. Even so, these broad mappings between rhythmic attending and the pleasures of play provide a useful summary of the possible major affective forces that can be at work during a playful rhythmic experience.

Mastering and Competing: There is pleasure to be found in playfully developing a skill and performing something skilfully. It is also pleasurable to try to achieve a defined goal, no matter whether that goal is set by the player, another person or an interaction design. These goals and skills might be physical or intellectual. In both cases, it will be more pleasurable from a play perspective if the skill or goal is neither too easy nor too hard to master or achieve. The player might also enjoy competing

Table 12.1 A mapping between the processes of playful rhythmic attending and the pleasures of play

Processes of playful attending		Pleasures of play
Experience Rhythm	Finding patterns	Exploring and discovering. Feeling and sensing
	Learning patterns	Mastering and competing. Exploring and discovering
	Predicting patterns	Imagining and acting out. Acting up and taking risks
	Completing patterns	Making and building. Mastering and competing
	Sharing patterns	Leading, following and collaborating. Feeling and sensing
Perform Rhythm	Repeating patterns	Mastering and competing. Leading, following and collaborating
	Expressing patterns	Feeling and sensing. Imagining and acting out
	Combining patterns	Leading, following and collaborating. Making and building
	Creating patterns	Making and building. Imagining and acting out
	Breaking patterns	Acting up and taking risks. Exploring and discovering

The table lists only the major and most common pleasures that would possibly be felt during a particular mode of attending

with or against another player, a perceived entity within the work, or the system of the work itself. Again, it will be more pleasurable if there is a balance between the two sides that are competing, so that the experience is neither too easy nor too hard. During playful rhythmic experience, the pleasure of mastering something can occur when players learn and complete patterns in order to perceive a rhythm. A pleasurable sense of mastery can also be involved when a player tries to repeat a learned rhythm. All three, learning, completing and repeating rhythmic patterns, can also involve the pleasure of competition, especially if there is a goal and/or an opponent involved.

Making and building: Players experience pleasure from the power to create or building something while interacting with a design. They also get pleasure from being able to express themselves creatively. For example, players might feel pleasure at being able to shape and manipulate a visual element of a work or to produce a musical rhythm from the sounds they are performing. This pleasure could come from the aesthetic qualities of their creation or equally come from the simple pleasure of feeling in control of the creation of something. In a playful rhythmic experience, the pleasure of making and building can occur when players complete a rhythm by chunking its patterns into groups and when they perceive structural beginnings, continuations or endings. This pleasure can also be strongly felt during the performative actions of combining and creating rhythmic patterns.

Imagining and acting out: Acting out something that mimics real-life or is a creation of the imagination is pleasurable. For example, players might get pleasure from the way their physical interaction mimics the real-world experience of rocking a baby to sleep. Players might also get pleasure from acting in a world where their avatar can perform fantastical physical feats that they cannot achieve in real life. Additionally, within the safe boundaries of play, something that in the real-world might cause negative feelings can, when acted out or imagined during play, can instead cause pleasure. The pleasure of imagining and acting out can be involved as we anticipate and predict rhythms because we will imagine rhythmic outcomes and often act out the paths of rhythmic movements in our imagination. This pleasure can also be felt as we expressively perform or create rhythmic patterns, imagining new patterns and acting them out with communicative expression.

Exploring and discovering: It is pleasurable to explore something and also to make a discovery or work something out. Exploration is often linked with discovery, but not always. Sometimes it is fun to just explore and to anticipate discovery. Because interactive designs often present players with unfamiliar situations, most will involve some degree of exploration and discovery. However, such exploration and discovery might not be pleasurable in some designs or play only a relatively minor part. For others, it may be the key pleasure of the experience. The pleasures of exploring and discovering can most commonly occur during the playful experience of finding and learning patterns. Taking pleasure in exploring and discovering can also be felt when players break patterns, especially when they do this in a way that creates novelty.

Leading, following and collaborating: Players can get pleasure from feeling captivated by something or from feeling as if another entity has control over them. The pleasure of being controlled might be caused by intense levels of engagement that can captivate in a way that reduces or expands a player's sense of self. If someone or something is leading players actions, they can enjoy following along. They might also develop a relationship of collaboration with an interactive system or other players, and may then enjoy leading others. During playful rhythmic experience, the pleasures of following and collaborating can occur when a playful experience asks players to draw on their shared cultural understandings of rhythmic patterns. The pleasures of following and collaborating can also be felt strongly when a player repeats a pattern during performance. All three, leading, following and collaborating can be involved when a player combines patterns during performance with another player or the system, especially when this involves the collaborative conversation of improvisation.

Feeling and sensing: The physical sensations an interaction design evokes, such as touch, body movements, hearing or vocalising, can be pleasurable. Players can also get pleasure from empathetically sharing emotional or physical feelings with something. Additionally, they might sympathetically feel a represented movement and also sense, and get pleasure from, their own physical movements as they interact.

The two together can create the common visceral physical pleasure of controlling an avatar's movement. The pleasure of feeling and sensing can be evoked during the processes of finding and sharing rhythmic patterns because players will empathetically sense and feel rhythms in order to perceive and understand them. This pleasure will also occur during expressive rhythmic performance as players feel and sense the rhythms they are performing.

Acting up and taking risks: Within play it can be thrillingly pleasurable for players to feel scared, surprised, in danger, or as if they are taking a risk. This feeling can be as mild as a sense of unease or as strong as a sense of threatening fear. During play it can also be pleasurable to break rules or to watch others break them. An aspect of a design or a player's action might pleasurably subvert the meaning of something or involve behaving mischievously. Players might also feel subversive pleasure simply from behaving in ways that they perceive as being "against the rules" of the world set up by a work or perhaps against their own personal rules of behaviour. In a playful rhythmic experience, the pleasure of acting up and taking risks can be involved when players predict rhythmic patterns. This is because there is always a risk that players will get their predictions wrong and, if wrong, there can then be subversive pleasure in the way a design or other player has challenged players' predictions. The pleasure of acting up and taking risks can also be felt strongly during any performative play that involves breaking rhythmic patterns.

The combination of the pleasures of play and the experiential and performative modes of attending to a rhythm is a useful tool for thinking about a playful design and the rhythmic experience it might elicit. An interaction designer might, for example, decide to focus on particular modes of playful attending and their associated pleasures during concept development and build a design that aims to evoke these. They might use them as a language for communicating with and questioning users during prototype evaluation. They could also use them to diagnose the key areas of strength and weakness within the rhythms of a design. As we saw earlier, to use rhythm as a diagnostic tool involves using multiple types of representation in order to emphasise temporal relations, reveal complexity and develop kinesthetic empathy. These, together with the other strategies for designing rhythmic experience that we have covered in this book, give designers a complex palette of tools for designing any kind of playful rhythmic experience. This is a palette of tools for creating architectures of rhythm that have a vitality and expressiveness and it is through this rhythmic movement that an interaction design and its users will then be able to play together.

I am now eager to try out some of these rhythmic design strategies. I want to know what an interactive experience that works with the Balinese gamelan brother/sister rhythms (described by Manolete Mora in Chap. 2) might feel like. I want to play around with Greg Sheehan and Rhiannon Newton's mathematical approaches from Chaps. 9 and 10, to see how they might operate within a multiplayer environment. I want to work with extremes of slowness and George Khut's idea of control as a form of gradual influencing from Chap. 7. I also want to work with the extremes of speed and layered tempos that Patrick Cook and Ilija Melentijevic talk about in Chap. 8. Inspired by Andrew Johnston and Andrew Lancaster in Chap. 11, I plan to create a design that produces the interactive conversation of rhythmic improvisation. I also plan to think more deeply about the rhythmic textures and transitions in my designs, using the compositional strategies of Andrew Schultz, and those of musicians Roger Mills, Bree van Reyk and Alon Ilsar. I have been given new insights into ways to shape the entrances and exits into and out from a rhythm by Clare Grant in Chap. 6 and the perspectives of Simon McIntyre and Joe Agius in Chap. 4. Lastly, inspired by Simon Barker in Chap. 3 and Nalina Wait in Chap. 5, I want to create designs that have a palette of physical interactions that are rhythmically expressive and pleasurable to perform. I do not doubt that you will have your own list of inspirations and I'd love to hear about any playful rhythmic experiences you go on to create. One thing I am certain of is that you will see, hear, feel and, in all other ways possible, sense rhythms with a heightened awareness after reading this book and that this awareness will now permeate your design thinking.

References

Costello B (2007) A pleasure framework. Leonardo 40(4):370–371
Costello B, Edmonds E (2007) A study in play, pleasure and interaction design. In: Designing pleasurable products and interfaces. University of Art and Design Helsinki, 22–25 Aug 2007, ACM, pp 76–91
Costello B, Edmonds E (2009) A tool for characterizing the experience of play. Paper presented at the proceedings of the sixth australasian conference on interactive entertainment, Sydney, Australia, Article 2, 10 pages. https://doi.org/10.1145/1746050.1746052
Koster R (2005) A theory of fun for game design. Paraglyph Press, Scottsdale
Moriarty B (1998–2002) Entrain. http://ludix.com/moriarty/entrain.html. Accessed 13 Jan 2006

Appendix
Biographies of Interviewees

Joe Agius

A Director of the leading international architecture firm COX since 2006 Joe Agius is part of the practice's national executive group, guiding strategy and design direction. He has worked on projects for both the Sydney and Beijing Olympic Games, undertaken public projects in every major Australian city and developed master plans guiding major Australian universities. Achieving strong public domain and civic outcomes supportive of public life are central to his design and philosophical approach. His projects include the carbon, energy and water neutral Sustainable Buildings Research Centre for Wollongong University; the Adelaide Studios for the SA film Commission; NeuRA an independent neuroscience research institute; and the Australian Film Television and Radio School. Joe Agius sits on the NSW Minister for Finance & Services Business Advisory Group and the Dean's Advisory Board for both the University of Technology Sydney and Canberra University architecture faculties.

Simon Barker

Drummer, composer and lecturer in Jazz Studies at the Sydney Conservatorium of Music in the University of Sydney Simon Barker studied in Australia with John Collins, and in New York with John Riley, Keith Copeland, Marvin "Smitty" Smith, Kim Plainfield and Mike Clarke. He has performed and conducted workshops throughout Australia, Europe, Asia and the USA with a wide range of artists. In 2005 Simon created Kimnara Records, an independent record label presenting new music by Australian improvisers. In addition to his solo performances and recordings, Simon co-leads several internationally recognized collaborative ensembles including Trace Sphere, Chiri, Showa 44, and Band of Five Names. Simon Barker also performs with many of Australia's most established ensembles including the Matt McMahon trio, the Phil Slater Quartet, and several groups led by Scott Tinkler. He has done extensive research into Korean rhythmic forms. The 2010 documentary by Emma Franz, *Intangible Asset No. 82*, records his search for an enigmatic South Korean shaman and documents Simon's collaboration with

© Springer International Publishing AG, part of Springer Nature 2018
B. M. Costello, *Rhythm, Play and Interaction Design*, Springer Series on Cultural Computing, https://doi.org/10.1007/978-3-319-67850-4

singer Bae Il-Dong. In 2015 he published a book on this research titled *Korea and the Western Drumset: Scattering Rhythms*.

Patrick Cook

Head of Game Design at SMG Studio an indie game studio in Sydney, Australia and avid gamer Patrick Cook has been making games for almost twenty years. In his day to day work at SMG, Patrick is also involved in many areas of game development, including code, art, sound and animation. This diversity matches his professional experience outside of game design, which has included work in a range of creative areas from cell painting for animation to digital compositing, web development, 3D art and music. A career in music nearly overtook all of these when he signed a record contract. But his deep interest in the psychology of games, play and the motivations for human actions lead him back to game design where he has maintained this diversity of creative practice. Patrick Cook has developed several acclaimed games with SMG including *OTTTD* (2014), *Thumbdrift* (2016) and *Death Squared* (2017).

Clare Grant

Performer, director and dramaturg Clare Grant is involved in the creation of new works for theatre, performance, radio and film. She worked with KISS Theatre Group in Europe and was a founding member of The Sydney Front, which was awarded the Sydney Theatre Critics Prize for Best Fringe Theatre Company in 1992. Clare was Co-director then Artistic Director of Playworks and has served on the Theatre Committee of the NSW Arts Advisory Council and the Theatre Fund, Australia Council. She has also lectured for many years at the University of New South Wales in Sydney, Australia. Clare has been associated with several Sydney companies engaged in the devising of new works for theatre, including Sidetrack and One Extra Company. Clare Grant's other performance work includes *Burn Sonata* (1998), *Inland Sea* (2000), and *Laquiem* (1999). In 2007 she received an award recognising her leading role in the field of experimental theatre from the Cairo International Festival of Experimental Theatre.

Sue Healey

Multi-award-winning choreographer, educator, filmmaker and installation artist Sue Healey was a founding member of Nanette Hassall's Dance Works in Melbourne and performed and choreographed with the company from 1983 to 88. She then continued her training in New York with such luminaries as Merce Cunningham and Trisha Brown Companies. Returning to Australia, she became Artistic Director of Vis-à-Vis Dance Canberra (1993–96) and Sue Healey Company (1996–present). Experimenting with form and perception, Sue creates dance for theatres, galleries and the camera. She is an acknowledged pioneer of dance on screen and her films have won many awards, screening in over 30 countries. Sue Healey has also toured her work throughout the USA, UK and Asia. She received the prestigious Creative Fellowship in 2013–14 from the Australia Council for Arts, and was recently made an Honorary Fellow of the Victorian College of the Arts, University of Melbourne. She has also won four Australian Dance Awards.

Alon Ilsar

An Australian drummer, composer, sound designer and instrument designer Alon Ilsar is co-designer of a new interface for electronic percussionists called the *AirSticks*. Alon has played the *AirSticks* in collaborations such as The Sticks, Tuka (from Thundamentals), Kirin J Callinan, Velize and Cephalon. During his career Alon was a musical director for *Circus Monoxide* and was also heavily involved in theatre and film as drummer, composer and sound designer. His diverse projects include Belvoir Theatre's *Keating! the Musical*, Sydney Theatre Company's *Mojo*, a Scottish production for deaf and hearing audiences *Kind of Silence*, and *Meow Meow* with the London Philharmonic, Alan Cumming, Jake Shears, Eddie Perfect and Tim Minchin. While an artist in residence at Brooklyn College's PIMA in New York Alon Ilsar worked on collaborations with musicians, visual artists and dancers such as Trevor Dunn, David Grubbs, Jim Black, Briggan Krauss, and Hannah Cohen of Neshamah Dance Company.

Andrew Johnston

Researcher and interaction/software designer Andrew Johnston is based in Sydney, Australia. His work focuses on the design of systems that support experimental, exploratory approaches to interaction, and the experiences and practices of the people who use them. He has qualifications in music and computing, and a Ph.D. combining the two. As a musician he has performed professionally with ensembles such as the Melbourne and Sydney Symphony Orchestras and many other ensembles. Andrew has had a long and productive collaboration with Stalker Theatre, a Sydney-based dance and physical theatre company. With Ph.D. researcher Andrew Bluff, he developed large scale interactive projections for the productions *Encoded* and *Creature: A Retelling of Dot and the Kangaroo*, which have toured nationally and internationally to the Netherlands, South Korea, the United Kingdom and Hong Kong. Andrew is an Associate Professor in the School of Software, Faculty of Engineering and IT at the University of Technology Sydney (UTS). He is also Research Director of the UTS Animal Logic Academy and co-directs the Creativity and Cognition Studios, an interdisciplinary research group working at the intersection of performance, art and technology.

George Poonkhin Khut

Artist and interaction designer George Khut works across the fields of electronic art, interaction design and arts-in-health. Khut's body-focussed interactive and partic-ipatory artworks use bio-sensing technologies to re-frame experiences of embodi-ment, health and subjectivity. In addition to presenting his works in galleries and museums, George has developed new audiences for interactive and participatory art with exhibitions and research projects in hospitals, starting with *The Heart Library Project* at St. Vincent's Public Hospital in 2009, and more recently with the *BrightHearts* research project—a collaboration with Dr. Angie Morrow, Staff Specialist in Brain Injury at The Children's Hospital at Westmead, Kids Rehab. Recent group exhibitions include *Group Therapy: Mental Distress in a Digital Age* curated by Vanessa Bartlett at FACT in Liverpool, UK; *CUSP: Design into the Next Decade*, curated by Object Gallery (Australian Design Centre); *Wonderland:*

Contemporary Art from Australia at the MoCA Taipei; and *Strange Attractors: Charm between Art and Science*, Zendai Museum of Modern Art, Shanghai, China.

Andrew Lancaster

Australian director and composer Andrew Lancaster is based in London and Sydney. He graduated from the Australian Film, Television and Radio School where he directed and composed the short films *Palace Cafe* and *Universal Appliance Co.*, which between them have won fifteen awards world-wide. His directing style combines cinematic vision with a strong emphasis on music, sound, choreography and rhythm. In 2010 he founded the music collective Sonar Music and joined Photoplay Films as commercial director. He won the 2012 AACTA award for Best Original Music for *The Hunter* and his micro documentary *The Town of Speed* won two Gold awards at the ADMA, Gold at Spikes Asia Awards, and two Silver CLIOs and Gold awards at the New York Festival Awards. Andrew Lancaster's debut feature film, *Accidents Happen* (starring Geena Davis) premiered at Tribeca Film festival 2009 and has won prestigious festival awards at Giffoni Italy, Stiges Spain, and the Netherlands. His second feature *The Lost Aviator* premiered in 2014 at the BFI London Film Festival, Miami, and received a special Jury mention at the Sydney Film Festival.

Simon McIntyre

A Faculty of Art & Design Associate Dean of Education at the University of New South Wales, Sydney, Simon McIntyre is also a member of the Scientia Education Fellowship. He is a multi-award winning educator, passionate about improving the effectiveness, quality and relevance of the student learning experience, and about pedagogically driven use of technology to innovate learning and teaching practices. Simon has led the design and management of several innovative professional development and educational programs; working with teams of dedicated academics and collaborators. He leads internationally successful open education initiatives such as the widely used open education resources, the multi-award winning *Learning to Teach Online* Massive Open Online Course (MOOC), and the *Transmedia Storytelling: Narrative worlds, emerging technologies, and global audiences* MOOC. In 2015, Simon McIntyre was one of 14 Australian educators to be awarded the Office of Learning and Teaching Excellence Award.

Ilija Melentijevic

Art lead Ilija Melentijevic is a founding member of SMG, a small but prominent Sydney game studio. Born in Belgrade, Yugoslavia in 1975, he had his first solo art exhibition at the age of five. Having conquered the art world so early, he then turned to new challenges and started writing terrible text adventures on the ZX Spectrum. Also at this time, the first of many pixels were pushed, by drawing on graph paper and then typing in strings of 0s and 1s. Arguably the world was not ready for him yet, as it wasn't until 1996 that the first commercial title Ilija worked on was published. Many more would follow, for home computers, game consoles, mobiles and the web. Today, Ilija Melentijevic makes games with SMG, a small studio behind some big titles, including *One More Line* (2014), *Thumbdrift* (2016), *Risk:*

Global Domination (2016) and *Death Squared* (2017). Outside of the game development scene, he has completed illustration and graphic design for numerous books and clients such as McDonalds, Microsoft and National Geographic. Ilija lives in the Blue Mountains, and in his spare time makes even more games, board games, pixel art and music.

Roger Mills

Musician, sound artist and writer Roger Mills practices and researches with a focus on networked music performance, improvisation, music composition and experimental radio. He has also worked as a composer and sound designer for both stage and screen. Roger's credits include sound design for the multiscreen cinema film *Hindsight* (Ignition Films, UK), the score for BAFTA award winning dance theatre performance *At Swim Two Boys* (Earthfall, UK), and a Golden Eye Award for his multi-stream radio performance *Idea of South*. He is the musical director of the internationally acclaimed Ethernet Orchestra, a networked music ensemble exploring new approaches to inter-cultural telematic improvisation. The ensemble informs Roger Mill's research at the University of Technology, Sydney (UTS) where he is examining cross-cultural collaborative interaction in networked and digitally mediated environments. Roger's performances, exhibitions and presentations include Medi@terra, Athens, ISEA, Istanbul, Sonic Circuits, Washington DC, O-Town Sound, New York, blackhole-factory, Braunschweig, Germany, Loop Space Gallery, Newcastle, NIME++2010, Memory Flows and Don't Look Gallery, Sydney.

Manolete Mora

Ethnomusicologist Manolete Mora convenes the Music program at the University of New South Wales (UNSW) in Sydney, Australia. At UNSW, Associate Professor Manolete Mora researches the musics of South East Asia and Africa and also leads the Balinese Gamelan ensemble. Previously, he was a faculty member at the Department of Music of The University of Hong Kong and an Andrew Mellon Research Fellow at the Department of Music, University of Pennsylvania. He is also an Honorary Fellow at The University of Melbourne Conservatorium of Music. Manolete specializes in Philippine Music, including popular music, epics and ritual songs, musical ethnography, and music of Bali, Ghana, and Cuba. Manolete Mora has produced ethnographic CDs (for Rykodisc and UNESCO) and is the author of the 2005 book *Myth, Mimesis and Magic in the Music of the T'boli, Philippines*.

Rhiannon Newton

Sydney-based dancer and choreographer Rhiannon Newton's work draws together dance and repetition to focus on social and environmental processes of change. Rhiannon's works have been presented at Dance Massive Festival and Dancehouse (Melbourne), Brisbane Festival and Metro Arts (Brisbane), Critical Path, Shopfront Arts, Firstdraft and PACT (Sydney), The Lock-up (Newcastle), The Judson Church (New York), Performing Arts Form (France), Nagib On Stage (Slovenia) and Tanzhaus Zurich (Switzerland). Rhiannon has been a part of international forums such as the Australian Eastern European Choreographic Exchange, Avignon Festival Seminar and the Swiss/Australian Reciprocal Residency. Today Rhiannon works as a performer with artists such as Rosalind Crisp, Mette Edvardsen, Martin Del Amo, Paea Leach and Brooke Stamp. She also co-facilitates First Run Sydney, is on the board of ReadyMade Works Studio and lectures in dance at the Australian College of Physical Education.

Bree van Reyk

Australian percussionist, drummer, composer and sound artist Bree van Reyk has toured and recorded extensively throughout Australia and around the globe with the likes of Paul Kelly, Holly Throsby, Sarah Blasko, Lior, Katie Noonan, Darren Hanlon, the Australian Chamber Orchestra, and many other songwriters and ensembles. Bree is long-standing member of Ensemble Offspring, Associate Director of Synergy Percussion, and was 2015 Artist in Residence at Campbelltown Arts Centre. With visual artist Lauren Brincat, Bree created large-scale performative works including 2014s *No Performance Today* which featured the NSW Police Band, and 2013s *Blood & Fire* with 50 tambourine players. As a composer, Bree van Reyk has been commissioned by Shaun Parker Company, Bell Shakespeare, Sydney Dance Company, the Museum of Contemporary Art (Sydney), NOMAD Percussion, and fashion designer Bianca Spender. In 2016, Bree created the soundtrack installation for *The Pool* exhibited at the Australian Pavilion during the Venice Biennale.

Andrew Schultz

A composer of operas, chamber music and orchestral works Andrew Schultz's music has been performed, recorded and broadcast by leading groups and musicians. He has held residencies and academic posts in Australia, Canada, France, UK and the US. Andrew has written a series of large-scale dramatic works, several of which incorporate parts for Australian indigenous singers. His three operas (*Black River, Going Into Shadows* and *The Children's Bach*) have been presented live and on film internationally. Black River (1988) was awarded the Australian National Composer Opera Award and, in its film version, the Grand-Prix, Opera Screen at Opera-Bastille, Paris. Andrew Schultz's orchestral music includes a series of works commissioned by the Sydney Symphony Orchestra: *The Devils' Music* (premiered with Jakov Kreizberg in 1989), *Diver's Lament* (Edo de Waart, 1995), *little tree* (Lyn Williams, 2003), and *Sound lur and serpent* (David Robertson, seven city China tour, 2014). Andrew has been the recipient of various awards and honours in Australia and overseas, including five Australia Council Fellowships, Fulbright Award, Commonwealth Scholarship, Maggs Award and the APRA Music Award. Recent successes include the Schueler Award, the Paul Lowin Prize and the premiere of his *Symphony No. 3—Century* in front of an audience of 150,000 to celebrate the centenary of Australia's capital, Canberra.

Greg Sheehan

One of Australia's premier and most innovative percussionists Greg Sheehan is recognised internationally as a leader in his field. Greg has experimented with and explored many instruments—tuned and un-tuned, man-made and earth-made. His rhythm diamond system for playing rhythmic phrases in a displaced, mathematical sequence has been a major influence for many artists. Greg is also an inspiring educator and teacher of rhythm to people of all ages, running body percussion workshops and appearing on the children's television show *Playschool*. With Bobby Singh and Ben Walsh he forms the percussion trio Circle of Rhythm. As a performer, he is significantly represented in the last three decades of Australian contemporary music as both a live band member and studio musician on hundreds of recordings. Greg Sheehan has performed with Blackfeather, Goanna, Kev Carmody, Blue King Brown, Sinead O'Connor and Cat Empire. Greg's debut solo album, *The Life Of My Time*, was published in 2009. He has performed at Womadelaide, Womad U.K., Woodford, various Festivals worldwide. Greg was honoured and celebrated at the 2013 Mullumbimby Music Festival and also presented and performed for TEDxSydney in 2012 and 2013.

Nalina Wait
Dance artist Nalina Wait works as a performer, choreographer and filmmaker. Her choreography often involves collaboration with sound artists and includes the dance film *Sole* (2003) with Gail Priest which screened in festivals in Australia, Israel and the US. As a performer she has worked extensively with Sue Healey (2003–present) including performing in all of the *Niche*, *In Time* and *The Curiosities* series. Nalina also performed in Healey's 2015 *On View: Quintet*, which was nominated for Ausdance award for Outstanding Achievement in Independent dance. Nalina was a founding member of Sydney Performance Group (2006–2011) working with Belgium choreographer Hans Van Den Broeck (SOIT) in *Settlement* (2007), *NO-MADS* (2008) and *HOMELANDS* (2011). She danced with Rosalind Crisp (1999–2002) performing in *The View From Here* (2000), *Accumulation (1–40)* (2000), *Scrapbook Live* (2001) and the work *Traffic and Kink* (2001), which toured to Antwerp, Paris and Berlin. In 2013, Nalina Wait re-performed works by Joan Jonas and Marina Abramović in the Sydney living sculptures exhibition *13 Rooms* and currently embodies a Tino Sehgal work for Kaldor Public Art Projects.

Index

© Springer International Publishing AG, part of Springer Nature 2018
B. M. Costello, *Rhythm, Play and Interaction Design*, Springer Series on Cultural Computing, https://doi.org/10.1007/978-3-319-67850-4

Printed in the United States
By Bookmasters

Printed in the United States
By Bookmasters